Last Saturday

BEFORE JESUS CHRIST RETURNS

JAREN L. JONES

LifeRich Publishing is a registered trademark of The Reader's Digest Association, Inc.

LifeRich Publishing books may be ordered through booksellers or by contacting:

LifeRich Publishing
1663 Liberty Drive
Bloomington, IN 47403
www.liferichpublishing.com
844-686-9607

Authorized King James Version
~ 68 Bible References

ISBN: 978-1-4897-3622-2 (sc)
ISBN: 978-1-4897-3623-9 (hc)
ISBN: 978-1-4897-3628-4 (e)

Library of Congress Control Number: 2021911069

Print information available on the last page.

LifeRich Publishing rev. date: 06/04/2021

Contents

Preface

Many years ago, I read a quote about Last Saturday, and realized it would be a good basis for a book about the Last Days. I began collecting articles, reading stories, and keeping notes. I hoped to present my information and thoughts in a future book.

I recently began organizing all my information and putting my ideas together for sharing with others. In this book, I cite scriptures, stories, current news, and other quotes as a realization of Last Day scriptural prophecies. Sometimes, I include quotes to emphasize the evidence that we live in perilous times. The references reveal signs of the times that are happening around the world.

If a quote or source is new or unfamiliar to you, I encourage you to look it up. This is easy to do with the technology we have at our fingertips.

I believe the events and signs preceding the Second Coming of Jesus Christ to the earth can be seen every day. Jesus Christ will soon come to earth again. I hope you learn something you didn't know, or at least discover something new to think about.

1

Last Saturday

Where were you last Saturday?
What were you doing last Saturday?

Most of us probably have trouble remembering what happened yesterday, let alone last Saturday. Yet surely, Saturday is often named as a favorite day of the week. Everyone makes plans for Saturday, sometimes weeks and months in advance. After all, when you think about it, Saturday is the weekend.

Those who work a nine-to-five job live for Friday nights, when the weekend begins. The calendar clearly shows that Sunday is the beginning of the week. So Saturday must be the weekend. Now we know why Saturday is such a great day; when we talk weekend, we are talking and thinking about Saturday. Let it rain and snow during the week, but we always want Saturday to be a perfect day. Richard and Karen Carpenter even recorded a hit song about "ever lovin' Saturday."

Saturday is usually a day of activities, recreation, and selected work. Saturday is the day we head to the mountains, beaches, tennis courts, parks, and other places for fun and sun. There seems to be an unwritten law that Saturday is the day to clean the house, mow the lawn, wash the car, and have a barbeque. After five days of work, school, Cub Scouts, piano lessons, and the ward dinner, perhaps the last day of the week should be free time for everyone.

Saturday is defined as the seventh day of the week. The name is derived from the Latin *Dies Saturni* (Saturn's Day), the last day of the Roman week. This day honored the god of agriculture. Oh, *that's* why we work five days of the week and do yard and garden (agriculture) work on Saturday.

Some reflections of Saturdays over the years by Latter-Day Saints would reveal to us another truth about Saturdays. Besides being a day of fun and relaxation, the last day of the week includes many activities that actually prepare us for the start of the week, Sunday. Everyone knows why we have a Saturday night bath. Many kids know why their hair must always be washed on that night. We clean the house, the car, our clothes, and even ourselves, in preparation for the Sabbath day.

Let's retreat for a minute and consider this very important day of the week. Think carefully for a minute about last Saturday. Where did you go? What did you do? How did you use your free time?

What happened last Saturday?

Oh, I slept until about ten thirty. Then I got up and watched cartoons for about an hour, even though my children grew up long ago. About eleven thirty, I took a shower and got dressed in my faded Levi's. I decided it was too late for breakfast, so I read the newspaper until lunchtime.

After lunch, it was too hot to mow the lawn, so I found a football game on TV. I spent three hours watching that but missed the third quarter, when I took a little nap. My wife wanted me to go shopping with her. I sat on a bench, while she marched up and down the mall. We came home, and I watched a couple of TV shows before dinner.

I cleaned out the car and then watched a couple of favorite TV shows. I read a few pages in the exciting novel I am currently reading. After the local TV news, I prepared my Sunday school lesson at ten thirty. It was a busy Saturday.

For many years now, I have faithfully tried to keep a journal. I find that I can't ever remember one Saturday from another. I have to keep notes in a daily planner and refer to them when I write in my journal. Most of us have pretty busy Saturdays and accomplish lots of important things. But just how important, and valuable, are your Saturday activities?

The last Saturday we should really think about and remember is a thousand times more important than those that have been described. Suppose we look at things with the same perspective as our Father in heaven. If we consider our lives, families, activities, and pursuits in the context of the plan of salvation, we might clearly see the importance of last Saturday.

THE EARTH'S SABBATH

In programming the world's mortal or temporal existence, God gave it a time allotment of 7,000 years (see Doc. & Cov. 77:6–7).

1,000 years to represent each of the seven days of creation. The first 4000 years began at the fall of Adam and ended at the birth of Christ. To this have been added [all the] years that have passed since that time, so that on the divine calendar we are now living in the year of the world "5990", which is the "late Saturday evening" of the world's history. This divine time table, as well as God's signs of the times, indicate that the earth's Sabbath, which is the seventh 1,000-year period is about to be ushered in. (Sill 1967, 35)

Biblical scholars agree that from Adam to the birth of Christ, four thousand years passed. The fifth millennium, or fifth dispensation of time, would be from Christ's birth (the year 4000, 0 BC, or AD 0) to the year 1000 (5000). The sixth millennium (thousand-year period) is the years from 1000 to 2000 (6000). It has been more than two thousand years since Christ was on the earth. The year 2000 should begin the final millennial period of the earth's history and should open the door for the Second Coming of Jesus Christ.

We cannot assume that the timetable for each dispensation of the earth's existence is set to the exact day, or even year. We can only

3

conclude that the year 2000, give or take a few years, is the beginning of the seventh and final millennium. The earth's Sabbath is about to begin. Jesus Christ may return to the earth tomorrow.

Is it indeed the Last Saturday? The day just before the final thousand years of the earth's temporal existence? Is the Lord about to return in his glory? We know and universally accept that we live in the Dispensation of the Fulness of Times.

DISPENSATION OF THE FULNESS OF TIMES

The Dispensation of the Fulness of Times is the final dispensation for this earth. Dispensations are periods of time, in which the gospel of Jesus Christ is administered by holy prophets called and ordained by God to deliver his message to the inhabitants of the world. The central work of the "dispensation of the fulness of times" consists of bringing together all gospel ordinances and truths of past dispensations. (Packer n.d.)

The apostle Paul tells us that in a future time, all things will be gathered. He says everything in heaven and earth will eventually be gathered together. The gathering of all things in the last dispensation will include some things that are exclusive to the Last Days. He called this future period of time the "dispensation of the fulness of times" (see Ephesians 1:10).

If today is the Last Saturday, if it is almost the midnight hour, what state would the world be in? Surely the signs of the times would indicate that the Savior's Second Coming is at hand.

1.1. KEYS, POWER, KNOWLEDGE

We may ask if any knowledge has been revealed in the last decade or so. If it has, then such knowledge could be a witness of not only the dispensation in which we live, but also that today is the Last Saturday. Statements in *The Encyclopedia of Mormonism* appear to include secular knowledge, not just religious, or things pertaining to God's church and Kingdom.

New information, knowledge, and inventions have been created in abundance over the last several decades. I remember first hearing about computers as a teenager. Lasers came into existence at about the same time. The world of technology has exploded during my life. Artificial hearts, worldwide communications, videocassette recorders, microwave ovens, space exploration, cell phones, and smartphones are just a few of the areas in which knowledge and information have been revealed in the Last Days.

Much of the knowledge and enlightenment that has occurred can be discovered by reviewing new products and conveniences we now have in our lives. We now have smartphones, smart televisions, and now even smart refrigerators. We may soon have smart (self-driving) cars. There are advances in medicine, health care, and fitness. Today, there are drones and robots used in many fields and industries.

Global positioning systems can pinpoint your location within a couple of meters. Barcodes have streamlined purchases and shopping. Even light bulbs have become more advanced, efficient, and smarter.

The age of technology began when Herman Hollerith marketed a mechanical tabulating machine and founded the Tabulating Machine Company, which later became IBM (see wiki/Herman Hollerith). The term *computer* came into existence in the 1950s and 1960s. Since then, the knowledge, development, and growth of technology can be seen in virtually every sphere of civilization and the world.

William Joy, who was involved in the tech revolution, wrote about the power and scope of this technological advancement.

Joy was a cofounder and chief scientist of Sun Microsystems. He was extensively involved in the rapid advancement of technology and concluded that humans won't be needed in the future. Genetic engineering, nanotechnology, and artificial intelligence are creating power and means to seriously change the world.

In 1998, Joy became anxious about dangers we could face in the twenty-first century. He spoke at a conference with two other men. Here is what one of them said:

WHY THE FUTURE DOESN'T NEED US

> "The rate of improvement of technology was going to accelerate and that we were going to become robots or fuse with robots or something like that" …

> Accustomed to living with almost routine scientific breakthroughs, we have yet to come to terms with the fact that the most compelling 21st-century technologies— robotics, genetic engineering, and nanotechnology— pose a different threat than the technologies that have come before. Specifically, robots, engineered organisms, and nanobots share a dangerous amplifying factor: They can self-replicate. A bomb is blown up only once— but one bot can become many, and quickly get out of control. (Joy n.d.)

Technology is providing the masses with instant access to the world. Such extreme, extensive opportunities may pose serious problems and challenges.

The Lord's church, with all of its power, authority, doctrine, truths, and offices, would need to be in existence sometime before the Lord returns.

Paul, in his Epistle to the Ephesians, states that the Lord's church will be restored in the last dispensation.

> That in the dispensation of the fulness of times he might gather together in one all things in Christ, both which are in heaven, and which are on earth; *even* in him. (Ephesians 1:10)

Paul says that all things in Christ will be gathered together. The Lord's church, authority, power, indeed all things will be gathered, restored.

In a revelation given to Joseph Smith in August of 1830, the Lord again states that he will gather all things together. This will be done for the last time. This will be done on the Last Saturday.

> Unto whom I have committed the keys of my kingdom, and a dispensation of the gospel for the last times; and for the fulness of times, in the which I will gather together in one all things, both which are in heaven, and which are on earth. (Doc. & Cov. 27:13)

Isaiah, the Old Testament prophet, frequently describes the events and conditions of the Last Days:

> Zion shall be redeemed with judgment, and her converts with righteousness.
>
> And the destruction of the transgressors and of the sinners *shall be* together, and they that forsake the LORD shall be consumed. (Isaiah 1:27–28)

Isaiah says that Zion, the Lord's kingdom, city, or people, will be redeemed or restored and saved. The people of Zion will be righteous, and those who "forsake the Lord shall be consumed."

Bruce R. McConkie, a former apostle of the Church of Jesus Christ of Latter-Day Saints, made this statement about the knowledge to be revealed in the Last Days:

> All of the knowledge that has ever been revealed (plus some held in reserve to be revealed initially in the last days) will in due course come to light in this final dispensation. (McConkie 1966, 200)

The restoration of the Church of Jesus Christ through the prophet Joseph Smith started the restoration of all knowledge. The Book of Mormon is a major part of increased knowledge about Jesus Christ, his teachings, his doctrine, his Atonement, and the Plan of Salvation. This is knowledge revealed in this final dispensation.

The Doctrine and Covenants contains prophecies and information about the organization, administration, and management of the restored church of Christ; it contains even more knowledge that has been restored.

Knowledge of the Gospel and the Lord's latter-day kingdom continues to be restored through church publications. Continuing counsel, warnings, and revelation from the living apostles and prophets of the Church of Jesus Christ of Latter-Day Saints are also part of modern-day knowledge.

The Lord, through Joseph Smith, has said that saints who are faithful and obedient to the Lord's commandments "shall find wisdom and great treasures of knowledge, even hidden treasures" (see Doc. & Cov. 89:18–19). Faithful saints are truly receiving marvelous knowledge about the Last Saturday.

1.2. SECOND COMING

Christians believe that Jesus Christ will return to the earth. This return of Christ is known as the Second Coming.

SECOND COMING

The Second Coming (sometimes called the Second Advent or the Parousia) is a Christian and Islamic belief regarding the future return of Jesus Christ after his incarnation and ascension to heaven about two thousand years ago. (Second Coming 2019)

Historical documents concerning Jesus are quite extensive and reveal that He will come to the earth again. The English Nicene Creed most commonly used today includes these statements about Jesus:

He ascended into heaven and is seated at the right hand of the Father. He will come again in glory to judge the living and the dead, and his kingdom will have no end … We look for the resurrection of the dead, and the life of the world to come. (Christian 2019)

Many scriptures speak of the return of Jesus Christ to the earth. One of the most referenced and quoted is found in the book of Acts:

> And when he had spoken these things, while they beheld, he was taken up; and a cloud received him out of their sight.
>
> And while they looked steadfastly toward heaven as he went up, behold, two men stood by them in white apparel;
>
> Which also said, Ye men of Galilee, why stand ye gazing up into heaven? this same Jesus, which is taken up from you into heaven, shall so come in like manner as ye have seen him go into heaven. (Acts 1:9–11)

The earth's Sabbath, the final one-thousand-year period of its history, is often referred to as the Millennium. This is the period during which "Christ will reign personally upon the earth as King of kings and Lord of lords" (see Improvement Era, June 1967, 35).

Many of the church leaders and disciples of Jesus believed, and hoped, that he would return while they still lived on the earth. However, as the years passed, they came to realize that they didn't really know when he would return.

Peter, in his Second Epistle, concluded (or was told by the spirit) that the Lord will not return for some time. He reveals that in the Last Days, some will mock and reject the Lord's Second Coming:

> Knowing this first, that there shall come in the last days scoffers, walking after their own lusts, And saying, Where is the promise of his coming? for since the fathers fell asleep, all things continue as they were from the beginning of the creation. (2 Peter 3:3–4)

Peter indicates that those who have no faith, the unbelievers, will claim that a long time has passed, and Jesus hasn't returned. Nothing has changed. He is not coming back.

Of course, Christ's reign during the final thousand-year period will be preceded by his glorious Second Coming. That means that before the earth's Sabbath begins, the world must be cleansed. The Gospel must be preached to every nation. The wicked must be destroyed.

> Blow ye the trumpet in Zion, and sound an alarm in my
> holy mountain: let all the inhabitants of the land tremble:
> for the day of the Lord cometh, for it is nigh at hand.
>
> A day of darkness and of gloominess, a day of clouds
> and of thick darkness, as the morning spread upon the
> mountains: a great people and a strong; there hath not
> been ever the like, neither shall be any more after it,
> even to the years of many generations. (Joel 2:1–2)

Will the earth be cleansed and the wicked destroyed in one day, or one year? Most likely not. The cleansing and destruction may take many years. This may not even happen or be completed before Christ returns. We don't know.

Throughout the history of the earth, the Lord has on occasion cleansed the earth of the wickedness that defiled its face. Floods, wars, famine, pestilence, and disease have been used to destroy the wicked and unrighteous. The Lord has indicated that in preparing for the earth's Sabbath, it will be cleansed by fire.

> For behold, the day cometh that shall burn as an oven,
> and all the proud, yea, and all that do wickedly shall
> burn as stubble; for they that come shall burn them,
> saith the Lord of Hosts, that is shall leave them neither
> root nor branch. (Joseph Smith-History 1:37)

The scriptures are filled with statements and prophecies concerning the Second Coming of Christ and events that will take place on the Last Saturday of the earth's temporal existence. If we look at those prophecies and scriptures, if we examine them as they relate to the world today, we may come to realize how late it is on the Last Saturday. We should be able to make some decisions about our lives, the choices we are making, and the paths that we are taking.

The Lord, speaking to ancient Israel in Ezekiel chapter 14, states that he will not answer the wicked. If anyone in Israel, or any stranger in Israel, separates himself from the Lord, the Lord will not listen. When a man sets up idols in his heart and puts the stumbling block of his iniquity before his face, the Lord will not answer him when he comes to a prophet to inquire of the Lord. The Lord will cut him off from among the people.

How many people are there, even within the church, who are not receiving answers from the Lord, who are not blessed with the companionship of the Holy Spirit, who have never heard or listened to the still small voice? Have the people of the world, and even the Latter-Day Saints, separated themselves from the Lord?

Have we set up idols in our hearts and in our lives? Where do people and members of the Church of Jesus Christ of Latter-Day Saints spend their time, money, energy, and talents?

1.3. APOSTASY

Paul told the Thessalonians in his Second Epistle to them that they should remain faithful. The Lord will come again, but not until after a "falling away," or apostasy, has occurred.

> Be not soon shaken in mind, or be troubled, neither by spirit, nor by word, nor by letter as from us, as that the day of Christ is at hand.

> Let no man deceive you by any means: for that day shall not come, except there come a falling away first, and that man of sin be revealed, the son of perdition. (2 Thessalonians 2:2–3)

Paul tells the Thessalonians, who thought the day of Christ was at hand, that they should not be concerned or anxious about the return of Christ. He knew that before Christ comes again, the Gospel and Kingdom of God would be lost. Paul gave them a sign of the Second Coming, a sign they never saw. We, however, know that Paul's prophecy has been fulfilled.

History indicates that a falling away has already taken place. The Lord's church and many of his teachings, principles, and commandments were forgotten, intentionally changed, and lost upon the earth.

We know that after the deaths of the apostles, the world fell away from the teachings of Christ, which gave birth to the numerous religions found in the world today. Was the "man of sin revealed" during, or as a result of, the apostasy that took place after the death of Christ and his apostles?

The religious Reformation of the sixteenth century is a recorded and documented event in history. Encyclopedia Britannica describes some of the conditions that brought the Reformation about. The revolution led by Martin Luther and John Calvin had major effects on religion then and now.

The Reformation came about because the pope and Roman Catholic Church became involved in government, business, and everyday life. People became defiant and left the church because of its influence, power, and wealth. Reformers believed the religious doctrine and practices of their day were not in harmony with the teachings and Gospel of Jesus Christ.

Apostasy of the Lord's Kingdom had already occurred. The desires and actions of the reformers, however sincere in intent, did not restore the Lord's true teachings, authority, and church to the earth. Churches and religious teachings continued to become scripture mixed with the precepts and beliefs of humans.

Did this apostasy reveal the man of sin? Who is the man of sin? Who is the son of perdition? Holy scriptures teach us that he is Satan. He, more than any other being, wants to change God's plans and destroy the kingdom of Jesus Christ. Surely, he played a role in bringing about the apostasy. Was he not revealed by this act? Did men begin to sin without the true teachings and church of Christ?

During Joseph Smith's first vision and conversation with the Father and the Son, the Lord confirmed that His teachings and doctrines were no longer being taught. The Lord's church was no longer on earth. We had changed and corrupted His teachings.

> I was answered that I must join none of them, for they were all wrong; and the Personage who addressed me said that all their creeds were an abomination in his sight; that those professors were all corrupt; that: "they draw near to me with their lips, but their hearts are far from me, they teach for doctrines the commandments

of men, having a form of godliness, but they deny the power thereof." (Joseph Smith, History 19)

When Joseph Smith was born, and during his early life, the Lord's kingdom was not here. He acted, under divine direction, to bring it back to the earth.

Peter's reference to a falling away also describes events and conditions of the Last Days. We may need to see a falling away from Christianity and righteousness in the Last Days before the Lord is again sent from heaven. Has there been a falling away from Christ's teachings in recent times? Have Latter-Day Saints fallen away from the church? Is there more wickedness and evil in today's world than there was just a few years ago? Have truly righteous people become the minority?

1.4. WICKEDNESS AND EVIL

Signs of the Last Days may include apostasy from righteousness by man, societies, and even followers of Christ. Will wickedness and evil be prominent just before the Lord comes again?

> Verily, verily, I say unto you darkness covereth the earth, and gross darkness the minds of the people, and all flesh has become corrupt before my face.
>
> Behold, vengeance cometh speedily upon the inhabitants of the earth, a day of wrath, a day of burning, a day of desolation, of weeping, of mourning, and of lamentation; and as a whirlwind it shall come upon all the face of the earth saith the Lord. (Doc. & Cov. 112:23–24)

The Lord in these latter days has declared that darkness, weeping, and desolation shall come upon the earth. The scripture says that darkness covers the earth. What kind of darkness? Are days, even sunny ones, darker than they used to be? Does greater darkness exist in our minds, hearts, and lives? The darkness spoken of here may not only be the difference between physical light and dark.

Is the world currently in a day of burning, desolation, weeping, mourning, and lamentation? Is the whole face of the earth filled with evil, crime, and wickedness? Sophocles, the ancient Greek playwright, wrote about Philoctetes, the ancient archer; he makes an interesting statement about wickedness:

> The soul that has conceived one wickedness can nurse
> no good thereafter. (Sophocles n.d.)

If Sophocles is correct, then evil and wickedness are growing and constantly increasing. We should see greater wickedness and evil as Last Saturday is ushered in.

Today's headlines, more than ever before, are about children being killed:

> CHILDREN ARE BEING KILLED, BECAUSE
> SOME ADULTS THINK LIFE IS A GAME.

> Something is amiss.

> When children shoot up other children in school, it's a national tragedy, and a week of mourning.

> When grown men are killing unarmed young, yes unarmed young, it bespeaks the leagues of fear residing in these men's hearts; …

> If adults don't truly grow up, then their young may never get the chance. (Beau n.d.)

Many of these children are being killed at school. Since the 1999 massacre at Columbine High School in Littleton, Colorado, school shootings have increased. This event alone indicates that wickedness is escalating.

However, children are not the only ones being killed. People are randomly and wantonly killing others without provocation or cause. They even do it without conscience or in secret.

POLICE: SUSPECT KILLS ELDERLY VICTIM ON FACEBOOK; LIVE MANHUNT CONTINUES

CLEVELAND, Ohio. Police say a man killed someone on Facebook Live and a manhunt is underway Sunday.

The suspect broadcast the killing on Facebook Live around 2 p.m. ET, police said, and has claimed to have committed multiple other homicides which are yet to be verified …

In the video, which has been removed from Facebook, the suspect pulls up to an elderly man who is walking on the side of the road. He tells the man to say a woman's name and pulls out his gun. The elderly man repeatedly tells the suspect he doesn't know the woman—believed to be [the suspect's] former girlfriend—but the suspect pulls the trigger, shooting the man in the head, leaving him bloodied in the street. (CBS News 2017)

Increasing evil and wickedness is not occurring only in the United States.

VIDEO RELEASED OF SUSPECTS IN TEEN'S SLAYING AT PIZZA PIZZA

TORONTO. A group of teenage friends were having a bite to eat at a pizza shop early last Sunday when two gunmen suddenly burst in and opened fire.

Jarryl Hagley, 17, was killed in the "frenzied attack." (Doucette 2016)

UNION BOSS CALLS FOR TERROR SUMMIT
AFTER "DEVICE" IS BLOWN UP ON TUBE

A TUBE union boss today demanded an emergency "summit" between transport chiefs, police and City Hall to discuss security after a terror alert at North Greenwich.

Manuel Cortes, leader of the white-collar TSSA, demanded assurances about the safety of passengers and staff—and warned he would demand the Tube network be closed if they were not forthcoming.

His comments came as one source claimed that the alert was sparked after a Tfl worker discovered an abandoned bag "full of wires" on an eastbound Jubilee line train yesterday morning. (Davenport 2016, 2)

Evil and wickedness are manifest throughout the world.

1.5. RESTORATION

Peter, the apostle, reveals to us that Christ will reside in heaven until the times when his teachings are restored to the earth.

Repent ye therefore, and be converted, that your sins may be blotted out, when the times of refreshing shall come from the presence of the Lord.

And he shall send Jesus Christ, which before was preached unto you:

Whom the heaven must receive until the times of restitution of all things, which God hath spoken by the mouth of all his holy prophets since the world began. (Acts 3:19–21)

Peter says there will be a time of refreshing. Jesus Christ will be sent back to the earth, during or at the beginning of "the times of restitution of all things." According to Merriam-Webster Dictionary, *restitution* is "an act of restoring or a condition of being restored." Therefore, Peter is declaring that there will be a restoration of all things spoken of by all of the Lord's prophets.

Isaiah, the Old Testament prophet, also speaks of the restoration of the Lord's church, gospel, and kingdom in the Last Days:

> And it shall come to pass in the last days, that the mountain of the Lord's house shall be established in the top of the mountains, and shall be exalted above the hills; and all nations shall flow unto it.

> And many people shall go and say, Come ye, and let us go up to the mountains of the Lord, to the house of the God of Jacob; and he will teach us of his ways, and we will walk in his paths: for out of Zion shall go forth the law, and the word of the Lord from Jerusalem. (Isaiah 2:2–3)

Isaiah also makes other declarations concerning a restoration of knowledge.

> For the earth shall be full of the knowledge of the Lord,
> as the waters cover the sea. (Isaiah 11:9)

The Lord's house, his kingdom or temple, has been established in the tops of the mountains. It is where people go to be taught and receive knowledge. The restoration of all things has been accomplished through the mission and work of the prophet Joseph Smith. The earth is now full of the knowledge of the Lord.

Have the prophecies of the restoration of all things been fulfilled? Yes.

Joseph Smith's efforts, work, and ministry, in the restoration of the Lord's house and knowledge of the Lord, are extensive and miraculous.

The world headquarters of the Church of Jesus Christ of Latter-Day Saints is in Salt Lake City, Utah. This church is the fruit of the restoration completed by Joseph Smith. Salt Lake City is surrounded by majestic mountains. It is easy to see that the Lord's house has "been established in the tops of the mountains."

Are people, businesses, and nations flowing to the Lord's house in the mountains?

America's Fastest-Growing Cities 2016

Last year the economy in the Salt Lake City metropolitan statistical area grew 6.93%, the fourth-fastest rate among America's 100 largest metro areas …

But Utah's fastest-growing cities are exhibiting impressive acceleration: Salt Lake City jumped seven spots on our list and Ogden returns to it after falling off in 2015. (Carlyle 2016)

Reports about the growth and progress of Utah and the state's capital city are numerous and easy to discover. The growth and prosperity of Salt Lake City are testaments that today is the day we are claiming it to be.

Utah Growing Twice as Fast as Nation as Whole

Utah's population grew by 6.08 percent since the last full U.S. census count in 2010, to 2,942,902 residents in 2014.

The United States as a whole expanded by 3.1 percent during the same period. The country's population is currently at 320.9 million, about 2.03 million above where it was July 4, 2014.

Utah's 6.08 percent gain made it the fourth fastest-growing state so far this decade, behind North Dakota (9.7%), Texas (6.8%) and Colorado (6.09%). (Semerad 2015)

The current growth of Utah and Salt Lake City indicates that nations are flowing to the Lord's house. Utah's growth is not just from Utah residents.

Utah Ranks No. 2 in Growth of Residents Who Speak a Language besides English at Home

During this decade, Utah sped along to the second-fastest growth rate for residents who speak a language other than English while at home, a shift driven by the children of immigrants.

That population grew by 20 percent between 2010 and 2016, second only to the 25 percent growth rate in Wyoming, according to a Center for Immigration Studies report released Wednesday, which relied on U.S. Census Bureau data. (Davidson 2017)

In Ezekiel chapter 37, the Lord instructed Ezekiel that he should take two sticks, one for Judah and the children of Israel, the other for Joseph, the stick of Ephraim, for all his companions in the house of Israel. These two sticks are to become one. The Bible is the stick of Judah, and the Book of Mormon is the stick of Joseph (see Ezekiel 37:15–19).

Ezekiel 37:20 says that "the sticks whereon thou writest shall be in thine hand before their eyes." Ezekiel is writing on sticks or scrolls. He is writing books.

These two books, the Bible and the Book of Mormon, both of which contain books, fulfill the instructions and prophecy given to Ezekiel.

They both testify of Jesus Christ. Both books contain the teachings of prophets and the Lord Jesus Christ. They become one as the Gospel restored by Joseph Smith spreads throughout the world.

As people around the world learn about the restoration of the Lord's Kingdom by Joseph Smith, they receive the Book of Mormon (the stick of Ephraim). The knowledge and truths of the Book of Mormon are merged with the knowledge and truths of the Bible. The two sticks spoken of in Ezekiel become "one in their hands."

Ezekiel's prophecy has come to pass. The book of Judah and book of Ephraim are signs that it is the Last Saturday.

The LDS Hymnbook contains a hymn titled "High on the Mountain Top".

> High on the mountain top, A banner is unfurled.
> Ye nations, now look up; It waves to all the world.
> In Deseret's sweet peaceful land,
> On Zion's mount behold it stand!
>
> For God remembers still, His promise made of old
> That he on Zion's hill, Truth's standard would unfold!
> Her light should there attract the gaze,
> Of all the world in latter days. (Johnson and Beesley 1998, 5)

Through the restoration of the Gospel and the re-establishment of the Lord's Kingdom here on earth, a banner has been unfurled. During the last twenty years, the world has seen the banner. Those who came to the Salt Lake City 2002 Winter Games saw the banner first-hand. Restored Gospel truths are being taught to many nations, kindreds, tongues, and people. The law and truth are going forth to all the world.

1.6. GATHERING OF ISRAEL

One of the most prominent prophecies found in the scriptures concerns the gathering of the Children of Israel.

GATHERING OF ISRAEL

> The Gathering of Israel … is the biblical promise of Deuteronomy 30:1–5 given by Moses to the people of Israel prior to their entrance into the Land of Israel (*Eretz Yisrael*).

During the days of the Babylonian exile, writings of the prophets Isaiah and Ezekiel encouraged the people of Israel with a promise of a future gathering of the exiles to the land of Israel. The continual hope for a return of the Israelite exiles to the land has been in the hearts of Jews ever since the destruction of the Second Temple …

The gathering of the exiles in the land of Israel, became the core idea of the Zionist Movement and the core idea of Israel's Scroll of Independence, embodied by the idea of going up, Aliyah, since the *Holy Land* is considered to be spiritually higher than all other land. The immigration of Jews to the land and the State of Israel, … has been likened to the Exodus from Egypt. (Gathering_of_Israel 2019)

Ezekiel the prophet frequently declares that the Lord will gather his people. He claims that the Lord will gather His sheep from wherever they have been scattered, into their own land.

For thus saith the Lord God; Behold, I, even I, will both search my sheep, and seek them out.

As a shepherd seeketh out his flock in the day that he is among his sheep that are scattered; so will I seek out my sheep, and will deliver them out of all places where they have been scattered in the cloudy and dark day.

And I will bring them out from the people, and gather them from the countries, and will bring them to their own land, and feed them upon the mountains of Israel by the rivers, and in all the inhabited places of the country. (Ezekiel 34:11–13)

The Lord indicates that during the Last Days, he will gather Israel. He will take them from among the heathens and bring Israel to its own land. He will give Israel a new heart and a new spirit (see Ezekiel 36).

The prophet Isaiah also revealed to us that the Lord will recover and gather his people.

> And it shall come to pass in that day that the Lord shall set his hand again the second time to recover the remnant of his people which shall be left, from Assyria, and from Egypt, and from Pathros, and from Cush, and from Elam, and from Shinar, and from Hamath, and from the islands of the sea.
>
> And he shall set up an ensign for the nations, and shall assemble the outcasts of Israel, and gather together the dispersed of Judah from the four corners of the earth. (Isaiah 11:11–12)

Isaiah claims that the children of Israel will be gathered from "the four corners of the earth." He further states that the Lord will gather his people for the second time. Have they been gathered before, or are they being gathered today for the first time?

GATHERING SCATTERED ISRAEL

> After generations of servitude, the Israelites were miraculously delivered by Moses. Their migration from Egypt back to the land of Canaan took place over a 40-year period of travail in the wilderness. The exodus from Egypt and subsequent settlement of the promised land was the *first gathering* of the people now called Israel. Moses sought not only to restore them to their land but also to recommit them to their faith in God. (Browning 1998)

Religious and secular records explain historical events where the children of Israel were scattered and consequently gathered.

The Hebrews requested that a king should rule them. The prophet Samuel warned them against this choice, and the book of Kings reveals the consequences of the Hebrews' actions. Saul, David, and Solomon became kings of Israel. After Solomon's death, Israel was divided into two kingdoms: the northern kingdom of Israel and the southern kingdom of Judah.

Due to the rule of wicked kings in both kingdoms, each was taken captive; the northern kingdom was conquered by the Assyrians, the southern kingdom by Babylon and Nebuchadnezzar. The people of the northern kingdom were spread throughout the Assyrian Empire and were lost from history. They are now known as the "lost ten tribes." The Babylonians moved the people but did not scatter them like the Assyrians.

Babylonian rule over the two southern tribes of Israel ended in 538 BCE and is described in the books of Ezra and Nehemiah. Cyrus the Great allowed the Jews to return (gather) to the homeland.

The Jewish people have been scattered in various degrees throughout their history. Prophetic scripture declares that they will be scattered and gathered as a people twice. The International Christian Embassy Jerusalem agrees that the Children of Israel will return home twice.

What Does the Bible Have to Say about the Return of the Jews to Their Homeland?

> The first return was predicted by the prophet Jeremiah to take place after Israel had been in captivity for 70 years …
>
> After 500 years of intermittent and partial sovereignty in the Land, the Jewish people were once again dispersed under the Roman Empire in AD 70 …
>
> The Second Return is from All Nations
>
> This second return was to be from every nation where they had been dispersed. (Michael 2018)

The first chapter of the book of Ezra, in the Old Testament, reveals how the Jewish people returned to their homeland, fulfilling the first return prophesy.

During the last century, over 3 million Jewish people have returned to their homeland, from nations all over the world. The prophecy of a second return is quickly becoming reality, as God promised (see Isaiah 43:5–6).

The Lord in modern revelation has spoken extensively about the gathering of Israel in the Last Days. These scriptures also declare that God's chosen people will be scattered and gathered from among all nations.

> Ye say that ye know that the end of the world cometh; ye say also that ye know that the heavens and the earth shall pass away;
>
> And in this ye say truly, for so it is; but these things which I have told you shall not pass away until all shall be fulfilled.
>
> And this I have told you concerning Jerusalem; and when that day shall come, shall a remnant be scattered among all nations;
>
> But they shall be gathered again; but they shall remain until the times of the Gentiles be fulfilled. (Doc. & Cov. 45:22–25)

Recent revelation also talks about gathering the Latter-Day Saints throughout the world. This gathering involves bringing people to the Lord's church in the Last Days. Members of the Church of Jesus Christ of Latter-Day Saints become adopted children of Israel. They become part of the gathering of Israel.

> Wherefore I, the Lord, have said, gather ye out from the eastern lands, assemble ye yourselves together ye elders of my church; go ye forth into the western countries, call upon the inhabitants to repent, and inasmuch as they do repent, build up churches unto me.

And it shall be called the New Jerusalem, a land of peace, a city of refuge, a place of safety for the saints of the Most High God;

And the glory of the Lord shall be there, and the terror of the Lord also shall be there, insomuch that the wicked will not come unto it, and it shall be called Zion. (Doc. & Cov. 45:64, 66–67)

When the saints of the restoration are gathered to the New Jerusalem, the Lord's glory will be with them. The Lord's terror will also be there, which will serve as a protection to the righteous and deter the wicked from gathering there.

And it shall come to pass among the wicked, that every man that will not take his sword against his neighbor must needs flee unto Zion for safety.

And there shall be gathered unto it out of every nation under heaven; and it shall be the only people that shall not be at war one with another.

And it shall be said among the wicked: Let us not go up to battle against Zion, for the inhabitants of Zion are terrible; wherefore we cannot stand.

And it shall come to pass that the righteous shall be gathered out from among all nations, and shall come to Zion, singing with songs of everlasting joy. (Doc. & Cov. 45:68–71)

These words of the Lord through Joseph Smith sound like the gathering of Last Saturday. We see increasing wickedness in the world today. Almost every wicked person is taking "his sword against his neighbor." The righteous may soon flee to Zion for refuge and safety.

When the iniquity of all nations is full, those who belong to the family of Israel will be gathered. If the iniquity of all nations is not yet full, it will be soon.

> Mine indignation is soon to be poured out without measure upon all nations; and this will I do when the cup of their iniquity is full.
>
> And in that day all who are found upon the watch-tower, or in other words, all mine Israel, shall be saved.
>
> And they that have been scattered shall be gathered. (Doc. & Cov. 101:11–13)

The Church of Jesus Christ of Latter-Day Saints acknowledges and is part of the latter-day gathering of Israel.

> We believe in the literal gathering of Israel and in the restoration of the Ten Tribes; that Zion (the New Jerusalem) will be built upon the American continent; that Christ will reign personally upon the earth; and, that the earth will be renewed and receive its paradisiacal glory. (Articles of Faith #10)

The prophet Nephi in the Book of Mormon prophetically confirms the dispersal and gathering of the Lord's chosen people.

> And as for those who are at Jerusalem, saith the prophet, they shall be scourged by all people, because they crucify the God of Israel, and turn their hearts aside, rejecting signs and wonders, and the power and glory of the God of Israel.
>
> And because they turn their hearts aside, saith the prophet, and have despised the Holy One of Israel, they shall wander in the flesh, and perish, and become a hiss and a byword, and be hated among all nations.

> Nevertheless, when that day cometh, saith the prophet,
> that they no more turn aside their hearts against the
> Holy One of Israel, then will he remember the covenants
> which he made to their fathers. (1 Nephi 19:13–15)

The children of Israel who were at Jerusalem will wander among all nations, be hated by them, and perish. When they turn their hearts to the Holy One of Israel, they will be gathered from the four quarters of the earth.

A quick review and search of history will confirm that this sign of the times has come to pass. To some extent, this prophecy is still being fulfilled in various nations and societies.

Scriptures received in these Last Days declare that the righteous must flee from Babylon and gather to the Lord's restored church. These scriptures speak of how people from all nations will hear and learn about the Lord (see Doc. & Cov. 133). These verses also contain interesting descriptions of events of the Last Days.

> And they who are in the north countries shall come in
> remembrance before the Lord; and their prophets shall
> hear his voice, and shall no longer stay themselves; and
> they shall smite the rocks, and the ice shall flow down
> at their presence.
>
> And an highway shall be cast up in the midst of the
> great deep.
>
> And in the barren deserts there shall come forth pools
> of living water; and the parched ground shall no longer
> be a thirsty land. (Doc. & Cov. 133:26–27, 29)

Many of these verses could have various meanings and interpretations. They do, however, refer to the Last Days. Those who "come in remembrance before the Lord" could mean that they will learn of him and the restored Gospel.

Have we seen ice "flow down at their presence"? Perhaps people who are gathered are no longer out in the cold. They receive the light and warmth of the Savior's teachings, hope, and love.

A highway will be "cast up in the midst of the great deep." How many saints crossed the Atlantic Ocean to join the saints in America? Many of them became pioneers and trekked across the plains. How many are crossing highways of the deep today? Many of those crossing today come from countries around the world. They may not be aware of why they are crossing to the United States of America.

"Pools of living water shall come forth," and "parched ground" is no longer thirsty. The prophecy of these scriptures has, and is, being fulfilled. Do we not consider that the desert Southwest of the United States, as well as other regions around the world, no longer thirsts for the Word of the Lord? The gathering of Israel and the Latter-Day Saints is taking place around the world. The people of earth are receiving the living waters of Christ.

In February of 2018, the United States announced that it would move its embassy in Israel from Tel Aviv to Jerusalem.

US WILL "MOVE ITS EMBASSY TO JERUSALEM BY MAY"

The US will move its embassy to Jerusalem by May of this year in time to mark the 70th anniversary of Israel's independence, Israeli media reported.

A US official said an official announcement is expected late on Friday, finally setting a date for Donald Trump's controversial decision to go into force. (Sanchez 2018)

The announcement ended a long period of American neutrality concerning the Israeli city. In February, the US confirmed that the embassy would be moved from Tel Aviv to Jerusalem. The embassy was moved later in 2018.

In 1995, the US passed the Jerusalem Embassy Act, which recognized Jerusalem as the capital of Israel. The US embassy was to be moved to Jerusalem before May 31, 1999. The embassy was not moved because of the conflicts between Israel and the Palestinians. The embassy move could be an indication of the gathering of Israel, signifying that we live in the Last Days.

Moving the US embassy and officially acknowledging Jerusalem as the capital of Israel could be signs.

If today is the Last Saturday, the Lord should be gathering the children of Israel to Jerusalem.

The ensign spoken of by Isaiah has been set up. The Children of Israel are gathering and being gathered. Many are returning to their homeland, being gathered physically, while others are being gathered into the restored Church of Jesus Christ. They are being gathered by the worldwide missionary efforts of the Church of Jesus Christ of Latter-Day Saints.

1.7. Armageddon

Ezekiel chapters 38 and 39 reveal some interesting things about the Last Days. The battle of Armageddon against Israel is described. The army of Gog and Magog, horses and horsemen, clothed with all sorts of swords, armor, bucklers, and shields, are to ascend and come like a cloud against Israel.

The Lord says that when Gog comes to fight Israel, his fury shall come up in his face. Then because of his jealousy and wrath, there shall be a great shaking in Israel.

> So that the fishes of the sea, and the fowls of the heaven, and the beasts of the field, and all creeping things that creep upon the earth, and all the men that are upon the face of the earth, shall shake at my presence, and the mountains shall be thrown down, and the steep places shall fall, and every wall shall fall to the ground.
>
> And I will call for a sword against him throughout all my mountains, saith the Lord God: every man's sword shall be against his brother.

And I will plead against him with pestilence and with blood; and I will rain upon him, and upon his bands, and upon the many people that are with him, and overflowing rain, and great hailstones, fire, and brimstone. (Ezekiel 38:20–22)

We may believe that the battle of Armageddon has not yet occurred. The fish and fowls have not yet been shaken, have they? But the signs indicate that the battle is close at hand, or at least the skirmishes leading to the main battle are under way.

For many years, the Middle East has been a region of conflict and strife. People in Israel may say that a "great shaking" is taking place because of the events and fallout of war. The shaking spoken of by Ezekiel may be more than the shaking of the earth. Today's artillery and weapons can make the earth shake.

Ezekiel says that the Lord "will rain upon him" [people]. We may ask, rain what on us? The rain may be many different things and not limited to natural events. Bombs, bullets, hate, evil, wickedness, and death could be rained down, and cause us to shake.

As we examine prophecy and the world today, it may well be time for us to shake because of the wickedness and evil pouring out upon the earth and in people's hearts.

If the rain is water, we are indeed seeing it rain down upon the earth.

MAJOR HURRICANE HARVEY

August 25–29, 2017. Harvey exploded rapidly from a tropical depression to a major hurricane in around 40 hours. After impacting the Yucatan Peninsula earlier in the month as a tropical storm, Harvey moved into the warm waters of the Gulf of Mexico late on Tuesday August 22nd …

On Thursday August 24th, Harvey's impact on the Middle and Upper Texas Coast seemed almost certain and potentially devastating. Not only was Harvey forecast to become a hurricane by Thursday evening, but it was expected to strengthen and make landfall as a major hurricane (Category 3 or higher) on Friday …

Many observing stations in South Texas with equipment measuring wind speeds were disabled before they could record the highest wind speeds …

Southeast Texas bore the brunt of the heavy rainfall, with some areas receiving more than 40 inches of rain in less than 48 hours! Cedar Bayou in Houston received a storm total of 51.88 inches of rainfall which is a new North American record. (Hurricane Harvey 2017)

If rainwater records are being broken, does that not clearly indicate that greater rain (water) is being poured down upon us? This fact, with record rain that we hear about in some parts of the world, is a sign of the Last Days and a fulfillment of scripture.

The rain referred to by Ezekiel may not be just water. The rain may be the wrath of God. It may be natural disasters. It may be the secret works of Satan. Is it famine? Is it hatred? "Rain down" may not necessarily mean something from the sky. The rain could be the evil and dishonest actions of people.

Are we indeed witnessing events that will soon lead up to the battle of Armageddon?

The earth shall quake before them; the heavens shall tremble: the sun and the moon shall be dark, and the stars shall withdraw their shining:

And the Lord shall utter his voice before his army: for his camp is very great: for he is strong that executed his word: for the day of the Lord is great and very terrible; and who can abide it?

> Therefore also now, saith the Lord, turn ye even to me
> with all your heart, and with fasting, and with weeping,
> and with mourning. (Joel 2:10–12)

Current world events and past news headlines should convince us that Armageddon is fast approaching. It is time for us to turn to the Lord with all our heart.

THE CATHERINE FULLER CASE: EIGHT YOUNG MEN AND THE MURDER THAT SENT THEM AWAY FOR LIFE

> The murder of Catherine Fuller rocked the relative calm of 1984 Washington DC. Fuller, a 49-year-old wife and mother, was sodomized with a pipe, and kicked and beaten to death for $40 and the cheap jewelry she wore. It was perhaps the most savage and senseless killing in District history. That's what the police said, anyway.

> Detectives quickly called it a gang attack. By the time their investigation ended they had arrested 17 people for the crime. (Lybdahl 2017)

A gang attacks, robs, and beats a woman to death. Such choices and actions are not isolated incidents in our world today.

In January 1996, six young men were charged with beating and killing a sixteen-year-old boy. The young man who led the attack testified against the others. The killing was brutal and apparently random. It shocked the peaceful neighborhood of northeast Philadelphia. The young men used baseball bats and steel-tipped boots in the attack (see https://apnews.com/1059e1c60ac2193856f9087c70fcb616).

It doesn't matter if an assault results in the loss of a single life or multiple lives. The act is still an omen of the Last Day's Armageddon.

LAS VEGAS SHOOTING: AT LEAST 59 DEAD IN MASSACRE TRUMP CALLS "ACT OF PURE EVIL"

A gunman turned a Las Vegas concert into a killing field Sunday night from his perch on the 32nd floor of the Mandalay Bay Resort and Casino, using at least 10 guns to rain down a steady stream of fire, murdering at least 59 people and injuring more than 520 others in the deadliest mass shooting in modern United States history …

Paddock reportedly had about 23 guns in his hotel room, according to police in an evening press conference. (Fox News 2017)

Las Vegas had bullets, terror, and chaos raining down one evening in October.

Fully automatic weapons manufactured after the 1980s are illegal in the United States. Guns made before 1980 may still be purchased, subject to heavy regulations and background checks. However, semi-automatic weapons can be illegally converted to automatic weapons.

In the Old Testament, Ezekiel gives a further indication of how terrible this battle in the Last Days will be. The Lord states that the inhabitants of the cities of Israel will go forth to burn the weapons of this battle. This they will do for seven years. The dead will then be buried for seven months (see Ezekiel 39).

News and information about this terrible battle would surely be spread throughout the world. We can, as of today, feel confident that this great battle has not yet happened. We hear, and can read, about the battles leading up to it almost daily.

The days just before the Lord again appears on earth will be great and terrible. But those who hold to the rod and walk in the Lord's light will abide and will receive great blessings and rewards.

1.8. SAINTS KNOW SIGNS

The Lord's apostle Peter speaks of those in the Last Days who will doubt and scoff at the Lord's Second Coming:

> That ye may be mindful of the words which were spoken before by the holy prophets, and of the commandment of us the apostles of the Lord and Saviour:
>
> Knowing this first, that there shall come in the last days scoffers, walking after their own lusts, And saying, Where is the promise of his coming? for since the fathers fell asleep, all things continue as they were from the beginning of the creation. (2 Peter 3:2–4)

We may not currently hear scoffers who are denying the return of Jesus Christ. However, all things are not like the beginning. The events, lives, and choices of many people today are indications of his return. The evidence is right outside your door.

Peter says we should remember the words spoken by prophets and apostles. He then speaks of the Lord's return and what we should do as prophecies come to pass.

> But the day of the Lord will come as a thief in the night; in the which the heavens shall pass away with a great noise, and the elements shall melt with fervent heat, the earth also and the works that are therein shall be burned up.
>
> Seeing then *that* all these things shall be dissolved, what manner of persons ought ye to be in all holy conversation and godliness, Looking for and hasting unto the coming of the day of God, wherein the heavens being on fire shall be dissolved, and the elements shall melt with fervent heat? (2 Peter 3:10–12)

Peter teaches that we should not doubt the return of Jesus Christ. We should be holy and faithful. We should be looking for and hastening the Lord's return.

No one knows the day, except by the signs of the times, as they are described in the scriptures. The apostle Paul in his Epistle to the Thessalonians indicates that the saints would, and should, know that the Savior's coming is near at hand.

> For yourselves know perfectly that the day of the Lord so cometh as a thief in the night.
>
> For when they shall say, Peace and safety; then sudden destruction cometh upon them, as travail upon a woman with child; and they shall not escape.
>
> But ye, brethren, are not in darkness, that that day should overtake you as a thief.
>
> Ye are all the children of light, and the children of the day: we are not of the night, nor of darkness. (1 Thessalonians 5:2–5)

The apostle Paul teaches us things we should know and understand. He tells us we should watch and be vigilant. In verse 8, he describes how we should be and what we should do:

> But let us, who are of the day, be sober, putting on the breastplate of faith and love; and for an helmet, the hope of salvation. (1 Thessalonians 5:8)

Paul teaches that we, as disciples of Christ, and latter-day members of his church, are not in darkness. We are children of light and should watch and prepare for the Lord's coming. Because of our knowledge and faith, we should "not sleep." We should look forward to and rejoice in the Lord's return.

The Old Testament prophet Isaiah talks about a "sealed book." people whose hearts are far from him, and a marvelous work to be done among the people:

> And the vision of all is become unto you as the words of a book that is sealed, which men deliver to one that is learned, saying, Read this, I pray thee: and he saith, I cannot; for it *is* sealed:

> And the book is delivered to him that is not learned, saying, Read this, I pray thee: and he saith, I am not learned.

> Wherefore the Lord said, Forasmuch as this people draw near *me* with their mouth, and with their lips do honour me, but have removed their heart far from me, and their fear toward me is taught by the precept of men:

> Therefore, behold, I will proceed to do a marvellous work among this people, *even* a marvellous work and a wonder: for the wisdom of their wise *men* shall perish, and the understanding of their prudent *men* shall be hid. (Isaiah 29:11–14)

We know these prophecies by Isaiah have been fulfilled and are signs of the times. Isaiah's words came to pass in 1828 when Martin Harris visited Professor Charles Anthon in New York City:

> I went to the city of New York, and presented the characters which had been translated, with the translation thereof, to Professor Charles Anthon, a gentleman celebrated for his literary attainments. Professor Anthon stated that the translation was correct, more so than any he had before seen translated from the Egyptian. I then showed him those which were not yet translated, and he said that they were Egyptian, Chaldaic, Assyriac, and Arabic; and he said they were true characters. He gave

me a certificate, certifying to the people of Palmyra
that they were true characters, and that the translation
of such of them as had been translated was also correct.
I took the certificate and put it into my pocket, and was
just leaving the house, when Mr. Anthon called me
back, and asked me how the young man found out that
there were gold plates in the place where he found them.
I answered that an angel of God had revealed it unto
him. (Joseph Smith - History 1:64)

Professor Anthon then took the certificate from Joseph and tore it
up. He said that ministering of angels no longer existed. When Joseph
told him the plates were sealed, Anthon said, "I cannot read a sealed
book," literally fulfilling Isaiah's prophecy.

Joseph then took the translated characters to Dr. Mitchell. He
verified and confirmed what Professor Anthon had said concerning
the characters and the translation.

The modern-day fulfillment of this ancient prophecy about a sealed
book occurred over one hundred and fifty years ago. It is a clear sign of
the times and evidence of the Last Saturday. The marvelous work and
wonder spoken of by Isaiah has happened, and is happening. The great
work and wonder is the restoration the Lord initiated through Joseph
Smith.

Joel, the prophet in the Old Testament, describes dark and glorious
events and conditions of the Last Days. His descriptions help us to
understand and acknowledge the signs of the Last Saturday:

And it shall come to pass afterward, that I will pour my
spirit upon all flesh; and your sons and your daughters
shall prophesy, your old men shall dream dreams, your
young men shall see visions:

And also upon the servants and upon the handmaids in
those days will I pour out my spirit. (Joel 2:28–29)

Joel says that the Lord will pour his spirit upon all flesh. People shall prophesy, have dreams, and see visions. He has done this with Joseph Smith, other modern-day prophets, heavenly messengers, Latter-Day Saints, and those who follow the Savior.

> And I will shew wonders in the heavens and in the earth,
> blood and fire, and pillars of smoke. (Joel 2:30)

He will show wonders in heaven and on the earth. These wonders are surely angels and messengers from heaven, who were part of the restoration of Jesus's Gospel and church. We have seen, and are seeing, wonders on earth. Natural wonders of fire and devastation, and wonders of human progress and achievements.

> The sun shall be turned into darkness, and the moon
> into blood, before the great and terrible day of the Lord
> come. (Joel 2:31)

Many locations around the world have problems with air pollution. This pollution can sometimes darken the sun. As crime and evil increase, becoming more frequent and prevalent, these acts also turn the sun into darkness.

Has the moon been turned into blood? If we are thinking literally into blood, the answer is no. However, pollution and atmospheric conditions that sometimes exist today can turn the moon red, figuratively into blood. The acts of violence and murder, now committed at night, have also turned the moon to blood.

> And it shall come to pass, that whosoever shall call on
> the name of the Lord shall be delivered: for in mount
> Zion and in Jerusalem shall be deliverance, as the Lord
> hath said, and in the remnant whom the Lord shall call.
> (Joel 2:32)

We can open our eyes, see, and recognize the signs of the Second Coming. How are we delivered from the dark and destructive events of the Last Days? We become true Christians and "call on the name of the Lord."

The Lord, through the prophet Isaiah, indicated that when the Gospel is restored, the desert will blossom and he will come. During this time, Israel will be gathered, and Zion will be established. Many of these prophecies have been fulfilled, and others are currently being fulfilled (see Isaiah 35).

David, in the book of Psalms, tells us that when Zion is built up, the Lord will come (see Psalm 102:16). We as Latter-Day Saints should look for and find peace in the signs of the times.

1.9. RIGHTEOUSNESS AND RELIGION

We know that wickedness and evil will increase as the Lord's Second Coming approaches. But what about truth and righteousness? Do we know that faith, religions, and righteousness will grow and spread? Will the gulf between the righteous and the wicked widen? Do we know what will happen to the Lord's Kingdom in the Last Days? Has Zion been built up? If today really is the Last Saturday, what do we expect to see happening in the church and the Kingdom of God?

Righteousness, or rectitude, is "the quality of being morally right or justifiable." This theological concept is sometimes found in Dharma and Abrahamic traditions. Various perspectives in Christianity, Judaism, and Islam consider it an attribute that implies that a person's actions are justified. It can also imply that a person has been "judged" or "reckoned" and is living a life pleasing to God (see Wikipedia: Righteousness, 04/22/2019).

We can look at the world today and decide if righteousness is increasing or decreasing. Are more and more people becoming morally right? Are people today "leading a life that is pleasing to God"?

Words of the Lord to Joseph Smith indicate what the state of religion and righteousness will be in the Last Days. It doesn't sound like righteousness will be growing throughout the world.

> Prepare ye, prepare ye for that which is to come, for the
> Lord is nigh;

And the anger of the Lord is kindled, and his sword is bathed in heaven, and it shall fall upon the inhabitants of the earth.

And the arm of the Lord shall be revealed; and the day cometh that they who will not hear the voice of the Lord, neither the voice of his servants, neither give heed to the words of the prophets and apostles, shall be cut off from among the people. (Doc. & Cov. 1:12–14)

The Lord declares what is going to happen sometime before he comes again. How do we know if the Lord is angry with us? We must look for and understand the events and conditions of the world. The unrighteous will be cut off.

The Lord then explains why unrighteous people will be cut off and why we will see (and possibly suffer) tribulations of the Last Days.

For they have strayed from mine ordinances, and have broken mine everlasting covenant;

They seek not the Lord to establish his righteousness, but every man walketh in his own way, and after the image of his own god, whose image is in the likeness of the world, and whose substance is that of an idol, which waxeth old and shall perish in Babylon, even Babylon the great, which shall fall. (Doc. & Cov. 1:12–16)

Studies by the Pew Research Center shed some additional light on religion and the righteousness of Americans.

US PUBLIC BECOMING LESS RELIGIOUS

Is the American public becoming less religious? Yes, at least by some key measures of what it means to be a religious person. An extensive new survey of more than 35,000 U.S. adults finds that the percentages who say they believe in God, pray daily and regularly go to church or other religious services all have declined modestly in recent years.

But the Pew Research Center study also finds a great deal of stability in the U.S. religious landscape. The recent decrease in religious beliefs and behaviors is largely attributable to the "nones"—the growing minority of Americans, particularly in the Millennial generation, who say they do not belong to any organized faith. (Pew Research 2015)

[Pew Research Center bears no responsibility for the analyses or interpretations of the data presented here. The opinions expressed herein, including any implications for policy, are those of the author and not of Pew Research Center.]

The Pew Research study did find that based on some standard measures, religious Americans are more faithful today than just a few years ago.

Based on scriptures concerning the Last Days, would we expect to see the righteous, the faithful, maintaining or strengthening their faith? Faithful Christians should be looking and waiting for Christ's return. As we see and acknowledge the witnesses and wonders of the Last Saturday, surely our faith should hold steady, or even increase.

AMERICANS SAY RELIGIOUS ASPECTS OF
CHRISTMAS ARE DECLINING IN PUBLIC LIFE

Shrinking Majority Believe Biblical Account of Birth of Jesus Depicts Actual Events

As long-simmering debates continue over how American society should commemorate the Christmas holiday, a new Pew Research Center survey finds that most U.S. adults believe the religious aspects of Christmas are emphasized less now than in the past—even as relatively few Americans are bothered by this trend. In addition, a declining majority says religious displays such as nativity scenes should be allowed on government property. And compared with five years ago, a growing share of Americans say it does not matter to them how they are greeted in stores and businesses during the holiday season—whether with "merry Christmas" or a less-religious greeting like "happy holidays." (Pew Research 2017)

There are some indicators that Christians are not necessarily losing their faith, but many feel that religion and righteousness are declining.

The Lord declares that his voice, his Gospel is for everyone and should be preached to all the world. The iniquities of the rebellious will be known, and all people will be warned. The Lord's voice is going throughout the world today.

> Or verily the voice of the Lord is unto all men, and there is none to escape; and there is no eye that shall not see, neither ear that shall not hear, neither heart that shall not be penetrated.
>
> And the rebellious shall be pierced with much sorrow; for their iniquities shall be spoken upon the housetops, and their secret acts shall be revealed.
>
> And the voice of warning shall be unto all people, by the mouth of my disciples, whom I have chosen in these last days. (Doc. & Cov. 1:2–4)

In our world of modern communication and advanced technology, the iniquities and secret acts of the rebellious are being declared from the housetops.

What would we expect the condition of religion to be on the Last Saturday? Should the world be more accepting and tolerant of different religions as the Savior's return nears? Review the headlines below that are related to religion today:

"I Would Be Afraid of Being Attacked": Why Some Jews Won't Put a Menorah in Their Window This Hanukkah

With anti-Semitism sharply on the rise, the Deseret News talked to more than 50 Jews around the world about whether they will put a menorah in their window this year.

SALT LAKE CITY. [Vicki] won't be putting a menorah in her window for Hanukkah this year. She didn't last year either. It's not because she doesn't celebrate the holiday. It's because she's afraid to do so publicly …

In a recent survey of American Jews by the American Jewish Committee, one in four respondents said they "avoid certain places, events or situations out of fear" for their "safety or comfort as a Jew." Nearly a third of the more than 1,200 respondents said they avoided "publicly wearing, carrying or displaying things that might help people identify" them as Jewish. (Friedman 2019)

The knowledge that some religious groups today live in fear provokes surprise and dismay. Aside from those feelings, we should ask ourselves if faith and religion today indicate that the number of days before the Lord Jesus Christ returns are few.

Today, news and information are everywhere. A significant amount of this information may be incomplete, inaccurate, or even completely false. We should seek the inspiration and guidance of the Holy Spirit in all matters, not just faith and righteousness.

Only a Fraction of Vatican's
Charity Fund Goes to the Poor

VATICAN (ChurchMilitant.com). The Vatican is spending the vast majority of its charitable funds not toward helping the poor but paying salaries and other administrative costs …

What the church doesn't advertise is that most of that collection, worth more than €50 million ($55 million) annually, goes toward plugging the hole in the Vatican's own administrative budget, while as little as 10% is spent on charitable works, according to people familiar with the funds. (Niles 2019)

We do not know the details concerning the finances and operation of the Vatican and its leaders. This is irrelevant in our Last Saturday context. What we want to determine is, does what we read here about Vatican finances confirm that it is the Last Days?

Why the Trumpet Watches Moral
Decline in Britain and America

The consequences of discarding a sacred moral code to govern the actions of individuals are far graver than most people realize …

Could *America* fall? Could *Britain* fall? Or are our societies too modern, too sophisticated, too enlightened for such a cataclysm? …

The longest-standing and most consistent forecast the *Trumpet* has made since Volume 1, Issue 2, in June 1990, has been that America and Britain *will* fall, and that the fundamental cause will not be birth rates, weather phenomena, superbug epidemics, gross domestic product or carrier strike groups. Fundamentally, it will be because America and Britain have rejected the foundation of national stability: the biblical *statutes*, *judgments* and *laws.* (Miiller 2017)

The Trumpet claims that two of the most powerful countries on earth will fall. Why? Because of the moral decline and disregard of biblical warnings within those countries. The Bible warns us about lawlessness, immorality, deceit, and wickedness. Yet these are all becoming more prevalent in the world today. This is like a neon sign that Christ will return tomorrow.

Some may not be convinced of the importance of biblical warnings, but secular history also confirms the grave dangers of national moral decline.

The Lord's Kingdom will go forth in the Last Days until it has filled the whole earth. What does the Lord say about the members of his Kingdom?

What about those who belong to the Lord's kingdom today? Is the faith of Christians today stronger than yesterday? Is the faith of those who belong to the Church of Jesus Christ of Latter-Day Saints growing stronger? What do scriptures say about the righteousness of Christians in the Last Days?

> Now the Spirit speaketh expressly, that in the latter times some shall depart from the faith, giving heed to seducing spirits, and doctrines of devils.
>
> Speaking lies in hypocrisy; having their conscience seared with a hot iron.
>
> Forbidding to marry, and commanding to abstain from meats, which God hath created to be received with thanksgiving of them which believe and know the truth. (1 Timothy 4:1–3)

The Last Days will see an increase in the Lord's spirit upon the earth. But all will not be well in Zion. Is the stone cut without hands rolling forth? Are Christians in general, and members of the church specifically, departing from the faith? Is the world filled with commotion and chaos? Can we see these signs of the Last Saturday? We only need to open our eyes and look around us.

1.10. PERILOUS TIMES

The website LetGodBeTrue understands and describes the great perilous times in which we live.

PERILOUS TIMES!

> The greatest threat to the kingdom of Jesus Christ today is the carnal, compromising, effeminate, and worldly Christianity the devil has spawned to destroy the faith once delivered to the saints. False teachers promote it on every side. The cure is simple, but few ministers will use it, since most hearers are demanding fables and entertainment instead. The importance of this prophecy cannot be overstated. You are living in the fulfillment of the perilous times! (Let God Be True 2000)

Let us examine the world in which we live and decide if we live in the "perilous times," described by the apostle Paul.

> This know also, that in the last days perilous times shall come.
>
> For men shall be lovers of their own selves, covetous, boasters, proud, blasphemers, disobedient to parents, unthankful, unholy.
>
> Without natural affection, trucebreakers, false accusers, incontinent, fierce, despisers of those that are good,
>
> Traitors, heady, highminded, lovers of pleasures more than lovers of God;

Having a form of godliness, but denying the power thereof; from such turn away.

For of this sort are they which creep into houses, and lead captive silly women laden with sins, led away with divers lusts,

Ever learning, and never able to come to the knowledge of the truth. (2 Timothy 3:1–7)

We can see and hear about these conditions every day in the news. If we pay attention to daily world events and analyze them against Paul's words, we will know that we live in perilous times. People today are ever learning. We are expanding our knowledge of everything faster and easier than ever before. But are we coming to a knowledge of the truth?

Do we live in perilous times? I used to work with a man who was born and raised in Brooklyn, New York. He told me he wouldn't go back; it was too violent and dangerous. He told me this over forty years ago. What is Brooklyn like today?

Elder Cecil O. Samuelson Jr. spoke of perilous times in October 2004:

PERILOUS TIMES

Brethren, it is both comforting and potentially worrisome to know that we live in an age and a time that was not only foreseen by the prophets of previous dispensations but was also clearly a focus of their concerns and their aspirations. The Apostle Paul said, "In the last days perilous times shall come" (2 Timothy 3:1), and then he went on to catalog and describe with remarkable accuracy much that we currently see daily in the media, in advertisements for entertainment, and almost everywhere in the world around us. As careful as we might and should be, absolute avoidance of much of the peril which is seemingly enveloping us is at best difficult and often near impossible to avoid. (Samuelson 2004)

47

In early 2020, a new infectious virus was identified and started spreading around the world. The virus raised great alarm and caused the World Health Organization (WHO) and many nations to monitor the outbreak and institute mandatory quarantine for people on airplanes and cruise ships.

WHO Says Hubei Cases Stabilized;
American Dies: Virus Update

An American and a Japanese man suspected of getting the virus died in Wuhan this week, officials said. The disease is spreading, with five Britons sharing an Alps chalet confirmed with cases, and two new cases on a Princess Cruise ship in Japan—largest center of infections outside China.

The virus reaches a milestone this weekend if deaths continue at the current pace. The toll of 724 after two months is shy of the 774 killed in the 2002–2003 [SARS] outbreak of severe acute respiratory syndrome over about eight months.

Key Developments

- American who died in Wuhan was a woman: New York Times
- China's sick doctors show breaches can fan coronavirus
- China death toll at 722; confirmed cases at 34,546
- Singapore confirms seven new cases, pushes total to 40
- Five Britons on ski holiday in French Alps are infected
- Carmaker VW delays restarting China joint ventures
- World's retailers take hit as Chinese shoppers stay home
- Death of a hero doctor sparks crisis of confidence in Xi's China. (Lin and Chen 2020)

This dangerous virus spread quickly and became a worldwide pandemic. Concern and risk for those with underlying health conditions and those over sixty-five years of age escalated swiftly. Health organizations and governments restricted gatherings of more than one hundred. Anyone over sixty was admonished to avoid groups of more than twenty.

Universities canceled classes; professional sports were canceled or postponed. Theaters and movies limited the number of people allowed or shut down completely. The Church of Jesus Christ of Latter-Day Saints suspended all church meetings and activities. Life suddenly changed around the globe. The entire world was in commotion for a while, as prophesied in sacred scripture.

Since 1900, the world has experienced seven events that were called pandemics, or epidemics. The first was polio, and the last was the Zika virus epidemic in 2015. Yet each new infectious incident is more virulent, spreads faster, and is more dangerous. Health pandemics and violent threats are clear evidence that we live in perilous times.

Pandemics and plagues have ravaged the world through the ages. But they are not the only events or actions that we should be anxious about.

Man Accused of Killing Two Called "Weird"

MADISON, Wis. (AP. A man accused of killing two people in a county building and wounding a third with a rifle had quarreled with police detectives over a charge against him just before the shootings, authorities said Saturday. (AP News 1988)

A sheriff's deputy helped disarm the gunman and asked him to surrender. The gunman responded by yelling, "I'm going to kill you and everyone else. I don't care if you kill me." When someone is in a state of mind like this, it is clear how perilous today is. We should plead for the Lord's return.

Perilous times: danger in the mall, at church, at school, at sporting events, in a theater, at the airport, in a plane, walking down the street, in your car, in your home; invasions, shootings, bombings. The times are perilous, no matter where we are, who we are with, or what we are doing.

In February 2020, two NYC police officers were shot. The first was shot in a patrol van, the second in precinct headquarters. Yes, precinct headquarters. We are not safe anywhere. Isn't that a definition of perilous times?

Indeed, today's media, advertising, and entertainment provide evidence of and fulfillment of the prophecy of perilous times. We live in dangerous, risky times, on the Last Saturday.

2

The World

The scriptures are full of prophecies concerning the Last Days. Many of these scriptures refer to the world, and the condition it will be in just before the Second Coming of the Savior. A review of these verses provides a clear picture of what we may look for and expect to see happening in the world during the Last Days.

Is the world to be filled with righteousness or wickedness, in the last dispensation? What sort of righteousness, or evil, will be prevalent during this period? Just what are the signs of the times that we may recognize or look for in the world, to determine if today is the Last Saturday?

One scripture is all it takes to give us a clear picture of what the world is to be like when the day of the Lord is at hand. In the Lord's words:

> Behold, the world is ripening in iniquity; and it must needs be that the children of men are stirred up unto repentance, both the Gentiles, and also the house of Israel. (Doc. & Cov. 18:6)

"The world is ripening in iniquity." Like an extremely overripe piece of fruit: an apple, peach, or plum. It is usually badly discolored, soft, and it may even smell bad. Overripe fruit may even have worms, maggots, and other bugs. If we look at the world today, will we see that it is ripe in wickedness?

> Therefore, what I say unto one I say unto all; "Watch, for the adversary spreadeth his dominions, and darkness reigneth.
>
> And the anger of God kindleth against the inhabitants of the earth; and none doeth good, for all have gone out of the way. (Doc. & Cov. 82:5–6)

Here the Lord tells us, in 1832, over 150 years ago, that the adversary is spreading, strengthening his power and influence. Darkness and evil are everywhere; none of the inhabitants of the earth are engaged in good works or righteousness.

Let's hope that since the Lord has re-established his church and Kingdom again on the earth, some of this has changed. Christians and members of the Lord's church are hopefully doing some good.

Switzerland Rated Best Place to Live

> WASHINGTON (AP). Switzerland, nestled in the Alps, is the world's most comfortable nation in which to live …
>
> A detailed analysis of human suffering worldwide released on Sunday rated Switzerland as having the lowest level of human discomfort …
>
> The United States finished fifth on the comfortable side of the list compiled by the Population Crisis Committee. (Schmid 1987, A8)

The study rated ten factors for their impact on human suffering. Western Europe, North America, and Japan had scores that supported favorable livability. Scores for countries in Africa, Latin America, and Asia are indicative of hunger, disease, and economic distress.

So the US ranks as the fifth-best place to live in the world. Should we expect it to be higher? Considering the events in our society today, are we surprised to be that high? Is the rest of the world filled with even greater crime, wickedness, suffering, and disasters?

At the start of this, the last dispensation, the Lord said:

> For all flesh is corrupted before me; and the powers of darkness prevail upon the earth, among the children of men, in the presence of all the hosts of heaven—
>
> Which causeth silence to reign, and all eternity is pained, and the angels are waiting the great commandment to reap down the earth, to gather the tares that they may be burned; and, behold, the enemy is combined. (Doc. & Cov. 38:11–12)

Is all flesh corrupted before the Lord? Some of today's headlines appear to affirm that our world is corrupt and violent.

JURY ASKS DEATH FOR FEMALE KILLER OF FIVE

LEXINGTON, Ky. A jury recommended the electric chair for a woman and life without parole for her lesbian lover in the murders of five people who were shot, stabbed and run over with a car. (Malloy 1987)

BESET PERU SEEKS TO STRENGTHEN COURTS

In January 1983, the eight Peruvian journalists and their guide set off for that community to investigate reports of clashes between guerrilla units and peasant bands. On arriving, the journalists were detained by local leaders. After a village council, the intruders were stoned and hacked to death, apparently mistaken for collaborators with guerrillas. (Smith 1987)

Some inconsistencies have arisen about what really happened to the journalists in Peru. They were killed, but questions about how, why, and by whom have been investigated. New questions and investigations are, however, outside our concern. These stories add evidence to the declaration we are working to verify.

There are very few places in the world that are not in some kind of conflict, places where we find no crime, corruption, assaults, injustice, or victims. The signs of the Last Days are not only limited to unrighteousness and evil. Times of turmoil, confusion, disorder, and conflict are also signs of the Last Days.

We have seen generations of "Do your own thing"; "Me, me, me"; and "God is dead." More recently, it has been "Me too" and "Black Lives Matter." We are again witnessing protests, marches, and calls for change.

Almost daily, we hear concerns expressed by various scientists and environmentalists about the earth's natural resources. They say we are destroying, polluting, consuming, and depleting them. Some even wonder how much longer the planet will be able to sustain not only human life, but life of any kind.

Growing Hole in Ozone Shield Is Discovered over Antarctica

A hole has opened in the atmosphere's ozone shield above Antarctica, scientists said yesterday the hole was growing at the same rate as one in 1987 …

"It's terrifying," said [a] program manager …

"If these ozone holes keep growing like this, they'll eventually eat the world." (Browne 1989)

Whether we believe the planet on which we live is being destroyed or not, the concern expressed about growing ozone holes are signs of the Last Days. We should also note that the world has not yet been eaten, in 2020. People do not know and understand as much as they sometimes think they do. Progress has been made in the last thirty years to preserve the ozone shield. However, ozone is critical to the world and major depletion would be catastrophic to life on earth. .

Surely one of the most dramatic signs that it is the Last Saturday is the way we live and our relationships with others, not only our own family and relatives, but other people in general. In many families today, things aren't going very well:

INCEST & MURDER: THE CHERYL PIERSON STORY

Cheryl Pierson was subjected to sexual abuse at the hands of her father …

Cheryl decided she would ask [a classmate] if he would kill her father for her. After informing her boyfriend of the plan, he collected $1000 which would be paid to [the classmate] once the job was done. On the afternoon of 5 February, 1986, [the classmate] hid behind a tree outside the Pierson household, armed with a .22-caliber rifle. When James stepped foot out of the door to go to work as an electrician, [he] shot him dead. (Thompson 2017)

Our purpose here is not to decide whether this young girl's act was justified or not. We are looking at this event, one of many such events happening today, as a sign of the Last Days. Families are turning against loved ones. A young high school student is willing to murder someone for a friend, for money. The action seems kind of extreme on the part of both the young girl and her classmate. But that seems to be the way more and more people feel problems should be solved: with violence and criminal acts.

Just ten or twenty years ago, this sort of violence was virtually unheard of. Today's new methods of communication, the internet, and social media are increasing the news sources of crimes and violence from around the world. All of these sources may be revealing that powers of darkness prevail.

2.1. WARS AND RUMORS OF WARS

Perhaps the most frequently mentioned sign of the Last Days is that of wars and rumors of wars around the world:

> Ye hear of wars in far countries, and you say that there will soon be great wars in far countries, but ye know not the hearts of men in your own land. (Doc. & Cov. 38:29)

Well, we might ask ourselves, are there any wars and rumors of wars anywhere in the world today? Have you read a newspaper in the last twenty years? South Korea has experienced war and conflict for many years.

THE GWANGJU MASSACRE, 1980

> Tens of thousands of students and other protestors poured into the streets of Gwangju (Kwangju), a city in southwestern South Korea in the spring of 1980. They were protesting the state of martial law that had been in force since a coup that previous year …
>
> Troops shot dead twenty girls at Gwangju's Central High School. Ambulance and cab drivers who tried to take the wounded to hospitals were shot. One hundred students who sheltered in the Catholic Center were slaughtered. Captured high school and university students had their hands tied behind them with barbed wire; many were then summarily executed. (Szczepanski 2019)

Ireland is another country that sees civil unrest and contention:

IRA OFFSHOOT SAYS IT KILLED TWO FORMER MEMBERS IN FEUD

BELFAST, Northern Ireland (AP). A Marxist offshoot of the IRA said Sunday its snipers killed one of its own

former military leaders and an associate, bringing to nine
the number of people assassinated in an internal feud.

The group, the Irish National Liberation Army (INLA),
identified the victims … It called [one of the victims]
a –self-appointed Dr. Death". (AP News 1987)

These news headlines are not about accidents or one-time events
of Mother Nature. They are intentional acts of terrorists. They are acts
of war.

Acts of war, sedition, treason, and civil unrest are easy to find all
around the world, which is an indication of the state of life currently
found in nations of the world. All of these situations become a clear
commentary and witness that the Last Days described in holy writ are
upon us.

Saboteurs Derail Train, Hurting 150

MADRAS, India (AP). Saboteurs blew up a railway
bridge Sunday in southern India, derailing an express
train and killing at least 22 people, police said. Police
reported 150 people injured, according to the United
News of India. (Greenville News 1987, 1)

Information found at the railway bridge revealed that Tamil
extremists destroyed the bridge. They were angry because India was
not helping them in their fight for a homeland in Sri Lanka.

News reports indicate that atrocities of war happen regularly in the
Philippines. However, that's not the only country where these types of
events are happening. The Philippines does have various wars taking
place at this time.

Wars, Conflicts, and Coups of the Philippines

NPA Maoist Rebellion (1969-Present). The New People's
Army (NPA), is the military wing of the Communist

Party of the Philippines, and began a guerrila campaign against the government in 1969.

Muslim Rebellion in the Southern Philippines (1969-Present): Muslim rebel groups seek autonomy/ independence from the mostly Christian Philippines.

Martial Law (1972-1981). Martial law over the entire nation instituted by President Ferdinand Marcos. (History Guy n.d.)

Philippines War on Drugs May Have Killed Tens of Thousands, Says UN

Tens of thousands of people may have been killed during Rodrigo Duterte's war on drugs in the Philippines …

The anti-narcotics crackdown in the Philippines, launched by the president after he won the 2016 election on a promise to rid the country of drugs … (Ratcliffe 2020)

The horrors of war are everywhere today. There are military wars, civil wars, drug wars, government wars, police wars, and terrorist wars; there are countless more.

BOMB KILLS 4, WOUNDS 39 AT ACADEMY

MANILA, Philippines (AP). A bomb wrecked a grandstand at the Philippine Military Academy while several dozen officers and civilians watched cadets march on the parade ground Wednesday, killing four people and wounding 39 …

Defense Secretary Rafael Ileto blamed it on people he described only as "terrorists." (Montgomery 1987, 9)

Wars of various forms and means are occurring regularly in various parts of the world. Acts of war and destruction are carried out by diverse groups of terrorists, radicals, and freedom fighters.

Tokyo Plagued by 25-Year-Old Airport Dispute: Aviation: Narita's Expansion Is Stymied by Farmers and Radicals

Eight farmers who refuse to sell their land are a major reason that work cannot go forward on planned construction …

In the nearly 25 years that the dispute has dragged on, more than 3,000 activists have been arrested in clashes with police at airport construction sites. Three policemen and two protesters have been killed. (Lazarus 1991)

PKK Claims Responsibility for Turkey Suicide Car Bomb Attack

Two militants set off a bomb inside their car near a police station at Pinarbasi in Turkey's central Kayseri province on Friday, killing themselves and one policeman and wounding 18 others.

The PKK has several times proposed peaceful solutions regarding Kurdish problem, Turkey has always refused saying that it will not negotiate with "terrorists." (Ekurd Daily 2012)

Through the prophet Ezekiel, the Lord has indicated that in the latter days Gog, King of Magog, will invade Israel and be defeated. This battle will usher in the Second Coming of the Savior. The Lord says he will come during a time of war. He further states that it will be a time when "every man's sword shall be against his brother." (see Ezekiel 38:1–23)

How Cold War II Could Play out Now That
Russia Has Cryptically Declared It's Ready

RUSSIA has declared via Twitter that Cold War II has begun.

The advent of this second Cold War was signalled by UK Prime Minister Theresa May's announcement this week that Britain will expel 23 Russian diplomats.

The decision follows the nerve gas poisoning of former Russian spy Sergei Skripal and his daughter Yulia on March 4 — which has set off a war of words between the two countries. (Sutton 2018)

There is clear evidence that we live in a time of war, when all living things on the earth are shaking and falling apart. Consider for just a moment, the nations and lands around the world that are at war. Review in your mind those countries that have been in some sort of military or civil conflict within the last ten years. Indeed, it is a time when every man's sword seems to be against his brother.

7 S. African Black Youths
Slain in Political Feud

JOHANNESBURG, South Africa. Seven black youths were found murdered near Durban on Tuesday in an apparent upsurge of a bitter feud between rival political groups there.

The bodies of the youths, aged 15 to 17, were found in a roadside ditch in Kwamashu, a black township outside Durban. ... They had been stabbed to death or shot after being abducted in a clash between rival groups Monday. (Parks 1987)

The following scriptures may be descriptions of current events around the world. It is a day of gloominess and thick darkness. Fortunately, the Lord has said the current conditions will end, and some, the righteous, will be saved.

> Blow ye the trumpet in Zion, and sound an alarm in my holy mountain: let all the inhabitants of the land tremble: for the day of the Lord cometh, for it is nigh at hand;
>
> A day of darkness and of gloominess, a day of clouds and of thick darkness, as the morning spread upon the mountains: a great people and a strong; there hath not been ever the like, neither shall be any more after it, even to the years of many generations. (Joel 2:1–2)

The Lord said long ago that unless the Last Days are shortened, there would not be anyone left to be saved.

> And except those days should be shortened, there should no flesh be saved: but for the elect's sake those days shall be shortened. (Matthew 24:22)

When I first read this scripture, I thought it was indicating that during the Last Days, each day would get shorter. I must admit that the older I get, the shorter the days seem.

However, the reality is that the Lord is saying that when the world becomes so filled with wickedness, wars, and evil, the days until His Second Coming will be reduced, meaning He will come sooner. It seems that with the conflicts and bloodshed currently found throughout the world, if the "day of the Lord" does not come soon, there may indeed be no flesh left to save.

Speaking further about these Last Days and the abundance of strife, war, and bloodshed, Jesus said,

> Immediately after the tribulation of those days shall the sun be darkened, and the moon shall not give her light,

and the stars shall fall from heaven, and the powers of the heavens shall be shaken.

And then shall appear the sign of the Son of man in heaven: and then shall all the tribes of the earth mourn, and they shall see the Son of man coming in the clouds of heaven with power and great glory.

And he shall send his angels with a great sound of a trumpet, and they shall gather together his elect from the four winds, from one end of heaven to the other. (Matthew 24:29–31)

The Lord says that just before his Second Coming, the sun and moon will be dark, and stars will fall from heaven.

The sun and moon have been darkened by clouds, fog, smog, air pollution, and atmospheric conditions found around the world today. Many of these conditions are now more intense and more frequent than in times past. Are meteor showers, when stars fall from the sky, more prevalent? Do solar and lunar eclipses occur more frequently than they used to?

A total solar eclipse on August 21, 2017, was called the Great American Eclipse. Within a band that spanned the United States from the Pacific to the Atlantic on that day, the sun was indeed darkened. On April 8, 2024, another total solar eclipse will occur and darken the sun in a narrow path across thirteen US states.

Of course, stars falling from heaven may also refer to those people who become wicked and reject the Savior of the world. Thus these stars, or disciples, fall from heaven. The destruction of the non-earthly cosmos could be symbolic, not literal.

After the tribulations of the Last Saturday, the Lord will come again. We can daily review those tribulations and conflicts. We can read and hear about the lives being lost, not only the military, but civilians, women, and children. We may ponder the suffering and heartache that the current situation in countries around the world brings to so many people. Is it time to look for the angels and listen for the trumpet?

DEADLY BOMBING IN KABUL IS ONE OF
THE AFGHAN WAR'S WORST STRIKES

KABUL, Afghanistan. A truck bomb devastated a central area of Kabul near the presidential palace and foreign embassies on Wednesday, one of the deadliest strikes in the long Afghan war and a reminder of how the capital itself has become a lethal battlefield.

In one moment, more than 80 lives ended, hundreds of people were wounded and many more were traumatized, in the heart of a city defined by constant checkpoints and the densest concentration of Afghan and international forces. (Mashal, Abed, and Sukhanyar 2017)

A quick review of virtually any newspaper or online news source will provide many stories and articles about wars and conflict.

ISRAELI TROOPS WOUND 15 IN
CLASHES WITH PALESTINIANS

JERUSALEM (AP). Israeli troops fired on hundreds of demonstrators in the occupied West Bank Saturday and Palestinian sources said 15 people were hit. In all, 24 people were reported hurt in clashes in the occupied territories.

Protests also rocked the Gaza Strip, shattering three weeks of relative quiet in the occupied territories, which were seized by Israel in the 1967 war. (Journal 1988, 4A)

Acts of terror occur regularly throughout the world. Some we know about; many we don't. These attacks have been happening for over forty years. We sweep some of them from our minds, while others are never-ending warnings of the earth's Final Days.

A 40-Year US Embassy Crisis

Unlike the terrorist attacks of 9/11, which we've memorialized and psychologized, we've generally buried memories of the string of flagrant assaults on U.S. diplomats and diplomatic missions in countries like Lebanon, Kuwait, and Sudan …

Unfortunately, backing away from the crime scene has become an American habit in the Middle East and North Africa, where for 40 years now our diplomats have been killed, kidnapped, and targeted for assassination, and our embassies have been bombed, besieged, and most famously, overrun and captured in Tehran. (Smith 2012)

The next scripture says the Lord speaks for his elect's sake. What does he say? Nations will be at war; there will be conflicts and natural disasters.

Behold I speak for mine elect's sake; for nation shall rise against nation, and kingdom against kingdom; there shall be famines, and pestilences, and earthquakes, in divers places. (Joseph Smith, Matthew 1:29)

Nations are rising against other nations. War and the signs of the Last Saturday are also rising within nations around the world.

Paris Attacks: What Happened on the Night

The attacks in Paris on the night of Friday 13 November by gunmen and suicide bombers hit a concert hall, a major stadium, restaurants and bars, almost simultaneously - and left 130 people dead and hundreds wounded.

The attacks were described by President Francois Hollande as an "act of war" organised by the Islamic State (IS) militant group …

"Three co-ordinated teams" were believed to have been behind the attacks. (BBC News 2015)

AQUINO ORDERS MILITARY: CRUSH ABU SAYYAF

Seven Marines were killed, including five who were found beheaded and mutilated, and 26 were wounded on Thursday when they tried to capture two Abu Sayyaf leaders in an assault on their jungle camp in Barangay (village) Panglahayan in Sulu's mountainous town of Patikul.

At least 13 Abu Sayyaf bandits were killed. (Alipala 2011)

In an angry speech, President Aquino ordered the country's military to crush the rebels who are seeking to destroy her government.

In another country, a threat is made to kill innocent students and teachers. A blast in the US destroys a school but does not injure any students. War can be found everywhere.

1,000 HELD HOSTAGE

SAN SALVADOR, El Salvador (UPI). An army deserter and a teenage girl, armed with rifles and grenades, seized a school Wednesday and threatened to kill 1,000 students and teachers. They freed their hostages five hours later after a visit from an archbishop and eventually surrendered peacefully. (News-Sentinel 1987)

Why Beirut's Ammonium Nitrate Blast Was So Devastating

Lebanese authorities say that the explosion, which killed at least 220 people, injured more than 5,000 and left an estimated 300,000 people homeless, was caused by 2,750 tonnes of ammonium nitrate, a chemical compound commonly used as an agricultural fertilizer, which had been stored for 6 years at a port warehouse. (Guglielmi 2020)

It is believed that the Beirut explosion was triggered by a nearby fire. That does not disqualify the event, or others like it, from being signs of the times. Last Day disasters may be caused by anything or anyone.

Yes, the world is filled with war. But not in the United States of America. Are we sure? We may not be witnessing any military conflicts in our country, but there is war here. Remember the war on crime, the war against drugs, and more recently the gang wars: gang against gang, police and law enforcement against gangs, and even citizens fighting gangs.

We have seen wars over pollution, the environment, and politics. Would you not say we saw a war over the Equal Rights Amendment? Wars over abortion, capital punishment, marriage, and civil rights continue today. There are wars in our own land. The wars predicted for the Last Days do not have to be military wars. The wars and rumors of wars prophesied for the Last Days are here.

2.2. DISASTERS, CALAMITIES, ACCIDENTS

The world is at war. But what other things might we look for to determine if today is the Last Saturday?

> But, behold, in the last days, or in the days of the Gentiles-yea, behold all the nations of the Gentiles and also the Jews, both those who shall come upon this land and those who shall be upon other lands, yea, even upon all the lands of the earth, behold, they will be drunken with iniquity and all manner of abominations—
>
> And when that day shall come they shall be visited of the Lord of Hosts, with thunder and with earthquake, and with a great noise, and with storm, and with tempest, and with the flame of devouring fire. (2 Nephi 27:1–2)

We know nation is rising against nation, but what about accidents, earthquakes, and other disasters? The Lord says there will be some of these things in the dispensation of the fullness of times, before the Lord comes again. Quite honestly, I have never been in a famine. I have experienced four or five minor earthquakes in my life. It might seem that the Second Coming isn't all that close. No, all we need to do is open our eyes to reality and see the signs of the times.

CENTER FOR DISASTER PHILANTHROPY
(CDP) DISASTER: 2020 NORTH
AMERICAN WILDFIRE SEASON

> Dozens of major fires are burning across North America. As of Oct. 29, according to the National Interagency Coordination Center (NICC), there are just over 8,000 firefighters and support personnel assigned to wildfires. The current 43 active fires—of which 27 are large, uncontained fires—have burned just under 4 million acres.
>
> NIFC reports that as of Oct. 29 there have been 47,053 wildfires that have burned 8,534,580 acres this year. This is approximately 2.2 million more acres burned than the 10-year average. As of Oct. 29, the majority of fires in the 10 states with large fires are burning in National Forests or National Parks. (CDP Disaster 2020)

The summer of 2018 brought extensive fires throughout the western United States. California experienced the largest wildfire in state history. Extensive fires in the western United States in 2020 again exceeded the damage and destruction of prior years.

Recently, many parts of the United States and the rest of the world have seen low rainfall. This has triggered more fires than I have ever seen in my life. I remember being in my yard one recent summer, and not only was the air filled with light smoke, but I discovered ashes falling all around me. This situation was caused by a fire in one of the canyons east of Salt Lake City. Authorities indicated that some of the smoke was from extensive fires in Yellowstone National Park.

Who can forget the image of Yellowstone burning to the ground a few summers ago? Fires were widespread; acres and acres of green forest were turning black. Indeed, an unbelievable amount of the park was burned, like never before.

We shouldn't only look for natural disasters as a sign of the Last Days. Surely, increased accidents and tragedies of any kind, throughout the world, are evidence that today is the final Saturday. Any event that causes suffering, heartache, and loss of life is a pestilence and tribulation.

KC-135 Jet Tanker Crashes

FAIRCHILD AIR FORCE BASE, Wash. An Air Force KC-135 jet tanker crashed Friday while practicing an aerial stunt over Fairchild Air Force Base, killing at least six people in a fiery explosion that engulfed a vehicle on the ground. (Warchol 1987)

Airplanes are one of the greatest achievements of modern times. Yes, flights can sometimes be expensive. Most airplanes are comfortable, and you can't beat how quickly you can arrive at your destination. Nevertheless, if something goes wrong, the result can be a disaster.

517 Believed Dead in Japan Air Crash: JAL 747 Down Near Tokyo; At Least 7 Survive Worst Single-Plane Disaster

TOKYO. A Japan Air Lines Boeing 747 jumbo jet carrying 524 people on a domestic flight crashed Monday in a mountainous area northwest of Tokyo after the pilot reported that a right rear door was "broken" and that he was "unable to control" the plane. Four survivors were found, a rescue party said today. (Jameson 1985)

We can look at air disasters and the loss of life as a sign of the Lord's impending return.

AIRSAFE.COM: RECENT US PLANE CRASHES

26 December 2019; Safari Helicopters; Eurocopter AS350 B2; Kauai, HI: The helicopter departed from Lihue, HI for a sightseeing flight over the island of Kauai. The aircraft crashed into a cliff … The pilot and all six passengers were killed …

23 February 2019; Amazon Prime Air 767-300; N1217A; flight 3591; near Anahuac, TX: The aircraft was on a cargo flight from Miami, FL to Houston, TX and crashed into Trinity Bay … The two crew members and one passenger were killed …

4 November 2015; Rais Group International BAe 125-700; N237WR; flight EFT1526; Akron, OH: The executive jet was on a nonscheduled domestic passenger flight from Dayton, OH, to Akron, OH, and crashed about two miles short of the landing runway … Both pilots and all seven passengers were killed. (AirSafe, n.d.)

Plane crashes and disasters, private and commercial, seem to occur weekly. Sometimes, it seems like there's one every day. This may be because there are more planes in the sky. It might be because older aircraft are still in use. There are, in reality, many plane accidents and crashes that most of us never hear about.

All types of disasters and accidents point to the Final Days before the start of the final millennium.

FERRY SINKS IN BELGIUM, 188 PEOPLE DROWN

A British ferry leaving Zeebrugge, Belgium, capsizes, drowning 188 people, on March 6, 1987 …

Within minutes, the *Herald* capsized. Many passengers were thrown into the sea and quickly drowned in the cold 30-foot-deep water. (Belgium 2020)

The Rising Death Toll in
Ecuador's Earthquake

> The strongest earthquake to hit Ecuador in decades has killed at least 350 people, injured scores more, and destroyed buildings and roads along the nation's northwestern coast …
>
> As many as 2,500 people were injured in the earthquake …
>
> "This wasn't just a house that collapsed, it was an entire town." (Koren 2016)

For our purposes here, the cause or reason for a catastrophe or accident is irrelevant. The Lord has said that in the Last Days, there would be numerous such events. The simple fact that there are many disasters in diverse places around the world testifies that today is the Last Saturday.

2.3. Weather and Elements in Commotion

Prophetic descriptions by Joseph Smith of the last dispensation indicate that the earth, other elements of nature, and humans will be in turmoil. These words provide us with additional information to verify that we are living in the late evening of the Last Saturday.

> For not many days hence and the earth shall tremble and reel to and fro as a drunken man; and the sun shall hide his face, and shall refuse to give light; and the moon shall be bathed in blood; and the stars shall become exceedingly angry, and shall cast themselves down as a fig that falleth from off a fig-tree. (Doc. & Cov. 88:87)

Here is another reference to stars falling from heaven. This revelation was given on December 27, 1832. The same reference was also made by John in the book of Revelation in the New Testament (Revelation 6:13).

Joseph Smith surely was familiar with the book of Revelation. However, he says, "not many days hence" and the stars shall cast themselves down. Apparently, just over eleven months later, in 1833, stars did fall from heaven.

STARS FALL FROM HEAVEN

The great star shower took place on the night of November 13, 1833. It was so bright that a newspaper could be read on the street. One writer says, "For nearly four hours the sky was literally ablaze." Men thought the end of the world had come. Look into this. It is most fascinating, and a sign of Christ's coming. (Bible Universe n.d.)

The Joseph Smith revelation continues with additional descriptions of conditions in the Last Days. The conditions presented here are in harmony with accounts provided by other prophets in other volumes of scripture.

For after your testimony cometh the testimony of earthquakes, that shall cause groanings in the midst of her, and men shall fall upon the ground and shall not be able to stand.

And also cometh the testimony of the voice of thunderings, and the voice of lightnings, and the voice of tempests, and the voice of the waves of the sea heaving themselves beyond their bounds. (Doc. & Cov. 88:89-90)

A wave on the beach can knock you down if you are not paying attention. Imagine what happens when the waves of the sea "heave themselves beyond their bounds." We have seen this happen with ever-increasing frequency.

HURRICANE ELENA AND ITS IMPACTS
ON THE GULF COAST (1985)

> Making landfall in September of 1985, Hurricane Elena was one of the most unpredictable tropical weather events in the United States. Elena repeatedly deviated from the projected hurricane path, making a two day anti-cyclonic loop in the Gulf of Mexico. The hurricane finally made landfall in Biloxi, Mississippi on September 2nd, 1985, resulting in one of the largest evacuations in United States history …

> At least a dozen tornadoes were reported in coastal counties of Mississippi as the eyewall crossed the coast. (Junker 2018)

Scriptures describe the weather and commotion we can find all over the world:

> And all things shall be in commotion; and surely, men's hearts shall fail them; for fear shall come upon all people.

> And angels shall fly through the midst of heaven, crying with a loud voice, sounding the trump of God, saying: Prepare ye, prepare ye, O inhabitants of the earth; for the judgment of our God is come. Behold, and lo, the Bridegroom cometh; go ye out to meet him. (Doc. & Cov. 88:91-92)

Every day, we can see the prophecies of things in commotion, men's hearts failing, and fear upon all people being fulfilled. In this dispensation, we have seen angels fly in the midst of heaven, including Moses, John the Baptist, Peter, James, John, and Moroni. These and others have come to earth as heavenly messengers for the restoration of the Gospel.

Some years ago, there was a worldwide effort to relieve extreme famine and starvation in various African countries. Television, magazines, and newspapers presented articles and pictures of starving men, women, children, and infants. Although help and assistance followed, the problem has not been eliminated.

The prophets have also described for us signs of the Last Days that may be seen in the weather. During the Last Days, the scriptures indicate that the natural elements may become quite volatile. The elements may become confusing and shifting; it may even be difficult to determine the seasons of the year.

The prophecies of extreme, extensive changes in the weather and nature, in general, are being fulfilled.

HEAVY RAINS AND AVALANCHES KILL DOZENS IN PERU

Heavy rains have caused dozens of rivers in Peru to overflow and triggered widespread landslides claiming the lives of at least 39 people and leaving at least 10,000 affected. Hundreds have lost their homes.

The floods have inundated entire villages, while avalanches of mud and stones have demolished homes, schools and medical facilities, while laying waste to thousands of hectares of arable land. (Uco 2019)

TERRIFYING FLOOD LEAVES 11 DEAD IN CHEYENNE

A freak hail and thunderstorm that hovered over Wyoming's capital city for three terror-filled hours has left at least 11 people dead while transforming the local streets into what an embittered victim called 'white Christmas in August.' …

Most of the victims "were literally sucked out the windows of their cars in raging torrents of water." (Coates 1985)

The National Weather Service described the event as the worst storm "to hit southeastern Wyoming since the time of Christopher Columbus".

Earthquakes may not be considered an element of weather, but they do put the earth in commotion. In March 1987, two earthquakes occurred in Auckland, New Zealand. They sent residents into the streets; one of the quakes toppled homes and buildings, twisted bridges, and injured more than twenty-five people.

We experienced an earthquake in the Salt Lake Valley in March of 2020. It was the strongest earthquake of my life and was quite distressing. I was afraid that the glass windows in our home were going to explode. Yet there was no damage to our home, and we were not injured.

One of the most disturbing aspects of earthquakes is you don't know how strong they are going to be. You also don't know how many aftershocks there will be. Earthquakes are terrifying sign of the Last Saturday.

I had an opportunity to sit in a hurricane tunnel at the Science and Industry Museum in Tampa, Florida. As the winds hit 75 miles per hour, we watched our hair stand up and felt the force of nature's destructive power. I have never been too interested in hurricanes or followed them much. But it seems that lately, I've been hearing about storms that are stronger and more destructive than ever.

In 1989, Hurricane Hugo invaded the southeast shores of the United States. When it left, many cities and towns were virtually gone. In September 1988, Hurricane Gilbert wore out his welcome in a similar destructive fashion.

It's Going to Be Another Busy, above Average Hurricane Season, Meteorologists Say

After a nightmarish 2017 hurricane season featuring monsters such as Harvey, Irma and Maria, many in the U.S. are hoping for a quieter year. A top forecasting group says that won't be the case …

A tropical storm becomes a hurricane when its wind speed reaches 74 mph. (Rice 2018)

Hurricanes are not an issue in the Salt Lake valley. Tornadoes are not an issue, nor are volcanoes. However, increasing occurrences of these weather events elsewhere in the world are signs that the prophesied return is near.

Could the major eruption of a volcano also be a sign that today is the Last Saturday?

HAWAII VOLCANO'S LAVA SPEWS "LAZE" OF
TOXIC GAS AND GLASS INTO THE AIR

> Lava from the Kilauea volcano is pouring into the Pacific Ocean off of Hawaii's Big Island, generating a plume of "laze"—which Hawaii County officials describe as hydrochloric acid and steam with fine glass particles—into the air …
>
> "Health hazards of laze include lung damage, and eye and skin irritation." (Domonoske 2018)

The pictures of this volcanic eruption were amazing, fascinating, and scary. Weather and other elements are in commotion and confusion around the world.

2.4. SOCIETY AND CIVILIZATION

What about societies and civilizations in the Last Days? Has the Lord made any statements through prophets and apostles about what the social order will be like on the Last Saturday?

We know that Cain formed the first secret combination and became known as Master Mahan. We also know that this combination was the work of Satan. Are there secret combinations and societies in the world today?

Secret combinations are the most abominable and wicked in God's sight (see Ether 8:18).

In the Book of Mormon, Nephi, the son of Helaman, describes the state of the Nephites. They were ripe in iniquity and wickedness, like the world today.

> But behold, it is to get gain, to be praised of men, yea, and that ye might get gold and silver. And ye have set your hearts upon the riches and the vain things of this world, for the which ye do murder, and plunder, and steal, and bear false witness against your neighbor, and do all manner of iniquity. (Helaman 7:21)

Nephi then declares the wicked abomination that they had embraced as the reason for their unrighteousness.

> Yea, wo be unto you because of that great abomination which has come among you; and ye have united yourselves unto it, yea, to that secret band which was established by Gadianton!
>
> Yea, wo shall come unto you because of that pride which ye have suffered to enter your hearts, which has lifted you up beyond that which is good because of your exceedingly great riches! (Helaman 7:25-26)

Do we see pride, greed, murder, plunder, and false witnesses in the world today? So much of this is reported daily in the news and media that we often cannot determine who is telling the truth.

> And there are also secret combinations, even as in times of old, according to the combinations of the devil, for he is the founder of all these things; yea, the founder of murder, and works of darkness; yea, and he leadeth them by the neck with a flaxen cord, until he bindeth them with his strong cords forever. (2 Nephi 26:22)

The current political condition in the United States is surely a battle between those who have power and those who want it. This battle creates the accompanying evils and behaviors of secret societies, all of which can be seen in life today.

Prophets from the Book of Mormon described the secret societies and combinations that will be built up in the days of the gentiles. Without much thought about the world and societies today, we can grasp that the words of these prophets describe our day.

> And the Gentiles are lifted up in the pride of their eyes, and have stumbled, because of the greatness of their stumbling block, that they have built up many churches; nevertheless, they put down the power and miracles of God, and preach up unto themselves their own wisdom and their own learning, that they may get gain and grind upon the face of the poor.
>
> And there are many churches built up which cause envyings, and strifes, and malice. (2 Nephi 26:20-21)

Book of Mormon prophets tell us that secret societies of the Last Days will spill the blood of the saints and seek to destroy the people. These groups and religions are built up by the devil and seek to "overthrow the freedom of all lands, nations, and countries." It is the Last Saturday and time for us, Latter-Day Saints and other righteous Christians, to wake up to the wicked conditions found in the world today. We must awake to our awful situation (see Ether 8:24-25).

Why are these secret combinations created?

> And behold, I am Giddianhi; and I am the governor of this the secret society of Gadianton; which society and the works thereof I know to be good; and they are of ancient date and they have been handed down unto us. (3 Nephi 3:9)

Satan blinds us, deceives us, and teaches us that his secret oaths and practices are good.

Secret acts and societies exist all over the world and are used to achieve numerous and wide-ranging goals.

SATANIC PANIC: HOW BRITISH AGENTS STOKED
SUPERNATURAL FEARS IN TROUBLES

> British military intelligence agents in Northern Ireland
> used fears about demonic possessions, black masses
> and witchcraft as part of a psychological war against
> emerging armed groups in the Troubles in the 1970s …
>
> They deliberately stoked up a satanic panic from 1972
> to 1974, even placing black candles and upside-down
> crucifixes in derelict buildings in some of Belfast's war
> zones. (McDonald 2014)

What happened in Britain? How many groups, organizations,
companies, people are consciously and intentionally working to sow
discord and panic in countries around the world?

The word of wisdom given to us by the Lord in Section 89 of the
Doctrine and Covenants includes some wisdom about the Last Days:

> Behold, verily, thus saith the Lord unto you: In
> consequence of evils and designs which do and will
> exist in the hearts of conspiring men in the last days, I
> have warned you, and forewarn you, by giving unto you
> this word of wisdom by revelation. (Doc. & Cov. 89:4)

We may quickly think of coffee, tea, and tobacco as evil designs
in our hearts. Indeed, science and medicine have confirmed that those
things are not good for you. The evil design of men may well be the
desire to get gain, money, and wealth at the cost of the health and well-
being of others.

But people today have created some additional evils, and as a
testament to what day it is, their hearts have been filled with designs of
wickedness and psychotic episodes.

MAN DECAPITATED BY SEAT MATE ON BUS

A man aboard a Greyhound bus repeatedly stabbed and then decapitated a fellow passenger, witnesses said Thursday …

"We heard this bloodcurdling scream and turned around, and the guy was standing up, stabbing this guy repeatedly, like 40 or 50 times," [a passenger] said from a hotel in Brandon, Manitoba. (CBS News 2008)

MAN HELD 10-YEAR-OLD GIRL CAPTIVE IN "TORTURE DEN" ATTIC AS HE PLAYED OUT SADOMASOCHISTIC FANTASIES

A man who held a 10-year-old girl captive in his "torture den" attic where he electrocuted her while playing out his sadomasochistic fantasies has been jailed for 22 years …

She confided in someone who reported the incidents to the police. (Independent 2018)

The next news story suggests that sometimes, accidents in our lives may not be real. A family member may believe that another family member intentionally caused a car accident in which someone else was injured. Meaning it was no accident.

INJURED BOY TO GET $4.9 MILLION IN SUIT AGAINST DAD, SISTER

MILWAUKEE (UPI). An 11-year-old boy injured in a traffic accident two years ago has received an out-of-court settlement of $4.9 million. (Detroit 1979, 19)

The boy's lawsuit was against his sister, his father (who was divorced from his mother), and three insurance companies. It is possible that the divorce of the father and mother was contentious, which created some anger and resentment. The financial settlement awarded here also reveals the greedy conditions of our society.

In latter-day scriptures, the Lord says he is not pleased with the wickedness of men. He tells us what he will do about it. Latter-day scriptures reveal some events and conditions of the Last Days:

> I, the Lord, am angry with the wicked; I am holding my Spirit from the inhabitants of the earth.
>
> I have sworn in my wrath, and decreed wars upon the face of the earth, and the wicked shall slay the wicked, and fear shall come upon every man;
>
> And the Saints also shall hardly escape; nevertheless, I, the Lord, am with them, and will come down in heaven from the presence of my Father and consume the wicked with unquenchable fire. (Doc. & Cov. 63:32-34)

How angry is the Lord? The wicked are not currently slaying each other today, but that could happen soon. The Lord clearly states that he will come down from the Father's presence to deal with the wicked.

Let's assume that the Lord is withholding his spirit from the earth. Without his spirit, then surely Satan will have greater influence. We will see more wickedness and evil acts committed in our society and around the world. It is the Last Saturday. Here is what we are doing to one another:

EIGHT-YEAR-OLD CHARGED IN
SHOOTING OF PLAYMATE

AUBURNDALE, Fla. (AP). Police arrested an 8-year-old boy on charges of attempted second-degree murder for reportedly shooting a playmate in the head. (AP NEWS 1987)

An eight-year-old boy shoots a twelve-year-old neighbor in the head. We don't know why. The fact that the deadly decision was made and acted upon is something we would expect to see in the Last Days.

Vandalism and destruction of private and public property is another behavior we should look for today. And we will find it.

Aircraft Vandalism Highlights Need for Airport Watch

During the night on July 13, 10 single- and multiengine aircraft and a Cessna Citation 550 were damaged at Monmouth Executive Airport in New Jersey. Many of the instrument panels were damaged, tires deflated, and fuselages graffitied. (AOPA 2008)

Vandalism at an airport is not considered a terrorist act, but it is criminal and occurs frequently.

Iowa Mother Guilty of Murder in Death of Infant Found in Baby Swing

A jury on Wednesday found a northeast Iowa mother guilty of murder …

Sterling was found dead on a mechanical swing, weighing less than seven pounds …

Feces in his diaper ate through his skin, allowing E. coli bacteria to enter his bloodstream and cause infection. (Nozicka 2019)

A mother places her baby in a baby swing. She leaves him there for several days. He ultimately suffers a horrible death. Now let's not judge the mother. We don't know much about her or the father or the family situation. Information in a news story is limited and often incomplete. However, can we imagine anyone treating an infant in such a manner?

Do we not believe that the light of Christ, which is in all people, would prohibit such an act? The Lord's spirit is being withheld today.

Early in this last dispensation, the Lord said this:

> There were among you adulterers and adulteresses: some of whom have turned away from you, and others remain with you that hereafter shall be revealed …

> And verily I say unto you as I have said before, he that looketh on a woman to lust after her, or if any shall commit adultery in their hearts, they shall not have the Spirit, but shall deny the faith and shall fear. (Doc. & Cov. 63:14,16)

The world today is a real challenge for people who want to live a moral life. The media is filled with images, stories, and information that entice men and women to lust after each other. We don't know how many adulterers and adulteresses are alive today. Since it is the Last Saturday, there is most assuredly a plethora of them in all nations.

> These six things doth the Lord hate: yea, seven are an abomination unto him:

> A proud look, a lying tongue, and hands that shed innocent blood.

> An heart that deviseth wicked imaginations, feet that be swift in running to mischief,

> A false witness that speaketh lies, and he that soweth discord among brethren. (Proverbs 6:16-19)

An Old Testament verse in Proverbs declares that adultery is a serious sin in the eyes of God. Living in the Last Days requires us to avoid the sin of adultery.

But whoso committeth adultery with a woman lacketh
understanding: he that doeth it destroyeth his own soul.
(Proverbs 6:32)

Especially in the Last Days, when the Lord withholds his spirit, we
will see men lusting after women and even greater signs of immorality. If
a man commits adultery in his heart, he shall not have the spirit. Oh, so
that's why we see so many men and women without the spirit. Today, there
are many more broken marriages, families, and homes than fifty years ago.

The Last Days will be filled with lying tongues, hands shedding
innocent blood, wicked imaginations, and rampant discord.

On Monday, June 1, 1987, Ann Landers announced in USA Today
that she was going to conduct a nationwide poll. She asked readers to
write in and tell her if they had committed adultery. Yes, she decided
to find out how many people in the country were unfaithful to their
wedding vows and betrayed their spouse. A majority of Americans
consider extramarital sex wrong. However, close to fifty percent have
discarded their wedding vows.

I remember reading The Scarlet Letter by Nathaniel Hawthorne as
an assignment in one of my English classes. I didn't like the novel, but
I do remember that in it, a young wife was convicted of adultery. Her
punishment, because it was such a horrible and unacceptable act, was
to wear a giant scarlet "A" around her neck. Many years have passed
since the setting of that novel, and without question, much has changed
in our modern times.

It seemed to me then, and seems to me now, being an adulterer had
been considered a very disgraceful thing. Now in our society, we accept,
tolerate, and almost encourage such things without alarm or concern. It
reminds me of a quote I first heard many years ago.

Vice is a monster of so frightful mien, As, to be hated,
needs but to be seen; Yet seen too oft, familiar with her
face. We first endure, then pity, then embrace. (Pope 1744)

The signs of the Last Saturday are very prominent in the areas of
morality. In my youth, sex and nudity were seldom seen in magazines,

in movies, and on TV. Then as I grew into adulthood, sex and nudity were seen occasionally in various forms of media. Today, sex, nudity, and violence are everywhere. Truly a sign of the times is how we have endured, then pitied, and now embrace immorality.

In 1987, Deseret News published an article about a teacher who was in a car with four boys. She asked them what they do after school. One of the boys told her they "make out." She asked them what they meant by make out. The boy chided her saying that she knows what it means to make out.

He stated that their make-out activities included touching. This woman had been teaching for seventeen years. She was still astonished by this calm disclosure made by boys in the second grade (Deseret News, May 27, 1987, C1).

On December 15, 1986, *USA Today* contained a full-page ad titled "Sex Education for Parents." The ad was promoting birth control procedures. Is this an evil design of men on the Last Saturday? Is immorality so rampant that some think the media can help resolve the issues?

EVERYONE KNEW; NO ONE TALKED; DOCTOR FONDLED PATIENTS FOR 3 DECADES

"Rexburg physician retires," proclaimed the front-page headline in the Idaho Falls Post Register ...

All over eastern Idaho, hands reached for phones. It had finally begun: the end, albeit slow and reluctant, to an uncommon 32-year-long public silence.

For three decades, women had whispered about [LaVar] Withers' conduct in examining rooms. Those who didn't have their own stories to tell about the friendly physician fondling [them] knew someone else who did. "The booby doctor," they called him. (Siegel 1996)

Does disseminating birth control information and family planning options increase immorality and sexual promiscuity? Will it decrease immorality? We may find that publicizing information about birth control is a bad idea.

The definition of family has changed and expanded in the last thirty years. Today, many children are being raised by a single, unmarried parent. These new families face many new challenges and trials.

MARRIED AND UNMARRIED PARENTS: A RESEARCH SUMMARY

It is estimated that almost half of children growing up today will spend some time living with an unmarried, cohabiting couple. This should be considered a national tragedy. (Popenoe 1998)

The whole earth shall be in commotion, the love of men shall wax cold, and iniquity shall abound. Does this sound like the Lord was describing today? Is this happening now?

RUNAWAY KIDS AND TEENAGE PROSTITUTION: AMERICA'S LOST, ABANDONED, AND SEXUALLY EXPLOITED CHILDREN

A growing number of suburban throwaway children are referred to as "rat packers." These teens are often forced to leave home due to family problems, financial burdens, incorrigibility, rebelliousness, and an inability to relate to parental authority figures. Rat packers often tend to substitute peers for family and have a strong dislike for the "establishment." …

Rack packers often leave home for weeks or months, staying with friends, neighbors, or even other family members. It is estimated that more than 30,000 teenagers from the middle and upper class become rat packer throwaways annually in the United States. One expert observed that these troubled youth "glory in anarchy and destruction,"

oftentimes stealing what they need to survive, engaging
in alcohol and drug abuse, and committing vandalism and
petty crimes. (Flowers 2001, 25)

The values, attitudes, and actions of many people today are twisted
and irrational. Satan's power and influence are so great, it is seen every
day in our society. Youth and adults are often convinced that living is
hopeless and things would be better if life came to an end.

Four Teens Make Suicide Pact, Die of Carbon Monoxide Poisoning

BERGENFIELD, N.J. (AP). Four teen-agers locked
themselves in a car and committed suicide by apparent
carbon monoxide poisoning Wednesday, after writing a
note on a brown paper bag asking to be buried together,
authorities said …

The bodies of the two girls and two boys, ages 17 to
19, were found in a locked car in an apartment complex
garage about 6:30 a.m. after a passer-by heard the car's
motor running and called police. (Dolan 1987)

-vViolence is a major concern for everyone these days. Violence
against one another, against property, on television, and in movies has
become very prevalent. The Last Saturday will be filled with such
violence.

And there shall be earthquakes also in divers places, and
many desolations; yet men will harden their hearts against
me, and they will take up the sword, one against another,
and they will kill one another. (Doc. & Cov. 45:33)

The sword is a weapon of war from days long past. So, are men
today taking up the sword against one another? It may not be a physical
metal sword, but people use many means to engage in acts of violence

and evil. Today, without even looking or listening for it, we see and hear about violence against family, friends, neighbors, and strangers.

COURT DOCS: MOTHER CHARGED WITH ARSON, ACCUSED OF GETTING DAUGHTER TO SET FIRE TO MOBILE HOME IN LEBANON

LEBANON, Ind. The mother of a 19-year-old who admitted to setting fire to a mobile home earlier this year now faces an arson charge as well …

[Daughter's comments implied the mother] prepared things for her to set the fire." (FOX59 2017)

A black homeless man who was mentally ill grabbed a white police officer's gun. Some young black people reportedly urged him to shoot the officer, while the officer pled for his life. The man shot the officer in the face at point-blank range and then was killed by police.

Law enforcement regularly keeps us safe and gets involved when violence and crimes are committed. When they are essentially involved in criminal activity, it is without question a sign of the times.

EIGHT WOMEN FOUND DEAD AFTER "POLICE SEX TRAFFICKED THEM TO MALE INMATES"

At least half a dozen women told authorities that deputies raped and trafficked them to male inmates inside a long-troubled jail in southwestern Louisiana, according to newly unearthed state and FBI records.

The records offer a harrowing account of sexual assault being traded as currency in a contraband ring that pervaded the Jefferson Davis Parish jail.

Three deputies were charged in the 2002 corruption case. One of them remains a small-town police officer in Louisiana, The Associated Press found …

The victims, ranging in age from 17 to 30, were killed between 2005 and 2009 in and around Jennings, Louisiana. (Yahoo! News 2019)

Racial, sexual, religious, and many other prejudices exist today, which indicates that we are not following Jesus Christ very well. Many people who claim to follow the Savior are far behind him, or way off to the side, which prevents them from seeing him, hearing him, or becoming familiar with his teachings.

14-Year-Old to Be Charged in Shooting Death of 9-Year-Old

PITTSFIELD, N.H. (AP). A small town's hopes that a missing 9-year-old boy would be found safe were shattered by the discovery of his body buried under leaves in [the] woods …

Authorities … planned to charge a 14-year-old with the slaying of Jason Elliott, who died instantly when he was shot twice in the head. (Mitman 1987)

Elder Thomas S. Monson spoke at a funeral I attended many years ago. He said that we cannot judge people who take their own life. We don't know or understand what is happening to them. We don't know who or what voices they are hearing. An evil voice can influence anyone, even a fourteen-year-old boy.

However, surely a father who jumps off a hundred-foot highway overpass, while holding hands with his two sons, is not hearing the Savior Jesus Christ.

"Miracle" Kids Survive Father's Deadly Leap off I-287, Holding His 2 Children

A 1-year-old boy has a bruised lung and his 3-year-old brother has a concussion after they survived a 100-foot jump off a New Jersey highway overpass ... while holding their father's hand. (Davis 2016)

The father was killed. The two sons, however, are expected to survive. We don't know what evil voices took over his mind.

FRENCH MOTHER RELIEVED AFTER ADMITTING TO BABY KILLINGS

The oldest of the babies is believed to have been born in 1989 ...

Stunned relatives voiced disbelief that [she] hid eight pregnancies and births and smothered the newborns, whose bodies were found in bin bags. (Times Malta 2010)

The mother killed her own children, eight of them. We may ask why? Surely such an act could only come from evil voices. A friend one day was telling me about the troubled youth he and his wife bring into their home to help. He told me I would be amazed at the voices some youth hear.

Voices who scream at them, telling them they are worthless. Voices who hound them, saying they are not male or female. They can choose to be whatever gender they want. Satan and his minions are working harder and stronger than most of us realize.

The violence of the Last Days is not limited to the wars and rumors of wars. It not only involves criminals and police. It strikes out at all people, all ages, all social classes, and all nationalities.

CHILDREN KILLING CHILDREN

During the 1990s two inexcusable acts of horrific violence made the nightly news on TV and headlines in newspapers around the world: the bludgeoning death of a 2-year-old British boy and the stabbing/burning killing of a 12-year-old Indiana schoolgirl. Crimes like

these, as heinous as they are, rarely attract so much
international attention, but these murders stood out
from other sensational murders because of one chilling
fact: They were committed by other children ...

After attempting to throw James down an embankment
into the river, they finally beat him to death with bricks
and left his body on the railroad tracks, where a train
cut his body in two. (Evertz 2005)

A mother in Detroit says her son was not involved with drugs or
gangs. He was an athlete. His shooter was convicted and spent several
months in jail. She asks why teenagers increasingly confront each other
with guns, or knives, instead of fists.

A Washington DC father asks why two young men killed his son.
When the father is asked how to stop the killings, he says, "Drugs are
killing their brains, and guns are killing the youth."

SMALL TOWNS FIGHT BIG-CITY CRIME

Boston. Well away from America's big cities, and a
turnpike away from suburban calm, many rural towns
and outlying counties are now grappling with an urban-
like intrusion: rising incidents of violent juvenile
crime ...

"We're seeing every kind of crime you'd see now in
Chicago or New York," says ... a solicitor in rural South
Carolina. "In juvenile court it's rare to see a 16- or
18-year-old kid with any parents there to be with him."
(Holmstrom 1995)

Violence involves young and old, male and female. In the summer
of 1987:

A twelve-year-old girl shot a thirteen-year-old boy in front of a
grocery store. (Columbia, SC)

A fifteen-year-old killed a ten-year-old female friend, then turned the gun on himself. (Whitefish, MT)

A sixteen-year-old boy was charged with killing a sixteen-year-old girl in a store parking lot. (Tacoma, WA)

A fourteen-year-old pled guilty to shooting five children execution-style and cutting the throat of a sixth. All the victims, ages four to fourteen, survived. (Belleville, IL) (see *USA Today*, January 14, 1988, 9A)

Headlines and news broadcasts are filled with violence and acts of cruelty, brutality, and death. The taking of one's own life is also occurring with greater frequency. It is no longer necessarily a solitary act. The times we live in, and signs of those times, are the increasing number of people who take their own life.

Two More Try in Suicide Garage

BERGENFIELD, N.J. A young couple tried to kill themselves with auto exhaust today in the same locked garage where four teenagers died in a suicide pact last week, police said …

They were described as boyfriend and girlfriend. [The female] was an acquaintance of Thomas Rizzo Jr., 19, one of the four youths who killed themselves last week. (UPI 1987)

Police Link Two Young Suicides with New Jersey Deaths

ALSIP, Ill. (AP). Two young women, one holding a rose and a stuffed animal, the other a photo album, were found dead in a garage, apparently victims of the same method of suicide used by four teen-agers in New Jersey, police said Friday …

Miss Grannan's brother … said he felt his sister probably was influenced by the New Jersey incident. (Tanner 1987)

A very telling sign of the Last Days is the changes that are occurring in civil laws at the local and national level. Laws are changing in the United States and around the world. These changes are indications of Satan's influence in the world today.

SUPREME COURT: MARRIAGE IS A FUNDAMENTAL RIGHT FOR GAY COUPLES

> In a historic development for gay rights and the institution of marriage, the Supreme Court has ruled that same-sex couples have the constitutional right to marry.
>
> Specifically, the 5-4 ruling in *Obergefell v. Hodges* declares that the 14th Amendment requires all states to perform same-sex marriages and recognize same-sex marriages performed in other states. (Condon 2015)

Most Christians adhere to the tenet that marriage is ordained of God and is between a man and a woman. We could get caught up in the definition or legal application of the term *marriage*, but let's not. Let's just agree that the legal change to the term marriage, after many centuries, adds to our evidence of Saturday, the earth's last one.

In a Joseph Smith translation of the book of Matthew, Jesus is speaking to his disciples about conditions in the world when he comes again:

> But as it was in the days of Noah, so it shall be also at the coming of the Son of Man;
>
> For it shall be with them, as it was in the days which were before the flood; for until the day that Noah entered into the ark they were eating and drinking, marrying and giving in marriage. (Joseph Smith, Matthew 1:41-42)

These verses say that in the Last Days, it will be like the days of Noah before the Flood. Societies will be "marrying and giving in marriage." Marriage, as defined by God, is between a man and a woman. Are we not now "giving in marriage" couples of the same gender? A Last Saturday prophecy is fulfilled.

Joseph Smith's Matthew translation further describes Noah-like conditions before Christ comes again. They didn't know that the Flood was coming, as we don't know when Jesus will return. People and families will suddenly be taken.

> And knew not until the flood came, and took them all away; so shall also the coming of the Son of Man be.
>
> Then shall be fulfilled that which is written, that in the last days, two shall be in the field, the one shall be taken, and the other left;
>
> Two shall be grinding at the mill, the one shall be taken, and the other left. (Joseph Smith, Matthew 1:43-45)

The events described here are prevalent today in all parts of the world. Families and friends are together, a hurricane comes. Some remain, and some are taken. Students are in school when suddenly some are taken and no longer there. People are in restaurants, movie theaters, concerts, office buildings, community centers, even at home when family and friends are suddenly taken.

Utah's "Free-Range Parenting" Law Said to Be First in the Nation

> It all started when [a mother] let her 9-year-old ride the subway home alone. She gave him a map, a MetroCard, a $20 bill and ... quarters for a pay phone call. Then she left him in the handbag section in New York's original Bloomingdale's. It was all his idea. He had begged [Lenore] Skenazy to just leave him somewhere and let him find his way back all by himself. (Flynn 2018)

This mother trusted that her son could figure out how to get home, and if he couldn't do that, he would ask someone for help. She finally let him do it on a spring day. Her son did get home and was "ecstatic with independence."

The story quickly went viral on social media. People wondered if she was naive or just a mother who had great trust and confidence in her son. She wrote a book and called her parenting practices free-range." She allows her son to engage in various activities without intense supervision. The State of Utah enacted a new law to protect free-range parenting.

We may question this mother's actions here. Not all kids could or should be given such an opportunity. In the context of the Last Saturday, we should realize that Utah felt a need to pass such a law. One to allow parents the freedom to permit appropriate children to engage in independent activities without the threat of child neglect or endangerment charges. Laws are now required to preserve some freedoms and protect other freedoms from being lost.

Nephi describes the conditions of societies and civilizations in the Last Days (actually today):

> Howl ye, for the day of the Lord is at hand; it shall come as a destruction from the Almighty.
>
> Therefore shall all hands be faint, every man's heart shall melt;
>
> And they shall be afraid; pangs and sorrows shall take hold of them; they shall be amazed one at another; their faces shall be as flames.
>
> Behold, the day of the Lord cometh, cruel both with wrath and fierce anger, to lay the land desolate; and he shall destroy the sinners thereof out of it. (2 Nephi 23:6-9)

Are people's hands faint today? Are men's hearts failing? Yes, because many are engaging in evil, without warning, taking lives, and sparing others. We live in a time when people are "amazed one at another." These are the days described by Nephi.

Are we afraid? Are our hearts melting? Yes, for those whose lives are taken and for those who still live. "Behold, the day of the Lord cometh."

3

Religion and Righteousness

The Lord's Kingdom will roll forth in the Last Days. The church will grow until it spreads throughout the world. Satan's influence and power will grow stronger as the Lord's Second Coming draws near. These two major forces of good and evil will undoubtedly have a major impact on the world. Today is the Last Saturday. An examination of religion and righteousness in today's world will reinforce or refute that today is the Last Saturday.

As the two forces of right and wrong grow, we would expect to see increased activity in both religion and righteousness, as well as evil and wickedness.

BATTERED WIFE GETS SIX YEARS
FOR KILLING HUSBAND

CHARLOTTE, N.C. A battered wife who was forced by her husband to eat out of a pet food dish and to work as a prostitute was sentenced. (UPI 1987)

The woman was charged with first-degree murder, but convicted of voluntary manslaughter. Charges were reduced because of the abuse her husband inflicted on her.

Let's not judge the battered wife. Let's grasp that Last Saturday signs are real and all around us. Signs are not just illegal or criminal. They include demeaning and abusive actions and control imposed on others.

What is religion today?

Religion Definition

DEFINITION OF RELIGION – WWW.DICTIONARY.COM

1 a set of beliefs concerning the cause, nature, and purpose of the universe, especially when considered as the creation of a superhuman agency or agencies, usually involving devotional and ritual observances, and often containing a moral code governing the conduct of human affairs. (dictionary.com, n.d.)

Religion is service and worship of God, or the supernatural. However, it is also a system of beliefs that are followed with ardor and faith. Religion can, therefore, be organized and structured, or no more than one person's principles and theories.

The definition of religion justifies the existence of many religions in the world today. What is happening to today's religions? Are churches growing? What is happening today in the name of religion?

3.1. WORLD RELIGIONS GROWTH/STATUS

The lack of organized religion in the lives of many people encourages those people to disregard the laws and accepted norms of respect, tolerance, and decency in society. It promotes general indifference towards fellow human beings, allowing some to feel justified in any course of action they choose. In these situations, we could say there is no religion and no moral code of conduct.

MAN FACES DRUG CHARGES IN POT-GROWING CASE

MINNEAPOLIS (AP). A man has been arrested for operating what authorities say is the most sophisticated and largest marijuana growing operation they've ever seen, in an underground greenhouse. (APNEWS 1987)

The estimated street value of the marijuana plants in the underground greenhouse was $2.5 million. Keep in mind here, that in 1987 marijuana of any kind, or any form was completely illegal everywhere. Everything is about money. The need, desire, and love of money foster evil and sin.

It seems like some of today's religions or groups are lobbying and working to legalize drugs, including marijuana. You can read about various forms of marijuana that are being legalized in many states. Do we not, as a society, see this as an "unrighteousness" sign of the times? Many groups are promoting their own desires and beliefs, many of which are not on the righteous side of religion.

Many years ago, a friend argued that illegal drugs should be legalized. This would end drug abuse and related crimes. He may have been right, but legalizing currently illegal drugs and behaviors can bring a whole new wave of problems, crime, and chaos. The current furor and alarm, expressed by many, concerning the prevalent use of opioid drugs may serve as a warning about legalizing many prescription drugs.

In 2010, the Pew Research Center published some statistics about the religions of the world:

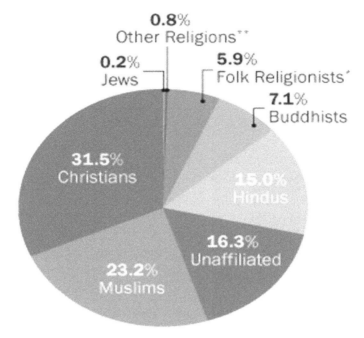

Size of Major Religious Groups, 2010
Percentage of the global population

0.8% Other Religions**

0.2% Jews

5.9% Folk Religionists´

7.1% Buddhists

31.5% Christians

15.0% Hindus

16.3% Unaffiliated

23.2% Muslims

* Includes followers of African traditional religions, Chinese folk religions, Native American religions and Australian aboriginal religions.

** Includes Baha'is, Jains, Sikhs, Shintoists, Taoists, followers of Tenrikyo, Wiccans, Zoroastrians and many other faiths.

Percentages may not add to 100 due to rounding.

Pew Research Center's Forum on Religion & Public Life • Global Religious Landscape, December 2012

(Pew Research 2012)

[Pew Research Center bears no responsibility for the analyses or interpretations of the data presented here. The opinions expressed herein, including any implications for policy, are those of the author and not of Pew Research Center.]

Christians are still the dominant religion and faith in the world. The concern, and question most related to our task, is how many of the world's Christians truthfully practice and live the teachings of Jesus Christ. As that number drops, time runs out.

Religion and righteousness are reflected by those who claim and practice a religion. It is also revealed by the actions and behavior of society in general. The extent to which we all exhibit civil obedience, lack of respect for social norms, and unkindness to one another are signs of righteousness and the Last Saturday.

RED-LIGHT ANARCHY REIGNS ON ALBANY ROADS

ALBANY. Green means go. Red means stop.

Simple rules, really. But George de Piro sees them ignored with abandon during his walks around Center Square. Traffic lights in Albany, he says, are merely suggestions …

Just 18 seconds in, a clear red is ignored by a mini-van, that symbol of suburban safety.

At the 1:15 mark, an Albany police cruiser fails to stop. No ticket for him!

A CDTA vehicle blazes through a red, too. (Churchill 2012)

When people ignore others and are blind to the laws and rights of others, then religion no longer exists. Anarchy and chaos will surely take root and grow.

Anarchism is the replacement of government with self-governed societies. Anarchy is found in a society without a high-level governing body. It results in confusion, chaos, and extensive civil unrest. Isaiah could be describing anarch in the following scripture.

Behold, the Lord maketh the earth empty, and maketh it waste, and turneth it upside down, and scattereth abroad the inhabitants thereof. (Isaiah 24:1)

Religious controversy and upheaval are being experienced worldwide.

Israel's Government Could Fall over Ultra Orthodox Enlistment

ASHDOD, Israel. A open-air market has become an unlikely battleground in a wider struggle that could potentially bring down Israeli Prime Minister Benjamin Netanyahu's government.

For weeks, shop owners in the Big Fashion mall have received warnings and fines for illegally opening on Saturday—the traditional Jewish day of rest. (Bruton 2018)

The Sabbath day is a long, ongoing dispute in Israel. The dispute is basically between the secular and religious populations in the country. It is also between the Orthodox and less faithful Jewish groups.

Devout Jews are opposed to secular Sabbath day activities like shopping and using public transportation. Issues related to whether ultra-Orthodox will participate in the country's military institutions also cause conflict. Some of the people would like to honor the Jewish Sabbath, but feel they are required to work on the Sabbath to feed their families. The issues provoke protests by those who are on both sides of the conflict.

What is the attitude of governments and nations today toward religion and churches?

Britain Puts Mormonism on Trial

A London court called the church's leader to account for "false" doctrines—the latest in a string of sensational charges leveled against Mormons since they first landed in Liverpool.

The president of the Church of Jesus Christ of Latter-day Saints has been ordered to appear before a British court to defend the Mormon faith against charges that it used false teachings to defraud church members.

The court order is the result of complaints filed by … a disaffected Mormon living in Portugal, on behalf of two men he says were induced to pay an annual tithing to the Church based on "untrue or misleading" claims. (Zeveloff 2014)

The claim filed by the disaffected individuals is not unusual. What is surprising is that the English magistrate is supporting the claim. He has ordered the president of the Church of Jesus Christ of Latter-Day Saints to appear in the Westminster judge's court to answer the accusations. Legal experts are perplexed by the magistrate's order.

Many individuals and groups will contend with organized religions, and those who believe in those religions. History bears witness of greater love, compassion, and tolerance when people faithfully practice a religion founded in a loving, caring supreme being.

Why Religion Matters Even More: The Impact of Religious Practice on Social Stability

A steadily growing body of evidence from the social sciences demonstrates that regular religious practice benefits individuals, families, and communities, and thus the nation as a whole. Policymakers at the federal, state, and local levels should therefore encourage an environment in which religious institutions and organizations can thrive and citizens can actively practice their faith. (Fagan 2006)

The longer man lives on the earth, has experiences, and increases his knowledge he becomes more enlightened. He believes and understands new exciting things. He then moves away from religion and faith. Sometimes he devises and teaches a new, his own, religion. All of which is evidence that these are the Last Days.

3.2. Wickedness

The prophet Enoch was an ancestor of Noah, son of Jared, and father of Methuselah. He was a righteous man who led the people of the city of Zion. The city was taken to heaven because of the faith and righteousness of those who lived there. Enoch saw the Savior ascend into heaven and asked the Lord "Wilt thou not come again upon the earth?" (see Moses 7:59).

> And the Lord said unto Enoch: As I live, even so will I come in the last days, in the days of wickedness and vengeance, to fulfil the oath which I have made unto you concerning the children of Noah;
>
> And the day shall come that the earth shall rest, but before that day the heavens shall be darkened, and a veil of darkness shall cover the earth; and the heavens shall shake, and also the earth; and great tribulations shall be among the children of men, but my people will I preserve. (Moses 7:60-61)

The Lord tells Enoch that he will return to the earth in the Last Days during a time of great wickedness. The earth shall eventually rest. But before that day the heavens and earth will be dark. Dark, as pertaining to the words and kingdom of God, like the Dark Ages.

Enoch even saw the day of the Savior's Second Coming. If he saw when that day would be, he didn't disclose it.

> And it came to pass that Enoch saw the day of the coming of the Son of Man, in the Last Days, to dwell on the earth in righteousness for the space of a thousand years. (Moses 7:65)

With all the wickedness in the world today, the day of the Second Coming must be near.

HORROR STORIES

Every few years, Hong Kong sees a murder so bizarre or gruesome that it captures the public's imagination. Over the past few weeks, we have recoiled in horror as we read the details of the black-magic killer case—yet most of us continued to follow the reports.

The combination of repulsion and curiosity create a compulsive fascination. It is a strange relationship, this flirting with the sheer horror of it all, and one that can only be indulged strictly in moderation. One such murder every three to five years is enough for public consumption. Too much and we would become desensitized …

The recent case of cannibalism in Germany, in which two men advertised on the internet for someone to torture and eat alive, received light coverage in Hong Kong. (Whitehead 2004)

Wickedness today is not just violent crimes, murder, and individual torture. Dishonesty, deceit, breaking the law, and all types of fraud are forms of wickedness. Everything that is not in harmony with God, and the teachings of Jesus Christ, is wickedness. We are either with the Lord or against Him.

CARNIVAL RACKETEERING AND ORGANIZED CRIME

Carnival racketeering is endemic throughout the United State and has been for years. Carnivals have close ties to not only organized crime but to local law enforcement. Carnival midways are the only venues in the United States where local police departments allow carnival lots to be free crime zones for illegal gambling, larceny, and fraud. Gaffed and chance-based games travel to thousands of carnival lots and fairs each year, raking in billions of dollars in ill-gotten gains with virtual impunity.

Have you ever played a carnival game and felt cheated?

A poll conducted by Carnival Biz, an Internet link to carnival business, reveals that over 70 percent of participants feel they are cheated on a carnival midway. Carnival game players lose "95 percent of the time" says a carnival game enforcement specialist. (Margittay 2015)

Does the life people choose to live, and the choices they make, provide insight into the Last Saturday? The lack of faith and religion in many homes and families.

In Leviticus, the prophets teach us about religion and an important aspect of wickedness. The actions described here are not in harmony with the teachings of God or his Son.

Thou shalt not uncover the nakedness of thy daughter in law: she is thy son's wife; thou shalt not uncover her nakedness.

Thou shalt not uncover the nakedness of thy brother's wife: it is thy brother's nakedness.

Thou shalt not uncover the nakedness of a woman and her daughter, neither shalt thou take her son's daughter, or her daughter's daughter, to uncover her nakedness: it is wickedness.

Neither shalt thou take a wife to her sister, to vex her, to uncover her nakedness, beside the other in her life time. (Leviticus 18:15-18)

The amount of sex, nudity, and violence found in all forms of media today destroys righteousness throughout the world. Thus, allowing wickedness to permeate the minds and lives of people everywhere. These Leviticus scriptures warn us about adultery, fornication, and all unholy sexual activity.

There was a recent news headline about a young girl who was shot to death by her nine-year-old brother. She wouldn't give him the video game controller. The boy found a gun and shot his sister in the head (see https://nypost.com/2018/03/19/teen-dies-after-brother-allegedly-shoots-her-over-video-game-fight/).

What day is it?

"Mommy, Don't!": Graphic Audio, Video Show Killing of Woman Who Stabbed Son 25 Times

HENDERSON, Nev. Graphic body camera footage, along with the audio of a desperate 911 call placed by a 6-year-old Nevada boy, show how the fatal police shooting of the boy's mother unfolded last month.

Henderson police officers were called just after noon Oct. 21 to the Equestrian on Eastern Apartments, where the boy, who had called for help, was found bleeding from multiple stab wounds. In a video statement released Thursday, authorities said the boy was stabbed 25 times. (Bonvillian 2019)

The mother here was seemingly shot by police, which is sad and tragic. Our focus here is why the mother stabbed her son twenty-five times. What kind of evil and wickedness was present? Was the boy misbehaving; was he threatening his mother? Was his mother angry with him? Was she using powerful medications or illegal drugs?

When the dispatcher answered the 911 call and asked about the nature of the emergency, he heard the boy speak up: "My mom is trying to kill me."

One of the commandments God has given us is "Thou Shalt Not Kill." Killing a child of God is truly an appalling act. Most of those who break and violate this commandment know what they are doing. Individuals who kill another person are signs of the times.

Serial Killer Myth #1: They're Mentally Ill or Evil Geniuses

Serial killers are rarely insane or brilliant — just deadly!

The sensationalized images of serial killers presented in both the news and entertainment media suggest that they either have a debilitating mental illness, such as psychosis, or they are brilliant but demented geniuses …

Very few serial killers suffer from any mental illness to such a debilitating extent that they are considered to be insane. (Bonn 2014)

Today is a day of wickedness.

3.3. The Promised Land

The Book of Mormon prophet Lehi was instructed by the Lord to flee Jerusalem. The Lord led Lehi through the wilderness to a seashore. He then led them across that sea to a new home, even a new land.

> And it came to pass that after we had sailed for the space of many days we did arrive at the promised land; and we went forth upon the land, and did pitch our tents; and we did call it the promised land. (1 Nephi 18:23)

Another group of people in the Book of Mormon also sailed for many days and arrived in a new land. They are known as the Jaredites and were led by Jared and his brother. Their records describe what they did when they arrived in the new land.

> And they did land upon the shore of the promised land. And when they had set their feet upon the shores of the promised land they bowed themselves down upon the face of the land, and did humble themselves before the Lord, and did shed tears of joy before the Lord, because of the multitude of his tender mercies over them. (Ether 6:12)

Many nations of the world, including the Promised Land where Lehi and his descendants lived, are not following the example of Lehi's or Jared's family. They do not bow down and humble themselves before the Lord. They do not shed tears of joy and do not see or understand the tender mercies of the Lord.

The lives, choices, and actions of those living in the Promised Land continually provide evidence that we live in the Last Days.

A man in Florida was sent to jail for marrying a woman in November and then marrying her eighteen-year-old daughter the following September. He pleaded no contest to charges of bigamy, forgery, and owning a firearm; he is a convicted criminal. He denied his guilt, but with the no-contest plea, he admits that evidence is sufficient to find him guilty.

Disregard for the laws of the Promised Land, as well as the laws of God, adds to the mountain of evidence we see that our days are the last.

DOMESTIC VIOLENCE AND ABUSE

Domestic violence and abuse are used for one purpose and one purpose only: to gain and maintain total control over you. An abuser doesn't "play fair." An abuser uses fear, guilt, shame, and intimidation to wear you down and keep you under their thumb.

Domestic violence and abuse can happen to anyone; it does not discriminate. Abuse happens within heterosexual relationships and in same-sex partnerships. It occurs within all age ranges, ethnic backgrounds, and economic levels. And while women are more often victimized, men also experience abuse. (Smith 2019)

Abuse of any kind or form, physical, sexual, mental, emotional, spouse, child, is wicked and evil. Abuse not only affects the victims but those who love them. Abuse destroys the soul of those who engage in it. It hampers the spiritual growth and emotional well-being of abusers and victims.

Those who abuse are seeking control and power. An abuse counselor says he knows of no abuse therapy that can teach someone how to love, respect, and cherish another person.

The widespread abuse that is reported, and unreported today, is a glaring declaration of the Final Days of wickedness that are upon us. The following scriptures further teach us about behaviors we will see at the end. Behavior around the world and even in the Promised Land.

Moreover thou shalt not lie carnally with thy neighbour's wife, to defile thyself with her.

And thou shalt not let any of thy seed pass through the fire to Molech, neither shalt thou profane the name of thy God: I am the Lord.

Thou shalt not lie with mankind, as with womankind: it is abomination.

Neither shalt thou lie with any beast to defile thyself therewith: neither shall any woman stand before a beast to lie down thereto: it is confusion. (Leviticus 18:20-23)

These scriptures describe some of the abominations that are being engaged in today. The list of evil, unheard of actions that are occurring today is steadily increasing. How much wickedness exists in the world, that never reaches news headlines or media outlets?

A FATHER GETS 60 YEARS IN PRISON FOR TRYING TO SELL HIS DAUGHTER FOR SEX. SHE WAS 4.

A jury ... convicted him of trafficking a child and compelling prostitution of someone under the age of 18 ... [he] caught the attention of Houston police officers who saw a Craigslist ad called "Play with Daddie's Little Girl." (Phillips 2018)

Selling a daughter for any purpose is a dreadful crime. Selling a four-year-old daughter for any reason is appalling. The action of this father is a sign of today's terrible times. This is surely an abomination condemned by the Lord.

Ye shall therefore keep my statutes and my judgements, and shall not commit any of these abominations; neither any of your own nation, nor any stranger that sojourneth among you. (Leviticus 18:26)

Satan is grabbing the hearts and minds of people with greater success each day. We read and hear of inconceivable acts that are being committed regularly by and to men, women, and children.

STABBING

RIVERSIDE (AP). [A girl] was found bleeding behind a shopping center Aug. 7. The little girl had been stabbed and left in a trash bin. (Desert Sun 1979, 2)

Two women found this little girl wandering in a neighborhood, wearing a bloody dress. She told the police she was awakened by her mother and was told they were going for a ride.

She had been stabbed in the stomach and dropped into a large trash container. The girl was taken to a hospital and was in stable condition after surgery.

We may think that many of the wicked, violent acts that are being committed today have been committed through the ages. However, they are increasing, expanding, and mutating. They are spreading across race, gender, age, religion, and station in life. Today we have politicians, celebrities, athletes, media moguls, and religious leaders who are accused of unrighteous acts and conduct.

The number of youths who are making poor choices and decisions in their lives is sometimes beyond comprehension. Trends and education often help what is considered negative and life-altering choices to decline. Each generation seems to have new and unique challenges. Why? Because the evil one constantly updates and alters his game plan to capture the hearts and souls of God's children.

ADOLESCENT PREGNANCY

Key facts:

- Approximately 12 million girls aged 15–19 years and at least 777,000 girls under 15 years give birth each year in developing regions.

- At least 10 million unintended pregnancies occur each year among adolescent girls aged 15–19 years in the developing world.
- Complications during pregnancy and childbirth are the leading cause of death for 15–19-year-old girls globally.
- Of the estimated 5.6 million abortions that occur each year among adolescent girls aged 15–19 years, 3.9 million are unsafe, contributing to maternal mortality, morbidity and lasting health problems. (World Health Organization 2020)

Pregnancy is a life-changing event and requires difficult decisions for the young people involved. The decisions include abortion or adoption. They may need to drop out of school, leave family, and ultimately go on welfare.

Childbirth outside of marriage may have a negative impact on life potential. It is a violation of God's laws and is prevalent in the Promised Land.

The Promised Land of Lehi's family, and the family of Jared and his brother, is not so promised now. The choices, lives, and practices of many living in this land now are not in harmony with the teachings of Christ. They are proof that today is the final day of the earth's existence as we know it.

3.4. THE WORLD WIDE WEB (INTERNET)

The World Wide Web today is truly a global source of information, data, news, events, instructions, and knowledge.

Here is an alarming, older article from the Meriden, Connecticut, *Record-Journal*. It explains the ever-increasing access to sex, nudity, and vulgarity in our world today:

PARENTS BEWARE: SOFTWARE IS
BECOMING "HARDCORE"

LOS ANGELES (AP). That personal computer your kid got for Christmas may be more educational than you think. Animated nudes, sex-filled bulletin boards, and files filled with dirty jokes are now accessible to most PCs. (Gutierrez 1988, 5)

The internet today provides access to more sexually explicit material than ever before. Sexual material includes artwork, games, images, jokes, adult pictures, and sexual messages. All of this can be readily found, viewed, and shared around the world.

Many people receive their news and information today from the internet. Access to the web has exploded worldwide since the term *internet* was first heard.

The following are a few of the most popular news websites from eBiz|MBA The eBusiness Guide, as of August 2020:

Popular News Sites as derived from our *eBizMBA Rank* ...

	eBizMBA Rank	Estimated Unique Monthly Visitors
1 | Yahoo! News	30	| 175,000,000
2 | Google News	35	| 150,000,000
3 | HuffingtonPost	38	| 110,000,000
4 | CNN	63	| 95,000,000
5 | New York Times	88	| 70,000,000
6 | Fox News	93	| 65,000,000
7 | NBC News	125	| 63,000,000

(see http://www.ebizmba.com/articles/news-websites)

Add up all the "Estimated Unique Monthly Visitors" to these news websites, and the number of people on the internet is astounding. The numbers themselves do not serve as evidence of the Last Saturday. What is important is the type and content of information that is being accessed, viewed, and shared via the World Wide Web, and other social media.

The access and tolerance of sex, nudity, foul language, crudeness, and violence accepted in our lives today is a behavior of Last Saturday.

It is offensive and an abomination to God. The World Wide Web may be the biggest tool of evil that we have ever seen.

Yet, the web also has much that is extremely uplifting, beneficial, and effective in promoting religious faith and righteousness. Stories and articles like the following ones can easily be found online or in print.

Husband Arrested after Wife's Body Found at Sea during Honeymoon Cruise

LOS ANGELES (AP). The body of a woman who was on a honeymoon cruise has been found in the Pacific Ocean, and her husband has been booked for investigation of murder …

[The husband] told authorities that high wind blew his wife off the deck near the ship's jogging track. (APNews 1988)

Searching for evidence of Last Saturday online will quickly produce overwhelming results. Many of the stories and articles we find in print came from or will be placed online. The web expands and multiplies the evidence of the Saturday we are examining.

Ex-Teacher, Coach Accused of Sexually Assaulting Students Faces Trial

A former teacher, coach and club adviser is headed for trial for allegedly sexually assaulting six students in Lehigh and Bucks counties …

The 40-year-old … is charged with 18 counts, including sexual assault by a sports official. (Cassi 2019)

A teacher/coach is charged with eighteen counts of sexual assault, with multiple students. This type of sexual relationship seems to be on the rise. Cases of sexual relations with high school students, and younger, are widespread today. Is this a new type of sexual involvement? Was it occurring before and never revealed or reported? Does it not support the claim that it is near midnight on the Last Saturday?

> THERE HAVE BEEN 5 FRATERNITY DEATHS THIS
> SCHOOL YEAR ALONE, BUT LITTLE IS BEING
> DONE TO CURB DANGEROUS FRAT BEHAVIOR

> A recent spate of deaths at American colleges has brought a focus back on dangerous behavior at fraternities.

> So far this school year, five young men have been found dead at fraternities, or after attending fraternity events, at schools across the country from New York to California. Two fraternity brothers died this week alone. (Collman 2019)

In our world, during these Last Days, many are deliberately making choices that are in opposition to the laws of God. When such actions are chosen, the wrath of God will soon fall upon them and us. God does not tolerate sin or choices of disobedience.

> ZEFFIRELLI DOESN'T UNDERSTAND
> OBJECTIONS TO SCREEN SEX

> HOLLYWOOD. Director Franco Zeffirelli is planning a May production start for "Endless Love," a film in which he hopes to prove "sexology does not have to be pornography." …

> [The director] is developing the "Love" screenplay … that, as he puts it, "it will have the full impact of a violent, almost deadly love of a 17-year-old boy and a 16-year-old girl who can't sustain the scorching effects of the relationship." …

> But what about the harm of encouraging teen-agers to indulge in premarital sex?

"What's wrong with that?" he asks. "Kids of 16-17 making love is something beautiful. It's the crowning expression of moral and spiritual greatness. (Salt Lake Tribune 1980)

It is important for us to realize that many people have no knowledge or understanding of the laws of God. They are oblivious to the challenges and social problems that violation of God's laws will bring. The voices of these individuals and groups will become louder in the Last Days.

News stories, articles, blogs, and posts that confirm it is the Last Days are never-ending. They can be found in newspapers and online with little effort.

After His Wallet Was Stolen, Man Chased Thief and Beat Him to Death, New Orleans Police Say

[He] snapped when a man swiped his wallet outside an Uptown gasoline station …

He chased the thief across the street and beat him to death with his fists and feet. (Vargas 2018)

News headline: A man beats and kills another man for stealing his wallet. Can that be true? The actions of people today are becoming more shocking. What day is it?

3 Arrested in Manila on Charges of Child Exploitation

MANILA, Philippines. Two metro Manila women, and a man face charges for exploiting three children for online sex shows and offering them for sexual abuse for a fee …

The arrests resulted in HSI and the NBI rescuing two children, ages 8 and 13 years old. (ICE Newsroom 2017)

115

Evidence of the Last Saturday is extensive and easily identified. The Last Saturday evidence on the World Wide Web is overwhelming.

Any subject, phrase, or single word can be researched on the web. The results, pages of information, and links about the subject are presented in about two seconds. Try "Serial Killers." Some information you see on the web can be positive, uplifting, and valuable, but other links and information may be false, depressing, harmful, or seductive.

The problem with the internet, and it is a major one, is that there is no real way to determine and verify what is true and what is not. However, the same can be said for many articles and news stories.

The internet can instantly present information, pictures, and videos about anything and everything. A search for "Evil Today" displayed about 675,000,000 results in 0.46 seconds. That's less than half a second.

What an extraordinary source of good, incredible, useful, bad, false, sinful information. This is one of the Evil Today results from the internet:

THE EVIL ONE AND TODAY'S SOCIETY

Today's Way of Thinking

> We define culture and today's way of thinking as *satanic*, as in the Hebrew word *satan*. The Hebrew noun *śāṭān* is a derivation of the root *s ṭ n*, which means being hostile, opposing and assailing, even if only morally, and also defaming and slandering.

> Our current society can also be defined as *diabolical* (from the late Latin *diabŏlus*) a word that was adopted from the Greek for *contradictor* or *opposer*, in order to translate the Hebrew *śāṭān*. (Carlin 2018)

Father Paolo Carlin has described the world today. His comments and observations attest to the fact that it is the end of days. It only takes seconds (or less) on the World Wide Web to find confirmation that today is the Last Saturday.

The World Wide Web provides positive and negative information to millions of people around the world. Yet all of that information is an insignificant part of the real internet. There are other unknown parts of the web, not accessed by most of the world's population.

Experian has provided information about how vast and sinister the web truly is. The Experian post discusses three levels of the web. The Dark Web is another indicator of Satan's power and influence in the world today.

What Is the Dark Web?

There are three levels—the publicly available world wide web, the deep web, and the dark web—and we'll explain a bit more here about each:

Public Web: Information that you would normally find on search engines. Comprises roughly 4%.

Deep Web: Information that is not indexed by search engines and does not require authentication. Comprises roughly 93%.

Dark Web. Information that is not accessible by normal internet browsers. Comprises about 3%.

Because of its hidden nature and the using special applications to maintain anonymity, it's not surprising that the dark web can be a haven for all kinds of illicit activity including the trafficking of stolen personal information. (Sirull 2018)

The public web is the internet you and most people surf, search, and use. The deep web consists of internal company sites, school intranets, online databases, member-only websites, and pages with controlled access.

The dark web is a hidden network of websites. The dark web incorporates and uses special applications to allow those who manage and use it, to do so anonymously. This allows the dark web to be a haven of illegal and illicit activity.

The dark web is where criminals hack, sell, and buy corporate, government, and personal information. They can make a living through the dark web using computer malware, scams, and viruses.

One can find enough negative, bad, inappropriate, and evil information and things on the public World Wide Web. Imagine the amount of bad, illegal, and wicked sites on the dark web.

3.5. SIN

In the New Testament, in his first general Epistle, John defines sin.

> Whosoever committeth sin transgresseth also the law:
> for sin is the transgression of the law. (1 John 3:4)

When we disobey the law of the Lord, we are committing sin. When we rebel against God's commandments, we are committing sin. When our life is not in harmony with the teachings, doctrines, and standards of God, we are committing sin. When we fail to follow the instructions of God, we are committing sin.

> Therefore to him that knoweth to do good, and doeth it
> not, to him it is sin. (James 4:17)

Here are some additional descriptions of sin:

THE SPIRITUAL LIFE: SIN

Sin is a transgression against divine law. Sin can also be viewed as any thought or action that endangers the ideal relationship between an individual and God; or as any diversion from the perceived ideal order for human living.

Sins are generally actions, any thought, word, or act considered immoral, selfish, shameful, harmful, or alienating might be termed "sinful". Each culture has its own interpretation of what it means to commit a sin. In Jainism, sin refers to anything that harms the possibility of the jiva (being) to attain moksha (supreme emancipation). In Islamic ethics, Muslims see sin as anything that goes against the commands of Allah (God). Judaism regards the violation of any of the 613 commandments as a sin. (Spiritual Life n.d.)

Each culture has its own interpretation of what it means to sin.

What is the state of sin today in the world? In the United States? In our neighborhoods? In our homes? Are sins occurring with more frequency and with increased visibility? Yes, they are.

DOCTOR SUGGESTS FAIRFAX CO. MOTHER CHARGED WITH KILLING 2 DAUGHTERS COULD BE MALINGERING

A court-appointed psychologist investigating the mental health of a Fairfax County mother charged with the 2018 murders of her two daughters suggests Veronica Youngblood is feigning or exaggerating mental illness.

Youngblood allegedly shot her daughters, 5-year-old Brooklynn Youngblood and 15-year-old Sharon Castro, in their McLean, Virginia, apartment in August 2018. She was indicted in May 2019 on two counts of murder. (Augenstein 2020)

The consequences of sin are serious and have destroyed people, families, societies, and nations.

When toleration for sin increases, the outlook is bleak and Sodom and Gomorrah days are certain to return (Kimball 1965).

The eleventh president of the Church of Jesus Christ of Latter-Day Saints spoke of sin and noted its growth in Babylon.

Admonitions for the Priesthood of God

I want to warn this great body of priesthood against that great sin of Sodom and Gomorrah, which has been labeled as a sin second only in seriousness to the sin of murder. I speak of the sin of adultery ...

and besides this, the equally grievous sin of homosexuality, which seems to be gaining momentum with social acceptance in the Babylon of the world. (Lee 1973, 106)

Sacred verses from the Bible frequently warn against sin. Sexual sin is often mentioned and forbidden. Sexual sin is a transgression against one's own body and God's commands.

Do not prostitute thy daughter, to cause her to be a whore; lest the land fall to whoredom, and the land become full of wickedness. (Leviticus 19:29)

There are many ways to commit sexual sins. Surely the following actions of a mother are most severe. She forces another person to engage in sexual activities:

Dad: Shaniya's Mom Trafficked Her to Settle Drug Debt

Nov. 20, 2009. The father of [a] 5-year-old told Oprah Winfrey today that the girl's mother trafficked the child to pay off a drug debt.

The allegation ... came a day after [a man] was charged with the rape and murder of Shaniya ...

The girl's mother ... has been arrested and charged with child prostitution. (Netter 2009)

Perhaps the family needed some additional money, so the parents decided they could earn it by exploiting their daughter. We don't know, and it is of no concern here. The actions of the parents are a significant sign of sin today. How many family members have been sold for sex around the world?

The world, including the United States, has become filled with sin and wickedness.

A Utah teacher Sexually Abused Children over His 31-Year Career. How Did He Hide So Long?

When it was their turn to speak, the victims and their family members didn't mince words.

During the Sept. 24, 2019, sentencing of former Washington County School District teacher …, one woman—the first of more than 30 accusers who came forward to police—spoke of how her sexual abuse as a child caused her enormous shame and now impacts the way she parents …

Colby Backman, a clinical mental health counselor based in St. George who has treated children with trauma, said perpetrators tend to be "very charismatic" and "very good salespeople," capable of putting on a show for the people around them to hide their abuse. The rapport they build with their victims can sometimes cause them to question if anything is wrong, he said. (Bancroft 2020)

In holy scripture, God forbids adultery consistently and frequently. Is adultery a crime? A New Hampshire court ruled on this in 1987. In these Last Days, the courts of the land may revoke God's command.

New Hampshire's Adultery Law on Trial

> MERRIMACK, N.H. (AP). An 18th-century law against
> extramarital sex faces a court test March 20, when a
> husband presses a charge of adultery against the boss
> of his estranged wife. [The husband's] complaint …
> has stirred debate among Christian fundamentalists,
> lawyers and civil libertarians. (Bernotas 1987)

If the boss is found guilty of adultery, the 1791 law imposes four possible punishments: Standing on a gallows for one hour with a noose, taking thirty-nine lashes, jail time for a year, and paying a one hundred pound fine.

This law is old, times have changed, and adultery receives very little attention now. If convicted, the odds are high that the defendant will receive a slap on the wrist.

Do you doubt that the law on trial in New Hampshire is a sign of the dire days we live in? In April of 2014, the New Hampshire Senate voted to repeal the state's anti-adultery law. The governor said she is likely to sign it. Whether she did is not the issue. The issue is that humans are over-ruling God.

Is adultery a crime? It is a law of God. God's law condemns and forbids the act of adultery. People have, over time, changed their attitudes concerning adultery. We have even defined our own laws and punishments for those who engage in this sin. How can we be blind to the fact that the end is near?

3.6. Cults

If you don't believe there are cults and secret societies in the world, the website www.forbiddensymbols.com may change your mind. This website presents over 150 signs and symbols of cults, gangs, and secret societies. There are also blogs, headlines, and info about these types of groups, organizations, and activities from around the world.

Are there more churches today than ten or twenty years ago? Has there been an increase in those searching for something meaningful in their lives?

The *Salt Lake Tribune*, back in 1980, published an article about the growth of religious cults and sects. Religious beliefs continue to change today as nations and societies advance, and Satan realizes that the Last Saturday is about to happen.

RELIGIOUS CULTS, SECTS ON THE INCREASE

SAN FRANCISCO. Religious cults and sects are rapidly increasing in this country as replacements for the declining traditional religions ...

A study of the nation's changing religious patterns reveals that there are about 1,000 cults and sects in operation ...

The study dismissed the notion of a "bible belt" in the South but it did find a "cult belt" along the entire West Coast and extending to Alaska. (Salt Lake Tribune 1980, 4F)

The group of sociologists who completed the study reported that many witchcraft and pagan groups are immersed in magic. They promise their followers supernatural power and the ability to manipulate the natural world.

Many years ago, an interesting article was published in *USA Today*. The article revealed the diversity of various cults, as well as the changing definition of religion. The article reported on a woman who manages a group called Conscious Connection in Mar Vista, California. She channels a spirit named Ramtha:

CHANNELS THE LATEST IN PSYCHIC CHIC

Bashar, "an extraterrestrial from the [planet] Essassani," sometimes drops by.

Don't snicker: Bashar and other new celebrities with names like "Ramtha" and "Lazaris" claim to be disembodied spirits who've come from distant ages, dimensions and planets to teach us about "ultimate knowingness." (USA Today 1987, 1D)

Those who believe the channeling spirits claim that we have evolved beyond religion. They declare that communicating telepathically with spirits from the past gives us eternal life.

Throughout history, people have flocked to religious leaders of all kinds. But this may be a first; they are listening to and following the counsel of "channels," through whom spirits from other worlds teach us about life and the future.

One would expect the channeling phenomenon to be short-lived. However, in 2014, a former follower of Ramtha made a shocking allegation against … the Ramtha School of Enlightenment. The former follower claimed members at the Ramtha School were encouraged "to drink a concoction of Dead Sea water mixed with Red Devil Lye to enlighten themselves."

Ramtha is still alive but facing some challenges. The channeling movement is still a sign of the Last Days. It draws people away from God the Father and his Son Jesus Christ (see https://q13fox.com/2014/04/18/shocking-allegations-from-jz-knight-follower/)

> Regard not them that have familiar spirits, neither seek
> after wizards, to be defiled by them: I am the Lord your
> God. (Leviticus 19:31)

There are countless groups who teach and follow their own precepts. Their beliefs and actions would astound and mystify us. They represent those who do not know the Savior or have rejected him and his teachings.

OFFICIALS RAID FROZEN-BODY LAB AGAIN

> Coroner's officials said Alcor continued to refuse to turn
> over the head of Dora Kent, 83, which was surgically
> removed Dec. 11 at the foundation's laboratory so that
> it could be frozen …

> But advocates of the idea that bodies can be frozen for
> revival at a later date—a practice called cryonics—believe
> that tests run by the coroner would so harm the skull and
> brain that Kent could never be returned to life …

"She's his mother," [an employee] said. "She's alive in there." (McGarry and Sahagu 1988)

The foundation that removed the mother's head says she was dead at the time. They argue that if the head is thawed, the skull and brain would be harmed. The mother would no longer have a future life.

Are not the ideas and concepts of many people today beyond belief? We should not believe them. We can and should see them for what they truly are: banners declaring that today is the Last Saturday.

How surprised would we be if we were to learn about all the cults around the world? How many inconceivable groups are there, and what are some of their beliefs, tenets, and practices? Many of them could serve as proof that our Final Days are here.

3.7. SATANISM: EVIL

In Deuteronomy, the Lord provides some insightful information. He very closely describes many of the movements and events of today.

> There shall not be found among you any one that maketh his son or his daughter to pass through the fire, or that useth divination, or an observer of times, or an enchanter, or a witch,
>
> or a charmer, or a consulter with familiar spirits, or a wizard, or a necromancer.
>
> For all that do these things are an abomination unto the Lord: and because of these abominations the Lord thy God doth drive them out from before thee. (Deuteronomy 18:10-12)

Here is a possible secret society that shows it is the Last Days. They are doing strange things that are most likely offensive to the Lord and the sanctity of life.

Woman Who Kept Husband's Body at Home Could be Part of a So-Called Health Cult

GALESBURG, Ill. (AP). A county sheriff said Sunday he's asked the FBI to help locate a dentist who might help authorities understand why a woman kept her husband's mummified body in their home for nearly nine years. (Herald 1988, 4)

A society that promotes nutrition and uses exorcism before medicine is not particularly noteworthy. The sheriff says they are almost a secret society. He says they were tending the body as he was alive. Secret societies are a sign of the end of days. It doesn't matter if the society is truly violent or evil.

In 1975, Gary Dahl created a bizarre fad. He started marketing Pet Rocks. It was just a rock in a box. Yet, for a few years, he raked in millions of dollars. Using rocks instead of modern-day medicine is also a sign of the times.

Dark Crystals: The Brutal Reality behind a Booming Wellness Craze

Demand for "healing" crystals is soaring–but many are mined in deadly conditions in one of the world's poorest countries. And there is little evidence that this billion-dollar industry is cleaning up its act.

In February, crystals colonised Tucson. They spread out over carparks and gravel lots, motel courtyards and freeway footpaths, past strip malls and burger bars. Beneath tents and canopies, on block after block, rested every kind of stone imaginable: the opaque, soapy pastels of angeline; dark, mossy-toned epidote; tourmaline streaked with red and green. There were enormous, dining-table-sized pieces selling for tens of thousands of dollars, lumps of rose quartz for $100, crystal eggs for $1.50 …

Five years ago, crystals were not a big deal. Now, powered by the lucrative combination of social media-friendly aesthetics, cosmic spirituality and the apparently unstoppable wellness juggernaut, they have gone from a niche oddity associated with patchouli and crushed velvet to a global consumer phenomenon. (McClure 2019)

One of the proponents of healing rocks and crystals says the body absorbs energies from the crystals. This action expels most "viruses, poisons, and germs" from the body.

Do rocks calm, cleanse, and jump-start the human body? The answer to that question is not what we are considering here. Our query is, are New Age rocks a sign of the times and evidence that today is the Last Saturday? Are New Age rocks evil? Are they a tool of Satan? Do they help him achieve his desires and thwart the plan of God?

Do New Age rocks distract people from righteousness, the Savior, and his teachings? Do New Age rocks take money from people, robbing them of their financial resources and limiting their ability to serve, share, and do good? Who is the author of anything that draws people away from faith, sacrifice, love, Jesus Christ, and God? Rocks are easily a modern-day sign of the devil's handiwork.

Battling Demons: The Reality of Satan

They sat in a circle, holding hands. The room was dark, except for the dim light cast by a flickering candle in the center of the ring. An aroma of incense floated through the air as Madam Zerkee chanted, "The one the candle flame points to will be the one through whom the spirit will speak" …

Meanwhile in another city, the chauffeur driving three members of a rock group asked what its name stood for.

"It means we're in Satanic service," replied one of the young men as their car sped toward a concert and a waiting audience of impressionable teenagers …

"Every full moon, one particular rock recording studio gathers up all the master recordings they've cut ...

A ceremony of incantations summons demons. These satanic emissaries are instructed to accompany every duplicate record sold anywhere in the world. (Cook 1982)

New Age rocks could be rather harmless compared to those who practice Satanism.

A man arrested and questioned is believed to be a California stalker. He was chased, beaten, and captured in East Los Angeles after attempting to steal a car.

A newspaper article reports some relevant information about this man:

STALKER SUSPECT ISN'T TALKING: RAMIREZ DESCRIBED AS PASSIVE AND COMPLIANT

Night Stalker suspect ... has remained silent during detectives' questioning about 16 slayings and 21 assaults that in recent weeks sowed fear from Mission Viejo to San Francisco, authorities told The Times on Sunday ...

A Northern California man who said he attended school with Ramirez in El Paso was quoted in Sunday's edition of the San Francisco Examiner as saying that [the suspect] was obsessed with what he believed to be satanic themes in the music of the rock group AC/DC's 1979 album "Highway to Hell." (Stewart and Freed 1985)

The Night Stalker may not be a worshipper of Satan, but he is evil.

AD/DC's Highway to Hell album includes a song titled "Night Prowler." The song includes these lyrics:

Was that a noise outside the window?

What's that shadow on the blind?

As you lie there naked

Like a body in a tomb

Suspended animation as I slip into your room.

News headlines and stories show that there is intense evil in the world. No question that there is more evil now than thirty or forty years ago. We also know who the author of evil and wickedness is.

New Trial Begins for "Cannibal" Who Raped and Butchered His Ex-Girlfriend

A new trial is now underway for an Indiana man accused of raping and butchering his ex-girlfriend before eating parts of her body—as jurors have already been warned they will be shown crime scene photos worse than any horror film …

An autopsy revealed Blanton died from multiple stab wounds and that parts of her heart, lungs and brain were missing. (Crane 2020)

The news is presented almost everywhere today. It is available on different electronic, print, and media devices. We can't always trust news sources or know if the news they report is true. However, a man killing and eating his ex-girlfriend is a notable indication of current evil in the world.

It is worth noting that the man was found mentally fit to stand trial. This would suggest that other choices and influences exist in his life. He is most likely a follower of evil. Could he be a follower of Satan?

We do not need to know if this man really did murder and eat parts of his ex-girlfriend's body. The fact that someone, any group or organization, would make this story public is a strong revelation about the condition of our world. The story itself, whether true or false, further reveals that is it the Last Saturday.

3.8. MINISTERS AND PREACHERS

The scriptures are filled with prophecies about the Last Days. Some of these prophecies reveal to us what religion will be like, how churches will function, and how ministers will preach.

> He commandeth that there shall be no priestcrafts; for, behold, priestcrafts are that men preach and set themselves up for a light unto the world, that they may get gain and praise of the world; but they seek not the welfare of Zion. (2 Nephi 26:29)

TV evangelists have experienced great fame and success over many decades. Many have been a source of controversy, deceit, and greed.

THESE TELEVANGELISTS HAVE SOME SECRETS
THEY DON'T WANT YOU TO KNOW

Jim Bakker

Jim Bakker eventually had to face the music when a former employee, Jessica Hahn, accused him of gross misconduct …

It is also believed that Bakker was taking home large chunks of his followers' donations.

Pat Robertson

Over the years, the preacher has generally offended people for the things he has said about certain religions and ethnic groups …

In 2010, in light of the Haiti earthquake, Robertson claimed that the Haitian people were cursed ever since their founders made a "pact with the Devil."

Jimmy Swaggart

Appearing on thousands of channels every week, Jimmy Swaggart was one of the most recognizable televangelists of the '80s …

In 1988, the preacher was caught with an escort by his side …

Gilbert Deya

After becoming the head of a number of churches [in the UK], Deya claimed that his powers were able to make infertile women have children. However, it was soon revealed that Deya and his family were actually kidnapping babies from their home country [Kenya] and using this as the cover up for his supernatural powers …

Robert Tilton

Success-N-Life catapulted Tilton into the '90s as one of the most successful TV preachers around, raking in a cool $80 million each year. However, … it was revealed that he was taking home the money that viewers submitted to have their prayers answered …

Oral Roberts

After locking himself in a tower, Roberts made an emotional announcement, saying that God would "call him home" if he couldn't raise $8 million worth of donations. (Hawthorne 2019)

We may think that as a church, we are the only ones who see the signs of the times. Others also see the corruption and dishonesty that can easily be found in religion and Christian groups today. The Soul Intention website has noticed the behavior of spiritual leaders today.

What's the difference between a Preacher, Priest, Pastor, Rabbi, Reverend, Deacon, Bishop, Minister, & Pope?

> In this day in age, many, but not all, who take Spiritual Leadership titles and roles have not yet tamed their ego, or "Shadow" self, which is one of the steps when wanting to fully immerse oneself in the Love of Christ Consciousness. Many carry one or more of the seven deadly thought forms (Pride, Envy, Gluttony, Lust, Anger, Greed, or Sloth) within their being, infecting their followers like a rampant virus. (Soul Intention 2015)

The US government is also interested in today's preachers and televangelists. Many TV preachers today live lavish, exorbitant lives. They request and collect money from their followers and supporters. Many preachers who receive money for teaching the word of God become quite wealthy. When they use that money for selfish, personal gain, it is called priestcraft, which the Lord condemns.

6 Outrageously Wealthy Preachers Under Federal Investigation

> Spreading the gospel has become a very profitable business for several well-known televangelists, affording them the opportunity to live in mansions, own private jets, take exotic trips, relax in hotel rooms that cost thousands per night, and even own second and third homes.

> Of course, these preachers are heads over nonprofit, tax-exempt organizations, so whenever one of them starts to flaunt their wealth, the government is going to take notice. And 6 of the wealthiest televangelists have been the subject of Senate investigations to ensure they aren't taking advantage of their nonprofit status. (Eric 2010)

We are not judging the actions or preaching of these ministers. We are not deciding if their ministries are correct, wise, or successful. Our query is, do these evangelists and preachers indicate that we live in the Last Days of the earth's mortal existence? Do their actions satisfy Last Day prophecies?

Are greed, sloth, wrath, envy, pride, and lust running rampant in the world today?

The apostle Paul in his First Epistle to the Thessalonians talks about how he and his companions were preaching the Gospel.

> For ye remember, brethren, our labour and travail: for laboring night and day, because we would not be chargeable unto any of you, we preached unto you the gospel of God.
>
> Ye are witnesses, and God also, how holily and justly and unblameably we behaved ourselves among you that believe. (1 Thessalonians 2:9-10)

It appears that the ministers of today have not read the Bible, or at least have not learned from the teachings therein. Compare how Paul and his fellow apostles preached the Gospel with modern-day preachers. Gospel preaching today is rocked with scandal, illicit sex, drug addiction, blackmail, and deception.

Throughout the history of TV, God and religion have been presented in positive and negative lights. Today, Christian TV is hard to find. It is being replaced with secular principles and feel-good morality.

THERE IS NO GOD ON TV, ONLY THE *GOOD PLACE*

> In a post-*7th Heaven* TV landscape, Christian-based TV is failing in favor of secular moral programming inspired by *The Leftovers* and *Lost*.
>
> God has a bad habit of getting cancelled. He (or she) is too specific. Or perhaps not specific enough. Either way, God is the Katherine Heigl of moral-driven television: a once

popular omnipresent being who just can't seem to get a show to stick these days. In the '90s, the balancing act was a bit easier—shows like *Promised Land* and *Touched By an Angel* had a solid place in the cultural zeitgeist …

But audiences that once gravitated to the miraculous manifestations of Christian-centric television just aren't showing up anymore. And Christian-focused morality shows have dropped in popularity since the mid-2000s. (Kirkland 2018)

The words of prophets coming true today are not only about evil and wickedness. The number of churches and religions also shows that the Savior will soon usher in the final millennial era.

For the time speedily shall come that all churches which are built up to get gain, and all those who are built up to get power over the flesh, and those who are built up to become popular in the eyes of the world, and those who seek the lusts of the flesh and the things of the world, and to do all manner of iniquity; yea, in fine, all those who belong to the kingdom of the devil are they who must be brought low in the dust; they are those who must be consumed as stubble; and this is according to the words of the prophet. (1 Nephi 22:23)

If someone who preaches the word of God violates one of God's commandments, what action should be taken? By whom? What would we expect? Are all of these events and actions signs of the Last Saturday? How? Why?

Televangelist Swaggart Admits Infidelity

BATON ROUGE, La. Television evangelist Jimmy Swaggart, who reportedly was photographed with a prostitute, confessed yesterday that he had sinned and said he would stop preaching …

Swaggart, who a year ago had scathingly denounced fellow Assemblies of God evangelist Jim Bakker for committing adultery, did not describe his misconduct. (Harvard Crimson 1988)

Scandals, marital infidelity, financial dishonesty, and myriad other issues may plague TV preachers. However, sometimes, the churches they belong to do not tolerate bad behavior. Sometimes, they do expel them.

Sometimes, churches do not expel preachers after misconduct, but the church leaders go to prison.

Ex-Pastor ... Gets Life in Prison in Child Sex-Trafficking Case; Victim Speaks

The former leader of Abundant Life Ministries looked to members of his family and mouthed an apology as he was sentenced to life in prison for two counts of sex trafficking children and one count of sexual exploitation of children for having sex with the girl at his church, his home, and hotels. He later had a threesome with the girl and one of her teenage friends at a hotel. (Dunn 2019)

Marital infidelity, financial dishonesty, and also child sex-trafficking. God is surely angry with life choices that are being made by people and ministers. He will send his Son to the earth again any day now.

The preachers don't always wait to be fired. Jimmy Swaggart eventually left the ministry after he confessed to "incidents of moral failure."

Back in 1988, an astonishing soap opera was unfolding that involved some of the most prominent TV evangelists of the day. Some of them are gone. They have been replaced, however, with new preachers, churches, and ministries. When prophecies become reality, we have strong signs of the times.

This is how the chosen servants of Christ preached and taught after his death. It is a vivid contrast from many of today's preachers.

For our exhortation was not of deceit, nor of uncleanness,
nor in guile:

For neither at any time used we flattering words, as ye
know, nor a cloak of covetousness; God is witness;

Nor of men sought we glory, neither of you, nor yet of
others, when we might have been burdensome, as the
apostles of Christ. (1 Thessalonians 2:3,5-6)

You may be interested to know that Oral Roberts did indeed raise
the $8 million. "A dog track millionaire put him over the top with [a]
$1.3 million check." He was not called home (see *USA Today,* March
26, 1987, 5D).

These holy wars literally fulfilled the prophecy given to us by Nephi
concerning such events during the Last Days. Many of these ministers
were brought "low in the dust" and consumed.

The extent to which today's churches and pastors will go to receive
money, fame, and praise is beyond belief:

South Africa Funeral Firm to Sue Pastor for "Resurrection Stunt"

A viral video of [the] Pastor shows him shouting "rise
up" to a man lying down in a coffin who then jerks
upright to cheers from worshippers. (BBC News 2019)

The funeral companies are charging the pastor because they feel
they were lied to and deceived. Followers of Jesus Christ around the
world would never really believe this stunt. The action performed here
denies the power and love of Christ. It is a wild sign of the times. Many
will resort to anything to gain notoriety today.

As a young man, Joseph Smith was told there are no such things as
miracles. Do you think that is true in this case? The funeral companies
may have been defamed.

The actions of this pastor sound like a spectacle. We, however, know
that miracles do exist and do happen. God himself has declared that he

is a God of miracles and is the same yesterday, today, and forever (see 2 Nephi 27:23).

What is one of the strongest commandments? Thou shalt not kill. When a minister, a man of God and follower of Christ, commits murder, is that not an important sign of the times?

Pastor Jailed for Murdering His Second Wife in Staged Accident Is Now Charged with Killing His First Who "Fell down the Stairs"

New details shed light on how a Pennsylvania pastor nicknamed the "Sinister Minister" staged a car accident to kill his second wife, as he started dating one of his married congregants.

Police in rural Reeders, Pennsylvania started investigating [a] Methodist Pastor, after the October 2008 suicide of congregant Joe Musante, who had recently learned that his wife Cindy was having an affair with the pastor.

While the pastor and his married mistress were ruled out as suspects in Musante's death, the suicide put enough attention on [the pastor] that police decided to re-investigate the mysterious "accidental" deaths of his two wives.

[His] second wife Betty died in a car accident just three months before Musante's death, and his first wife Jewel died falling down a set of stairs in 1999. (Collman 2014)

A minister doesn't want to be married anymore. He knows that to divorce his wife would bring personal disgrace and dishonor. So the solution to his problems is to kill his wife, more than once. His choices and actions demonstrate the degree to which evil and confusion exist in our world today. Using the minister's logic, murder is now a smaller scandal than divorce or adultery.

The West Side Christian Fellowship also feels that there are many problems and issues with today's preachers.

Where Are the Bold, Authoritative Preachers Today?

A friend recently asked, "Where are those with uncompromising power and God-given authority in our pulpits today?" His statement reminded me of the desperate need for passionate, spirit-filled preachers focused on pleasing God rather than man. Our culture's false perception of God as a cosmic ball of love, or a doting grandfather desperately needs to be challenged.

Unfortunately, difficult truths are often compromised, watered-down, or avoided altogether in the hope of "not offending," "securing an audience," or building a "mega-ministry." As a result, the church is a mile wide but only an inch deep; judgment is never mentioned, repentance is never sought, sin is often excused, and lives are not radically changed. (Westside n.d.)

Are difficult truths watered down today by pastors and preachers? Those who believe and follow Jesus Christ frequently have their lives changed. Christianity requires a change of heart and a contrite spirit.

Any preacher, minister, or church who does not teach and require a change of heart toward Christ is surely counterfeit.

Living the Law of Sacrifice

Our greatest blessings in this life and in the hereafter will come through our willingness to sacrifice as the Lord directs. Only through sacrifice and the faith it generates, the Prophet taught, can we achieve happiness in the eternities: "A religion that does not require the sacrifice of all things never has power sufficient to produce the faith necessary unto life and salvation; for, from the first existence of man, the faith necessary unto the enjoyment of life and salvation never could be obtained without the sacrifice of all earthly things. It was through this sacrifice, and this only, that God has ordained that men should enjoy eternal life." (Brough 2000)

Today is the Last Saturday. It also needs to be a day of sacrifice.

The law of sacrifice should be taught and practiced in every Latter-Day Saint home (see M. Russell Ballard, "The Blessings of Sacrifice," *Ensign Magazine,* May 1992, 77). We do this by making repentance a part of our lives, by faithfully paying our tithes and offerings, by obeying the commandments, by doing family history work and attending the temple, by being an example to others, and by being "willing to submit to all things which the Lord seeth fit to inflict upon [us], even as a child doth submit to his father" (Mosiah 3:19).

We as members of the Lord's restored church know and recognize the signs of the times. It is quite evident that we will soon see the Lord return. We are, however, not the only ones who see and acknowledge the signs of the times.

Televangelist Wonders if Liberal Whitewashing of Sin Is the "Great Apostasy" before Christ's Return

Georgia megachurch pastor and televangelist Michael Youssef fears that the tendency today among some Christian leaders to water down the Gospel to make it "palatable" for today's culture could be a sign of the "great apostasy before the return of Christ." …

"I feel and sense in my spirit, as well as experientially, I am seeing more and more evangelical pastors who are turning their back on the faith." (Smith 2020)

Preachers and ministers of various faiths are found throughout the world. Some of those of our Christian faith look for the coming of Jesus Christ, and they know the signs of the times.

3.9. Righteousness: Darkness

We live in an age when righteousness is scarce. Respect, fear, and even belief in God is surely at an all-time low. As a nation and world, we have lost our respect for life and a sense of human responsibility. This is evident in the beatings, murders, torture, and suffering that is daily afflicted upon innocent victims.

A major example of our clouded vision and distorted sense of values is most prominent in the battle over the unborn child. Right to Life and Right to Choose groups have presented, argued, and debated their positions for many years. All of this began in 1973, when the US Supreme Court announced the explosive ruling that legalized abortion.

Unplanned is a movie about abortion. It was meant to support pro-life principles, but is not an indictment against pro-choice supporters. The movie is about the reality of abortion; it depicts a Planned Parenthood worker whose experience causes her to quit her job and become a pro-life activist.

Unplanned Tells an Essential Truth about Abortion: It Is Violent

"The fetus was 13 weeks old and I could easily see its head, arms, and legs," she later wrote. "The abortion instrument—a suction tube—was on the screen as well. The baby jumped away from it but it was all for naught. The abortionist turned on the suction and I saw that baby get sucked apart right in front of me on the screen" …

Before it is anything else, the destruction of life in the womb is an act of violence. (Jacoby 2019)

Unplanned received an "R" rating, which dismayed the producers. The movie was rated on a single MPAA criteria: violence. Abortion violence.

It is not necessary to analyze your thoughts or feelings about the abortion issue right now. Whether we are in the Right to Life or the Right to Choose camp, we should ask, is all of this a sign of the Last Days?

Today, there are many religious groups, organizations, and churches in the world. Our religious landscape is covered with thousands of religious denominations.

What Is the Difference between the Major Christian Denominations?

The three major groupings of Christianity ... are Roman Catholic, Eastern Orthodox, and Protestant. Under the umbrella of Protestantism, there are numerous Christian denominations ..., such as Lutheran, Anglican, Presbyterian, Baptist, Methodist, and Pentecostal.

However, if we rewind in history to the time just after Jesus died, there were no Christians denominations. There were just Christians. As time went on, however, people started to disagree about who Jesus was, what He wanted from us, and how churches should be led. (Dahlfred 2019)

In January of 1988, 125 New Jersey parishes voted to accept homosexual and unmarried relationships. The vote of both clergy and laity was overwhelmingly in favor of blessing these relationships. Remember, our attitude about the action taken by these fellow Christians is not the issue here. Do their votes fulfill prophecy? Are their decisions and the changes they initiated signs that today is the Last Saturday?

Further evidence of the Last Saturday is the emotional division that can be found in many groups, organizations, and even churches. These groups have existed in unity and harmony for years. Internal separation is occurring in businesses, politics, and religion. This separation phenomenon is a major sign of the Last Saturday, because Satan is the father of contention.

The War against Pope Francis

Pope Francis is one of the most hated men in the world today. Those who hate him most are not atheists, or protestants, or Muslims, but some of his own followers. Outside the church he is hugely popular as a figure of almost ostentatious modesty and humility. From the moment that Cardinal Jorge Bergoglio became pope in 2013, his gestures caught the world's imagination …

But within the church, Francis has provoked a ferocious backlash from conservatives who fear that this spirit will divide the church, and could even shatter it …

This mixture of hatred and fear is common among the pope's adversaries. Francis, the first non-European pope in modern times, and the first ever Jesuit pope, was elected as an outsider to the Vatican establishment, and expected to make enemies. But no one foresaw just how many he would make. (Brown 2017)

Religious malice and bickering reveal that we live in the unrighteous and faithless times of the Last Days. Many today have strayed from Christianity. They have virtually rejected the teachings of Christ and Jesus Christ himself.

Officials Blame Differing Groups
of "Outsiders" for Violence

WASHINGTON (AP). As protests over the death of George Floyd grow in cities across the U.S., government officials have been warning of the "outsiders"—groups of organized rioters they say are flooding into major cities not to call for justice but to cause destruction.

But the state and federal officials have offered differing assessments of who the outsiders are. They've blamed left-wing extremists, far-right white nationalists and even suggested the involvement of drug cartels. These leaders have offered little evidence to back up those claims, and the chaos of the protests makes verifying identities and motives exceedingly difficult. (Balsamo and Hennessey 2020)

The views and beliefs of the people who protested during the 2020 pandemic are, in most cases, not the teachings of Jesus. Where do such thoughts and feelings come from? There are many cases of violent, non-Christian thoughts and actions today. They are signs of the times.

2 BUFFALO YOUTHS ARRESTED IN MURDERS OF 2 PRIESTS

The police charged two teen-agers today in the slaying of two Roman Catholic priests within the last 13 days ...

Both youths live on Buffalo's East Side—the same inner-city neighborhood where the priests were stabbed and blugeoned to death in the rectories of their parishes. (New York Times 1987, B2)

Many people will do anything for money. The love of money, which does not come from the Holy Spirit, is the underlying force behind a large measure of unrighteousness and crimes found in the world. All of which should awaken us to the many signs that it is near midnight on the Last Saturday.

LAKE COUNTY MOM WHO DROWNED HER 3 CHILDREN IN '80s MAY BE RELEASED TO HALFWAY HOUSE

On New Year's Day in 1980, supper was done and a young mother at a Leesburg trailer park readied her three daughters for their bath.

[She] was 23 but had been plagued with delusions and hallucinations nearly her entire life. In her daze, believing that she was the Virgin Mary and that her children were doomed for hell, she drowned them. Her 4-year-old twins ... and her 2-year-old died, and [she] walked out alone, muttering to her uncle, "They're better off in heaven." (Lelis 2013)

The court found the mother not guilty by reason of insanity. Since then, she has been a patient in the Florida State Hospital.

If we were to tap into police scanners in any city, we would constantly hear about doom and gloom. We would quickly understand how much spiritual darkness is around us. How much suffering today is inflicted on children by parents and family members?

Police say a New York mother thought her twenty-month-old son was possessed. She wanted to get the devil out of him. So she turned on the stove, scalded the boy with hot water, and placed him in the oven. The mother then burned his clothes on the stove. She was charged with first-degree assault. The truth was, of course, she needed to get the devil out of herself (see the Franklin, Indiana *Daily Journal*, Thursday, January 3, 1980, 9).

The cause of such darkness in teenagers and mothers can only come from one place. The thoughts and actions of those in the following headlines do not suggest that it is the Last Saturday; they painfully declare it.

NJ Mom Who Set Newborn on Fire Sentenced to 30 Years for Manslaughter

A ... woman who set her newborn daughter on fire hours after giving birth was sentenced Friday to 30 years in prison for aggravated manslaughter ...

The baby died from smoke inhalation and third-degree burns over 60 percent of her body, ...

[The mother] pleaded guilty last month to dousing her baby with WD-40 lubricating spray and using a lighter to set the girl ablaze on Simontown Road in Pemberton Township. (Burney 2016)

We don't know the circumstances related to this vicious act. Family members pleaded for leniency, declaring that the mother suffered from mental illness and the pregnancy was from a sexual assault. What we do know is that there is a lot of darkness all around us today.

The Bible frequently warns us about actions that are not acceptable to the Lord. We are given clear counsel about things we should never do. Yet these forbidden activities are manifest every day around the world. These activities are signs of the Last Days.

> Ye shall not steal, neither deal falsely, neither lie one to another.
>
> And ye shall not swear by my name falsely, neither shalt thou profane the name of thy God: I am the Lord.
>
> Thou shalt not defraud thy neighbour, neither rob him: the wages of him that is hired shall not abide with thee all night until the morning.
>
> Thou shalt not curse the deaf, nor put a stumbling block before the blind, but shalt fear thy God: I am the Lord. (Leviticus 19:11-14)

A stumbling block is a metaphor for any behavior or attitude that leads another to commit sin or engage in destructive behavior. Read today's news and headlines. You will find too many stumbling blocks to even count.

"Amish Madoff" Charged with Bilking Church Members out of $15 Million in Fraud

> A 77-year-old Amish man in Ohio … was charged with fraud by the SEC for running an investment scheme

that swindled thousands of Amish families and other investors …

[He] bilked fellow church members out of millions in a vast 25-year-long investment swindle. (Caulfield 2011)

He told investors he was buying low-risk government securities, while playing with high-stakes stock-market investments. He provided quarterly statements of phony returns and became known as a financial wizard.

He, in fact, deposited their money into his own accounts and then used the money to pay for his home, a swimming pool, pool table, and tennis. Add fraud and dishonesty to our list of signs of the Last Days.

America was founded by people who were seeking religious freedom, patriots who felt the king of Britain had imposed unjust laws and excessive taxes. Joseph Smith was a young teenager when he saw and experienced the religious fervor and excitement of his day. The times in which we live are notably different from those days. Our days are more like the Last Saturday.

WHAT MOST INFLUENCES THE SELF-IDENTITY OF AMERICANS?

"God, family, country" might be the oft-touted creed of country music, but most Americans scramble the order. Adults are most likely to point to their family as making up a significant part of their personal identity, "being an American" comes second and "religious faith" is in third …

While religious faith squeaks into the top three, there is a sharp drop from the first two factors in the number of Americans who say their faith is a major part of their identity. A majority of Americans agree their family and their country are central aspects of who they are, fewer than two out of five adults say their religious faith makes up a lot of their personal identity (38%). About the same proportion of adults give little or no credence to the idea that faith is part of their identity: 18 percent say faith doesn't make up much of their identity and one in five say it doesn't affect their identity at all. (Barna Group 2015)

The Barna study defined people who are "practicing" their faith as those who attended a church service in the past month. These people also said religious faith was very important to them. How important is your faith to you? As we look at our current state of affairs, we need to be doing more than just practicing our faith.

3.10. FALSE CHURCHES

In his book, *This Little Church Stayed Home: An Historical Overview*, Gary Gilley provides some insight into the state of churches today, including why there are so many. He shares a pastor's comments about his claim that the first priority of any church is truth. The pastor said,

> The Bible does not place a great priority on being right. We are to be holy and righteous, pure and just. We are to believe, understand, and proclaim the truth. But that is not the same as being right.

Mr. Gilley then says:

> Welcome to the world of postmodernism, where words don't mean what they mean, truth is subjective and contradictions in logic are perfectly acceptable. (Gilley 2006)

Surely so many churches exist today because of human beliefs and precepts, and the extensive interpretations of faith, righteousness, and truth. How many of these churches are right? How many can be right? Do they even care if they are right?

In the Book of Mormon, Nephi, the prophet son of Lehi, describes many of the events and conditions of the Last Days. He talks of "things which shall be written out of the book." They will be "of great worth unto the children of men." His words clearly describe the environment in which Joseph Smith lived, as well as many situations we find in our environment today:

> For it shall come to pass in that day that the churches which are built up, and not unto the Lord, when the one shall say unto the other: Behold, I, I am the Lord's; and the others shall say: I, I am the Lord's; and thus shall every one say that hath built up churches, and not unto the Lord—
>
> And they shall contend one with another; and their priests shall contend one with another, and they shall teach with their learning, and deny the Holy Ghost, which giveth utterance.
>
> And they deny the power of God, the Holy One of Israel; and they say unto the people: Hearken unto us, and hear ye our precept; for behold there is no God today, for the Lord and the Redeemer hath done his work, and he hath given his power unto men. (2 Nephi 28:3-5)

There are many good religions and churches in the world today. However, Nephi has given an accurate description of many that exist on the Last Saturday.

Nephi further describes the beliefs, actions, and lives of many people today:

> Yea, and there shall be many which shall say: Eat, drink, and be merry, for tomorrow we die; and it shall be well with us.
>
> And there shall also be many which shall say: Eat, drink, and be merry; nevertheless, fear God—he will justify in committing a little sin; yea, lie a little, take the advantage of one because of his words, dig a pit for thy neighbor; there is no harm in this; and do all these

things, for tomorrow we die; and if it so be that we are guilty, God will beat us with a few stripes, and at last we shall be saved in the kingdom of God. (2 Nephi 28:7-8)

False prophets, false doctrines, and pride in the Last Days are also declared by Nephi. Ponder the current religious, social, and political environment in your city, the United States, and the world today. As you read the following words of Nephi, see him with you now, speaking directly to you:

Yea, and there shall be many which shall teach after this manner, false and vain and foolish doctrines, and shall be puffed up in their hearts, and shall seek deep to hide their counsels from the Lord; and their works shall be in the dark.

And the blood of the saints shall cry from the ground against them.

Yea, they have all gone out of the way; they have become corrupted.

Because of pride, and because of false teachers, and false doctrine, their churches have become corrupted, and their churches are lifted up; because of pride they are puffed up. (2 Nephi 28:9-12)

Nephi further tells us that false prophets and churches rob the poor to build their sanctuaries and to obtain their fine clothing.

Nephi continues with strong condemnation of pride and other vices. If we could measure the amount of pride in people, communities, businesses, and government, how much would we find? Is there greater pride in the world today than there was twenty or thirty years ago?

When people become successful and prosperous, pride and prejudice grow. Affluence, wealth, and power persuade them to put themselves above others.

They wear stiff necks and high heads; yea, and because of pride, and wickedness, and abominations, and whoredoms, they have all gone astray save it be a few, who are the humble followers of Christ; nevertheless, they are led, that in many instances they do err because they are taught by the precepts of men.

O the wise, and the learned, and the rich, that are puffed up in the pride of their hearts, and all those who preach false doctrines, and all those who commit whoredoms, and pervert the right way of the Lord, wo, wo, wo be unto them, saith the Lord God Almighty, for they shall be thrust down to hell! (2 Nephi 28:14-16)

Nephi further condemns those who reject that which is just and good for things of naught. Those who revile against good, and say it is of no worth, are filled with iniquity and shall perish.

Nephi states that if men repent of their wickedness and abominations, "they shall not be destroyed" (see 2 Nephi 28:17). Is today the Last Saturday? We are men on earth. There are many falsehoods and great wickedness around us. We must stand strong and tall. We must daily seek the spirit. We must bring to pass much righteousness. We must prepare for the Lord's return. It is time for us to repent.

Headlines today confirm the existence of churches that are lost, that will do anything to gain followers, fame, and of course money. The more unbelievable and fantastic, the better.

SEE IT: Televangelist Claims to Cure Coronavirus through Television Sets

[A Texas preacher]—his right hand dripping with ointment—urged believers to put their hands on their screens and be cured of the coronavirus. (Niemietz 2020)

The claim of curing coronavirus is no more implausible than many other declarations made by other preachers today. The claim to cure coronavirus, when no known cure exists, prompts us to quickly discount the event.

What we should not discount is that the preacher's actions, and all those like it, strengthen the evidence of the Last Saturday.

Nephi offers a lot of insight into the state of faith and churches in our day. The scripture below directly states that there will be many churches in our day. His words also describe some faces of these churches:

> And the Gentiles are lifted up in the pride of their eyes, and have stumbled, because of the greatness of their stumbling block that they have built up many churches; nevertheless, they put down the power and miracles of God, and preach up unto themselves their own wisdom and their own learning, that they may get gain and grind upon the face of the poor. (2 Nephi 26:20)

We, as members of the Church of Jesus Christ of Latter-Day Saints, are not the only ones who are aware of the many churches today. Other people and groups understand the teachings and activities they promote. Here is what biblicalproof.wordpress.com has said:

PREACHING FOR THE MONEY

> There are many who have made religion into a business. Churches pop up all over with a variety of names and doctrines in hopes to make a living by spreading their version of Christianity. In fact, religion is the largest business in the world today. The contribution of Christians builds colleges, orphanages, hospitals, recreational halls, parsonages, and places of worship. Oddly, the percentage is very small which goes to the needs of the faithful Christian, for which the contribution was initially intended. (Biblical Proof 2014)

3.11. RELIGIOUS LIBERTY/OPPRESSION

Recently, I have heard and read of apostate groups and organizations opposed to the Church of Jesus Christ of Latter-Day Saints. In recent years, various groups have attacked the church, openly criticized church leaders, mocked church doctrine, and ridiculed sacred covenants.

Bishops sometimes receive anti-church literature in the mail. Truly public awareness of the church, both good and bad, has increased in recent years. Ridicule and scorn of religion and faith have increased in the recent past. Many churches and faiths have been openly persecuted and victimized in many parts of the world. Religious liberties and beliefs are being attacked and taken away.

The Continuing Threat to Religious Liberty

Two years to the day after the Supreme Court redefined marriage in Obergefell, the Court announced that it would hear a case about the extent to which private parties may be forced to embrace this new vision of marriage. The case involves Jack Phillips, a Colorado baker who declined to bake a wedding cake for a same-sex wedding reception …

He had previously turned down requests to create Halloween-themed cakes, lewd bachelor-party cakes, and a cake celebrating a divorce. Yet Jack was never reprimanded over those decisions. He found himself in hot water only with the same-sex-wedding cake …

While there has always been disagreement about what religious liberty requires in particular cases, the idea of religious liberty as a fundamental human right has more or less been a consensus in America. It became controversial only in recent years as the government tried to force religious conservatives to violate their beliefs on sex and marriage, and as liberal advocacy groups decided that civil liberties aren't for conscientious objectors to the sexual revolution …

Agree or disagree with Catholic Charities, its belief that mothers and fathers are not interchangeable, that moms and dads are not replaceable, has nothing to do with sexual orientation. And respecting conscience here wouldn't make a single concrete difference to same-sex couples, who would remain free and able to adopt from public agencies and other providers.

Yet lawmakers aren't just coercing agencies such as Catholic Charities; they're punishing states for declining to coerce those agencies. When Texas passed a law protecting the freedom of such agencies, California barred state employees from traveling to Texas on "non-essential" official business. (Anderson 2017)

Nations and governments are also aware of religious oppression and the loss of religious liberties. All this proclaims that today is the Last Saturday.

TRUMP SIGNS EXECUTIVE ORDER TO "VIGOROUSLY PROMOTE RELIGIOUS LIBERTY"

(CNN). President Donald Trump signed an executive order Thursday meant to allow churches and other religious organizations to become more active politically, though the actual implications of the document appeared limited.

The order … directs the IRS not to take "adverse action" against churches and other tax-exempt religious organizations participating in political activity that stops short of an endorsement of a candidate for office …

The order prevents the IRS from expanding its restrictions on political activity by religious groups. It also provides "regulatory relief" for organizations that object on religious grounds to a provision in Obamacare that mandates employers provide certain health services, including coverage for contraception. (Liptak 2017)

Modern history has many examples of religious brutality, oppression, and violence. Religious oppression and persecution are also addressed in media and news sources. Here, *Forbes* advocates that religious cruelty should be a concern to everyone, everywhere:

Religious Persecution: The Ever-Growing Threat To Us All

States and international communities continue to neglect the issue of religious persecution. This destructive force has many faces which depend on the perpetrator, which includes individuals, groups, states and their actors, or the severity of the crime ranging from discrimination to severe examples of violence …

It is easy to turn a blind eye when the atrocities do not happen under our nose. However, we cannot forget that religious persecution anywhere in the world is a security threat to everyone, everywhere …

Religious persecution in several countries in the Middle East and North Africa were not enough for the terror group [Daesh]. They called for acts of violence against Western values and culture all over the world. (Ochab 2018)

Persecution called for by Daesh led to extreme persecution in the UK, France, Belgium, Germany, and many other nations. The religious persecution that is happening in a foreign land usually comes home.

The targeting and persecution of Christians by other religions, and in some cases nations and governments, is justly a sign of the Last Days before the Savior appears descending from heaven. As Christians remain true to their beliefs and faith, the critics and scoffers will only increase.

CHRISTIAN PERSECUTION

The persecution of Christians is on the rise worldwide.

In recent years, Christian persecution has peaked, and its terrible impacts have only begun to be felt. In fact, according to Pope Francis, conditions for Christians are worse now than they were in the days of the early Church.

The merciless targeting of Christians—driven by hatred of Christians and the faith itself—emerges as a common denominator in hundreds of testimonies of persecution received by Aid to the Church in Need …

Today, according to ACN research almost 300 million Christians around the world—or 1 out of every 7—live in a country where they suffer some form of persecution, such as arbitrary arrest, violence, a full range of human rights violations and even murder. (Church in Need n.d.)

4

The Lord's Kingdom

The Lord, his prophets, and the scriptures have revealed that the Lord's church will be on the earth in the Last Days. They also describe the growth and condition of his church. The Lord has said that he wants those who follow him to gather together and live righteously.

> Behold, it is my will, that all they who call on my name,
> and worship me according to mine everlasting gospel,
> should gather together, and stand in holy places. (Doc.
> & Cov. 101:22)

This gathering of the faithful could be in congregations (wards/stakes), in his restored church, or from the nations of the world. The saints are being gathered in all of these ways today. Are they not?

Later in this same section of the Doctrine and Covenants (101), the Lord gives additional information and direction concerning the gathering of the saints.

> That the work of the gathering together of my saints
> may continue, that I may build them up unto my name

upon holy places; for the time of harvest is come, and my word must needs be fulfilled.

Therefore, I must gather together my people, according to the parable of the wheat and the tares, that the wheat may be secured in the garners to possess eternal life, and be crowned with celestial glory, when I shall come in the kingdom of my Father to reward every man according as his work shall be;

While the tares shall be bound in bundles, and their bands made strong, that they may be burned with unquenchable fire. (Doc. & Cov. 101:64-66)

This work of gathering must continue because the harvest time has come. The gathering will be done to crown the faithful with glory. The gathering is not to be done in haste nor by flight.

However, let us note that from time to time in recent years, the church has made significant announcements about changes to church programs and procedures. Many of these changes, or updates, have had the purpose of gathering the saints and hastening the work.

We believe all that God has revealed, all that He does now reveal, and we believe that He will yet reveal many great and important things pertaining to the Kingdom of God. (Faith #9)

What has God revealed? His restored church and kingdom in the Last Days. Organizations, programs, policy changes, new directives, new areas of focus, and efforts to gather, fortify, and strengthen the members of the church.

The doctrines and truths of the Gospel do not change. The means, processes, and tools we use to perfect the saints, redeem the dead, and proclaim the Gospel are improved and expanded. Today is the Last Saturday; the saints are being gathered before the Lord comes in His glory.

4.1. RESTORATION

The restoration of the Lord's church began in the 1820s with a young man named Joseph Smith. Joseph lived in those early days after the nation declared its independence from Great Britain and King George III. The United States was a new, young country.

The challenges of survival during the growth of the nation slowed the building of institutions. Churches were one of the first things built during this time of westward expansion. Religious leaders realized the potential for western settlements to become communities of immorality and chaos. Therefore, they reached out with energy and zeal to new settlers. Joseph Smith describes these times.

> Some time in the second year after our removal to Manchester, there was in the place where we lived an unusual excitement on the subject of religion. It commenced with the Methodists, but soon became general among all the sects in that region of country. Indeed, the whole district of country seemed affected by it, and great multitudes united themselves to the different religious parties, which created no small stir and division amongst the people, some crying, "Lo, here!" and others, "Lo, there!" Some were contending for the Methodist faith, some for the Presbyterian, and some for the Baptist. …
>
> In the midst of this war of words and tumult of opinions, I often said to myself: What is to be done? Who of all these parties are right; or, are they all wrong together? If any one of them be right, which is it, and how shall I know it? (Joseph Smith, History 1:5,10)

The first vision of Joseph Smith commenced the restoration of the Church of Jesus Christ in the Last Days, in the last dispensation, on the Last Saturday. The restoration of Christ's church fulfilled prophecies and restored many of Christ's teachings.

The prophet Nephi tells us that the words of the Lord will hiss forth to the gentiles. The words of Nephi refer to the restoration of the church of Christ and specifically the Book of Mormon. He describes the reaction of some who hear these words, some who learn about Joseph Smith and the Book of Mormon.

> And because my words shall hiss forth—many of the Gentiles shall say: A Bible! A Bible! We have got a Bible, and there cannot be any more Bible. (2 Nephi 29:3)

The experiences and work of Joseph Smith provide evidence that Nephi was indeed a prophet and his words were fulfilled.

> Some few days after I had this vision, I happened to be in company with one of the Methodist preachers, who was very active in the before mentioned religious excitement; and, conversing with him on the subject of religion, I took occasion to give him an account of the vision which I had had. I was greatly surprised at his behavior; he treated my communication not only lightly, but with great contempt, saying it was all of the devil, that there were no such things as visions or revelations in these days; that all such things had ceased with the apostles, and that there would never be any more of them. (Joseph Smith, History 1:21)

If God spoke to his apostles in ancient times, it is reasonable to believe that he would speak to people now, especially on the Last Saturday.

Joseph Smith, as a prophet of God, restored everything pertaining to the Lord's Kingdom for these days in which we currently live. The power, keys, and authority for the Lord's kingdom have been given to people on earth today.

> Revelation given through Joseph Smith the Prophet to Thomas B. Marsh, at Kirtland, Ohio, July 23, 1837, concerning the Twelve Apostles of the Lamb. This revelation was received on the day Elders Heber C. Kimball and Orson Hyde first preached the gospel in

England. Thomas B. Marsh was at this time President
of the Quorum of the Twelve Apostles. (Doc. & Cov.
112 Heading)

The revelation Joseph Smith received in 1837 included further
information concerning the restored keys of authority. The Lord
provides an additional explanation about how the restored priesthood
operates in the Last Days: today.

> Verily I say unto you, my servant Thomas, thou art the
> man whom I have chosen to hold the keys of my kingdom,
> as pertaining to the Twelve, abroad among all nations—
>
> And again, I say unto you, that whosoever ye shall send
> in my name, by the voice of your brethren, the Twelve,
> duly recommended and authorized by you, shall have
> power to open the door of my kingdom unto any nation
> whithersoever ye shall send them—
>
> For unto you, the Twelve, and those, the First Presidency,
> who are appointed with you to be your counselors and your
> leaders, is the power of this priesthood given, for the last
> days and for the last time, in the which is the dispensation
> of the fulness of times. (Doc. & Cov. 112:16, 21, 30)

Many may say that the Church of Jesus Christ of Latter-Day Saints
includes teachings and practices that were not part of the Lord's original
church. And that is correct. The full restoration of the Gospel includes
some of Christ's teachings and doctrines that were lost and forgotten,
things that have never been known, and things that have been hidden
and are being restored now.

An indication that the Second Coming of the Lord is near must
certainly be the statements about the Lord's Kingdom and restored
Gospel.

One of the events that are to take place during the Last Days is that
Elijah the prophet would restore priesthood power. The power to be

restored was the sealing power, necessary to perform sacred Temple ordinances and bind generation to generation.

> Behold, I will send you Elijah the prophet before the coming of the great and dreadful day of the Lord:
>
> And he shall turn the heart of the fathers to the children, and the heart of the children to the fathers, lest I come and smite the earth with a curse. (Malachi 4:5-6/Doc. & Cov. 2)

This prophecy and miraculous event have already been fulfilled. The event took place on April 3, 1836, in Kirtland, Ohio. Elijah has returned and restored the Lord's sealing power on earth. The visit of Elijah and restoration of this priesthood authority was recorded by the prophet Joseph Smith and is documented in the Doctrine and Covenants.

> After this vision had closed, another great and glorious vision burst upon us; for Elijah the prophet, who was taken to heaven without tasting death, stood before us, and said:
>
> Behold, the time has fully come, which was spoken of by the mouth of Malachi-testifying that he [Elijah] should be sent, before the great and dreadful day of the Lord come-
>
> To turn the hearts of the fathers to the children, and the children to the fathers, lest the whole earth be smitten with a curse-
>
> Therefore, the keys of this dispensation are committed into your hands; and by this ye may know that the great and dreadful day of the Lord is near, even at the doors. (Doc. & Cov. 110:13-16)

Not only has Elijah already returned to the earth to restore the keys and power which he held, but Moses has restored the "keys of the gathering of Israel from the four parts of the earth." Elias has also returned and "committed the dispensation of the gospel of Abraham" (see Doc. & Cov. 110:11-12).

The Last Saturday would have to be a day in which all priesthood keys and authority are on the earth. All priesthood power required to do the Lord's work, "to bring to pass the Immortality and Eternal Life of Man" (see Moses 1:39), must be part of the Lord's Kingdom and church.

The dispensation of the fullness of times must include the restoration of all priesthood keys. This major prophecy has also been fulfilled. Moses, John the Baptist, Peter, James, John, and Elijah have restored their priesthood keys to the earth.

> And again, in connection with this quotation I will give you a quotation from one of the prophets, who had his eye fixed on the restoration of the priesthood, the glories to be revealed in the last days, and in an especial manner this most glorious of all subjects belonging to the everlasting gospel, namely, the baptism for the dead; for Malachi says, last chapter, verses 5th and 6th: *Behold, I will send you Elijah the prophet before the coming of the great and dreadful day of the Lord: And he shall turn the heart of the fathers to the children, and the heart of the children to their fathers, lest I come and smite the earth with a curse.*
>
> For we without them cannot be made perfect; neither can they without us be made perfect. Neither can they nor we be made perfect without those who have died in the gospel also; for it is necessary in the ushering in of the dispensation of the fullness of times, which dispensation is now beginning to usher in, that a whole and complete and perfect union, and welding together of dispensations, and keys, and powers, and glories should take place, and be revealed from the days of Adam even to the present time. And not only this, but those things which never have been revealed from the foundation of the world, but have been kept hid from the wise and prudent, shall be revealed

unto babes and sucklings in this, the dispensation of the fullness of times. (Doc. & Cov. 128:17-18)

In the early part of this dispensation, the Lord described the reasons and need for a restoration of his church. The saving ordinances of the Kingdom of God must be performed on earth. These ordinances are performed in holy temples of the Lord. The Church of Jesus Christ was restored so everyone who has ever lived on earth may receive these ordinances vicariously.

As a young man being ordained a deacon, I understood that the priesthood was not available to all male members of the church. As full-time missionaries in South America, we had to deal with the priesthood issue on many occasions. Although we understood that one day the priesthood would be extended to all worthy males, we assumed that it would happen during the Last Days, just before or after the Lord's Second Coming.

We didn't realize that we were living in the Last Days. It has been several decades since the priesthood was extended to all worthy male church members over twelve years of age.

The authority and keys of the priesthood have been restored to earth, as required for the restoration of the Lord's Gospel and church.

KEYS OF THE PRIESTHOOD

The keys of the priesthood refer to the right to exercise power in the name of Jesus Christ or to preside over a priesthood function, quorum, or organizational division of the Church. Keys are necessary to maintain order and to see that the functions of the Church are performed in the proper time, place, and manner. (Parrish n.d.)

The priesthood keys to direct, lead, and perform ordinances in the Lord's church were restored to Joseph Smith and Oliver Cowdery in the Kirtland Temple. The latter-day apostles are given the restored priesthood keys.

The president of the Church of Jesus Christ of Latter-Day Saints holds the keys; he is the senior apostle. He presides and directs the work of the restored church.

All the keys, power, and authority required to bring to pass our salvation and exaltation have been restored to the earth in these Last Days.

A clear sign of the Last Days is that the Lord will establish his church once again on the earth. Is there any doubt that this has happened?

4.2. CHURCH ORGANIZATION

We know that the Lord would need to reveal many things about his church and Kingdom in the Last Days. The organization of the church would be a major consideration in today's extensive, populated, modern world.

Modern revelations to the prophet Joseph Smith provided extensive information and direction concerning the organization of the latter-day church of Jesus Christ. Included in this information was the structure of the church at its highest level.

> Of the Melchizedek Priesthood, three Presiding High Priests, chosen by the body, appointed and ordained to that office, and upheld by the confidence, faith, and prayer of the church, form a quorum of the Presidency of the Church.
>
> The twelve traveling councilors are called to be the Twelve Apostles, or special witnesses of the name of Christ in all the world—thus differing from other officers in the church in the duties of their calling.
>
> And they form a quorum, equal in authority and power to the three presidents previously mentioned.
>
> The Seventy are also called to preach the gospel, and to be especial witnesses unto the Gentiles and in all the world—thus differing from other officers in the church in the duties of their calling. (Doc. & Cov. 107:22-25)

When do we, as a church, expect "many great and important things" about the Kingdom of God to be revealed? Undoubtedly many things would be, and were, revealed as the church was restored to the earth. These revelations are found in the Doctrine and Covenants, and Pearl of Great Price. Necessity and logic would dictate that many revelations would be received as the day of the Lord draws near.

The growth of the church would require revelations concerning the church's organization and administration. Policies and procedures would need to change to reflect the changing social and economic conditions of the world in the Last Days. New counsel is surely required as the church grows around the world. Evil, violence, and financial chaos will demand that the Lord reveal new programs and wisdom. All of which will enable Latter-Day Saints to survive the Last Days and remain faithful.

We may look at the revelations that have been received in the last decade or so. If we do, it becomes evident that the Lord is revealing many things concerning His kingdom right now.

SEVENTY: OVERVIEW

In the April 1989 general conference, the Second Quorum of the Seventy was organized, with General Authorities called to temporary service. As additional General Authorities are required to administer the growing worldwide organization, it is assumed that additional quorums of seventy will be formed "until seven times seventy, if the labor in the vineyard of necessity requires it" (D&C 107:95-96). (Parrish 2007)

During the years following the creation of the second quorum of the seventy, additional quorums were created. We witnessed the creation of the third, fourth, fifth, sixth, seventh, and eighth quorums. These brethren today serve in the Presidency of the Seventy, in Area Presidencies, and other church headquarters administrative functions.

Faithful members of the Church of Jesus Christ of Latter-Day Saints should rejoice in the historic revelations which the Lord is giving his church.

Therefore, whosoever belongeth to my church need not fear, for such shall inherit the kingdom of heaven.

But it is they who do not fear me, neither keep my commandments, but build up churches unto themselves to get gain, yea, and all those that do wickedly and build up the kingdom of the devil-yea, verily, verily, I say unto you, that it is they that I will disturb, and cause to tremble and shake to the center. (Doc. & Cov. 10:55-56)

In April 2018, the Church of Jesus Christ of Latter-Day Saints announced changes to the High Priest groups and Elders Quorums. This significant information also included the end of the Home and Visiting Teaching programs. These programs were replaced with a new program called Ministering.

The Savior's ministry exemplifies the two great commandments: "Thou shalt love the Lord thy God with all thy heart, and with all thy soul, and with all thy mind" and "Thou shalt love thy neighbour as thyself" (Matthew 22:37, 39). In that spirit, Jesus also taught, "Ye are they whom I have chosen to minister unto this people" (3 Nephi 13:25).

In April 2018, the Lord, through revelation to his chosen servants, made organizational and program changes. Ministering like the Savior became a main principle in the church.

MINISTERING WITH STRENGTHENED MELCHIZEDEK PRIESTHOOD QUORUMS AND RELIEF SOCIETIES

To focus the efforts of Melchizedek Priesthood quorums and Relief Societies on ministering as the Savior taught, we announce the following adjustments:

At the ward level, one Melchizedek Priesthood quorum. Members of elders quorums and high priests groups are now combined into one quorum with one presidency. The quorum is designated the "elders quorum," and ward high priests groups are discontinued.

At the stake level, one high priests quorum. The stake presidency continues to serve as the presidency of the high priests quorum. Members of that quorum are only those high priests currently serving in the stake presidency, in bishoprics, on the high council, and as functioning patriarchs.

Ministering replaces home teaching and visiting teaching. (Official Letter 2018)

No doubt, it is the Last Saturday. The Lord is revealing changes and programs to effectively prepare for his Second Coming.

4.3. Missionary Work

The scriptures contain numerous references to the fact that during the Last Days, the Gospel will be preached to every nation, kindred, tongue, and people.

And this gospel of the kingdom shall be preached in all the world for a witness unto all nations; and then shall the end come. (Matthew 24:14)

The Lord has indicated through prophets and the holy scriptures that the Gospel will go to all nations before his Second Coming. The Book of Mormon must be taken to all people, and the repentant, pure in heart will be gathered into the Lord's Kingdom.

We live in the days when we are watching the complete fulfillment of these words spoken by the Savior during his mortal ministry. The year 1989 will long be known as the year of freedom. Many of the doors to preach the Gospel to all the world started to open during that year.

We watched, and listened, in amazement as European and Far East countries began to sound the cry for freedom. Countries that had been under Communist governments for many years began to accept democracy. This freedom will allow the restored Gospel to be taught and embraced within their borders.

All of this activity was quite astounding. Yet, we know that we live in the Last Days and that before the Lord will come again, all nations will have an opportunity to hear and understand his life and mission, and the mission of the prophet Joseph Smith.

In 1989, the *Church News* reported, "More converts were baptized in 1988 than were in the entire Church until 1897–67 years after the gospel was restored." This 1988 total is an amazing number of new church members and "means that 703 people came into the Church every day of the year."

Since 1989, the church has experienced continued growth and increasing church membership. This growth has come from within and without. The 1988 total is also 58 percent higher than the number of baptisms in 1978.

Membership in United States Christian churches has shown a decline in recent years. However, the Church of Jesus Christ of Latter-Day Saints continues to grow.

New Temple Highlights Mormon Church Growth, Bucking National Trend

At a time when many Christian denominations are experiencing declines in membership in the US, one sect's numbers have continued to grow: the Church of Jesus Christ of Latter-Day Saints, commonly known as the Mormon church …

But the steady increase still marks a significant contrast to many other denominations, as fewer and fewer Americans choose to identify with an organized religion. (Williams 2016)

Events of the Last Saturday will include extensive missionary efforts on the part of the church and its members. Missionary work has been discussed and encouraged by all church leaders. But in recent years, the subject has been emphasized even more. It has been named one of the stated missions of the church.

The Church of Jesus Christ of Latter-Day Saints has three main missions. President Ezra Taft Benson spoke about the importance of the three missions:

A Sacred Responsibility

What a privilege it is to serve in the kingdom of God. In this work it is the Spirit that counts-wherever we serve …

We have a sacred responsibility to fulfill the threefold mission of the Church—first, to teach the gospel to the world; second, to strengthen the membership of the Church wherever they may be; third, to move forward the work of salvation for the dead. (Benson 1986)

How seriously do we take the threefold mission of the church? What are we doing with our time and energy during this very important last dispensation of time?

The 3 Guiding Principles of the LDS Church in the Mormon Faith

As members of the Church, we sign on to help Him in this endeavor. We help Him by sharing the gospel with others, helping other members to be righteous, and doing genealogy and temple work for the dead …

Mormons take these responsibilities seriously. They spend astonishing amounts of time on the three missions and continue to do so throughout their lives. (Bruner 2020)

How many Latter-Day Saints take the threefold mission of the church seriously? Are we spending "astonishing" effort, energy, and time in the Lord's service? Now is the day to step forward and up.

Several years ago, the church embraced today's technology to spread the restored Gospel and expand missionary work around the world. Perhaps you know of the church's "'I'm A Mormon" campaign.

"I'm a Mormon" Campaign

> The Church's national media campaign called "I'm a Mormon" (launched in 2010) included television spots, billboards, and ads on buses and on the Internet. The ads give a glimpse into the lives of Latter-day Saints from all over the world and refer people to the mormon.org website, where they can read the profiles of tens of thousands of Mormons, chat live with representatives who will answer questions about the faith and watch dozens of videos about members of the Church. (https://newsroom.churchofjesuschrist.org/article/-i-m-a-mormon-campaign)

This media campaign was successful in raising interest in the church and introducing people to the restored Gospel of Jesus Christ. It provided a new medium to increase missionary work. The program demonstrates the growth and progress of the Lord's Kingdom in these Last Days. The campaign was launched in many countries around the world.

Other announcements are evidence of the growth and strength of the church today, late on the Last Saturday.

On October 6, 2012, President Thomas S. Monson announced a change in full-time missionary service. The age for missionary service was changed from nineteen to eighteen for men, and from twenty-one to nineteen for women.

BYU Reflects on Missionary Age Change, Five Years Later

> Since the missionary age change announcement on Oct. 6, 2012, there has been a 20 percent increase in young

adults who serve full-time missions, and a 21 percent increase of the number of missions worldwide …

BYU saw an 8 percent increase of male students who are returned missionaries and a 32 percent increase in female students who are returned missionaries from the fall semester of 2012 to Fall 2017 …

In Fall 2012, 46 percent of BYU's student body had served missions. This fall semester, 65 percent of BYU students have served missions—a 19 percent increase over the last five years. (Baker 2017)

Missionary work is indeed growing. Countries around the world are now accepting missionaries. Just a few years ago, most members never thought we would see missionaries in many of these countries. The number of missionaries continues to increase. The growth of the church and its expansion to a truly worldwide church is exciting and is the fulfillment of prophecy.

4.4. TEMPLES

Temples are an essential element of the Lord's work. Therefore, the pace of temple construction becomes a valid sign of the end of our finite physical earth.

There was tremendous growth of the church during the administration of President Spencer W. Kimball. This summary of various events and announcements during his years as president is quite incredible. Note the number of events related to the temples of the Lord.

A Decade of Growth

Area Conference in Scandinavia	August 1974
Dedicated Washington Temple	November 1974
Announced Sao Paulo Temple in Brazil	March 1975

Dedicated 28-story Church Office Building	July 1975
Announced Tokyo Temple in Far East	August 1975
Reactivated First Quorum of the Seventy	October 1975
Announced Plans for Seattle Temple	November 1975
Reorganization of General Authorities	October 1976
Announced Plans for Samoa Temple	October 1977
Announced plans for Jordan River Temple	February 1978
Priesthood Given to All Worthy Males	June 1978
Dedicated the Sao Paulo Temple	October 1978
Nauvoo, Illinois becomes 1,000th Stake	February 1979
LDS Edition of the Bible Published	August 1979
Canadian Area Conference	August 1979
Consolidated Meeting Schedule Begins	March 1980
Announced Seven New Small Temples	April 1980
Announced Nine New Temples Worldwide	April 1981
Scripture Triple Combination Published	August 1981
Reduced Full-Time Mission Length	April 1982
Local Building Participation Reduced	April 1982
Six Temples Dedicated	June–December 1983

(Growth 1984)

Since President Kimball, the church has experienced additional changes, greater growth, and worldwide visibility and recognition. Church membership is now over 15 million further testifying of the significant Last Days in which we live.

Review and ponder the church's progress under the leadership of President Gordon B. Hinckley and Thomas S. Monson. Those years alone more than verify what day today is:

A RIPE HARVEST, NEAR TEMPLE SQUARE

Converts from Many Lands Join in Record Numbers in Mission Zone Surrounding Salt Lake Temple

Missionaries working practically within the shadow of the Salt Lake Temple are baptizing families from many countries in record numbers.

Some 87 people from 18 countries were baptized in February ...

"There are so many people who are led by the Spirit to come to Salt Lake City," said Pres. Merrell. "The Lord brings them here to be befriended by a member, taught by a missionary, and fellowshipped by stake missionaries." (Hart 1989)

People come to Salt Lake City, find the church, join the church, and receive sacred temple ordinances. These ordinances join family members who are living and deceased. These ordinances demonstrate the love and mercy of the Father and his Son. The ordinances keep the earth from being smitten with a curse (see Doc. & Cov. 128:18).

4.5. Prophecies and Revelation

Prophecies and revelations about the Last Saturday can be found throughout the ancient and modern scriptures. Paul, in his Second Epistle to Timothy, Peter in his Second Epistle, the Old Testament Prophet Micah (chapter 4), and Moses in the Pearl of Great Price (chapter 60) have prophesied and revealed truths about the Last Days.

In 2 Nephi, in the Book of Mormon, Nephi reveals to us information about the Promised Land in the Last Days.

Wherefore, I, Lehi, prophesy according to the workings of the Spirit which is in me, that there shall none come into this land save they shall be brought by the hand of the Lord.

Wherefore, this land is consecrated unto him whom he shall bring. And if it so be that they shall serve him according to the commandments which he hath given,

> it shall be a land of liberty unto them; wherefore, they shall never be brought down into captivity; if so, it shall be because of iniquity; for if iniquity shall abound cursed shall be the land for their sakes, but unto the righteous it shall be blessed forever.

> And behold, it is wisdom that this land should be kept as yet from the knowledge of other nations; for behold, many nations would overrun the land, that there would be no place for an inheritance. (2 Nephi 1:6-8)

A study of the secular history of the United States indicates that the land was kept from the knowledge of the world. Columbus discovered the New World in 1492. In a historical timeline, that could be considered recent. Relatively speaking, Columbus came to the New World long after the Nephites in the Book of Mormon were destroyed.

The Lord revealed the New World in the Last Days to facilitate his work of the restoration and bring to pass his eternal purposes.

Jacob, the Book of Mormon prophet, tells us that the Jews will crucify Christ because of their iniquities. They will be scattered but not destroyed, like the Nephites. Eventually, they will learn about the restored Gospel and believe in Jesus Christ as the redeemer of the world.

> For should the mighty miracles be wrought among other nations they would repent, and know that he be their God.

> But because of priestcrafts and iniquities, they at Jerusalem will stiffen their necks against him, that he be crucified.

> Wherefore, because of their iniquities, destructions, famines, pestilences, and bloodshed shall come upon them; and they who shall not be destroyed shall be scattered among all nations. (2 Nephi 10:4-6)

All things happen and work to bring forth the purposes of our Father in heaven. The history of the Jewish people has not been one of peace, joy, and prosperity. They will eventually receive the Savior of the world and all the blessings they have been promised.

> But behold, thus saith the Lord God: When the day cometh that they shall believe in me, that I am Christ, then have I covenanted with their fathers that they shall be restored in the flesh, upon the earth, unto the lands of their inheritance. (2 Nephi 10:7)

History reveals that the children of Judah suffered all manner of destruction and bloodshed. If they are being gathered and start to believe in Jesus Christ, we know without question that the end is near.

On one occasion when Jesus was on the Mount of Olives, the disciples asked him what the signs of his Second Coming and the end of the world would be:

> And Jesus answered them and said unto them, Take heed that no man deceive you.
>
> For many shall come in my name, saying, I am Christ; and shall deceive many. (Matthew 24:4-5)

Have not many been deceived today, even some who belong to the Lord's restored church? News headlines today often cover stories about dissenters and former members of the church, who now protest and march against the church. In many cases, they seek to change some of the procedures and practices, and sometimes the doctrine of the restored Gospel.

An event of the last days concerning the United States was revealed by Joseph Smith. It is recorded in scriptures of the Last Days:

> I prophesy, in the name of the Lord God, that the commencement of the difficulties which will cause much bloodshed previous to the coming of the Son of Man will be in South Carolina.

It may probably arise through the slave question. (Doc. & Cov. 130:12-13)

This simple yet clear prophecy refers to the Civil War of the United States of America. History documents the prophecy and evidence that it was true.

Today's technological advancements, computers, satellites, videos, and others are surely revelations from God to help prepare the world for the Lord's Second Coming. These innovations enhance the Lord's work here on the earth. A consolidated meeting schedule was initiated. Several announcements and changes to the missionary program have been instituted within the last several years.

In January 1990, a new ward and stake financial program was adopted. This change was never anticipated but was surely brought about by church growth and revelation for the Last Days. A new financial program for missionaries was also implemented.

Great revelations about the Kingdom of God are at hand. The prophets have told us that in the Last Days, many will be deceived and fall away. Some of these will even be the very elect. Are saints falling away?

As a member of a Stake High Council, I attended numerous High Council Disciplinary Councils. A sign of the times, in and of itself. I can't be sure, but I don't think there were as many Disciplinary Councils when I was a young boy.

On more occasions than I would like to remember, I arrived at the building for such a council. I learned that the council was for someone I knew personally. Sometimes, they were from my ward. I would walk into the building and see Bishops, Elders' Quorum Presidents, or other High Counselors sitting in the foyer. To my sadness, these men were sometimes there to face the council. Yes, saints are falling away, even some of the elect.

4.6. Gathering Saints

The prophesied command to gather the Lord's elect, in the Last Days, was given directly to Joseph Smith and the saints of the restored Church of Jesus Christ.

> And ye are called to bring to pass the gathering of mine elect; for mine elect hear my voice and harden not their hearts;
>
> Wherefore the decree hath gone forth from the Father that they shall be gathered in unto one place upon the face of this land, to prepare their hearts and be prepared in all things against the day when tribulation and desolation are sent forth upon the wicked. (Doc. & Cov. 29:7-8)

The gathering of the Lord's people began as soon as the church was organized. Missionaries were sent out, and the new church members gathered to Kirtland and Nauvoo. The Lord's command to gather the elect was initiated when the early saints left Nauvoo and trekked to the Salt Lake Valley. Led by Brigham Young, Salt Lake City became the worldwide gathering place. It was in the Salt Lake Valley where the elect prepared their hearts and prospered.

> And it shall come to pass in the last days, when the mountain of the Lord's house shall be established in the top of the mountains, and shall be exalted above the hills, and all nations shall flow unto it. (2 Nephi 12:2)

The mountain of the Lord's house has been established in the mountains around Salt Lake City, Utah. People from around the world have flowed to Salt Lake City. Many have come to find the church and become Latter-Day Saints. One place that saints are being gathered could be the city where the church headquarters is located. However, the one place could also refer to the church as an entity or worldwide organization. We cannot doubt or question the gathering of the Lord's elect in these Last Days.

The Lord's house has been established on the earth, and nations are flowing unto it.

FULFILLMENT OF PROPHECY

> Over the years, presidents of the United States, kings, judges, prime ministers, ambassadors, and officials from many lands have come to Salt Lake City and met with our leaders. President Nelson hosted leaders of the National Association for the Advancement of Colored People ...

> Many more have come to Temple Square and met in council with Church leaders. For example, this past year, to name just a few, we welcomed the United Nations 68th Civil Society Conference, a global gathering and the first of its kind outside of New York City. We have met with Vietnam's Committee for Religious Affairs and ambassadors from Cuba, the Philippines, Argentina, Romania, Sudan, Qatar, and Saudi Arabia. We also welcomed the secretary general of the Muslim World League. (Rasband 2020)

President Russell M. Nelson has taught us the following in a General Conference address (the gathering of Israel to their homeland and to the Lord's latter-day kingdom is a major mission of the Church of Jesus Christ of Latter-Day Saints):

THE GATHERING OF SCATTERED ISRAEL

> As prophesied by Peter and Paul, *all* things were to be restored in this dispensation. Therefore, there must come, as part of that restoration, the long-awaited gathering of scattered Israel. It is a necessary prelude to the Second Coming of the Lord.

This doctrine of the gathering is one of the important teachings of The Church of Jesus Christ of Latter-day Saints. The Lord has declared: "I give unto you a sign … that I shall gather in, from their long dispersion, my people, O house of Israel, and shall establish again among them my Zion." The coming forth of the Book of Mormon is a sign to the entire world that the Lord has commenced to gather Israel and fulfill covenants He made to Abraham, Isaac, and Jacob. We not only teach this doctrine, but we participate in it. (Nelson 2006)

The active gathering of the Children of Israel includes children from the lost ten tribes, or families of Jacob. This gathering is not only a Church of Jesus Christ of Latter-Day Saints doctrine and effort. The gathering of Israel is acknowledged, promoted, and supported by other organizations and religious groups.

"Operation Exodus" Helping US Jews Return to Israel

Earlier this year, immigrants from North America landed at Tel Aviv's Ben Gurion International Airport to make Israel their home.

Seeing Jewish people return to Israel is literally watching Bible prophecy unfold. Isaiah, Jeremiah, and Ezekiel speak of the Jewish return to their ancestral homeland.

"It says several times in Isaiah, 'I will lift up a banner to nations'—to the gentiles. They shall bring your sons and your daughters back," Operation Exodus head Debra Minotti told CBN News …

"If I can just give glory to God because this is His work," Minotti said. "In 1948, Israel had 800,000 Jewish people in the land, and they became a nation in one day like Isaiah said. Now there's over 6 million, so that is

incredible over 67 years. And so they're going back by
the plane loads yearly." (Aaron 2016)

Israel is truly being gathered in many ways in these "Times of the
Gentiles."

Nephi, the prophet/author of 3rd Nephi in the Book of Mormon, also
reveals to us that the remnant of the house of Israel will be gathered
from the four quarters of the earth in the Last Days. He further states
that because of the unbelief of the children of Israel, "in the latter-day
shall the truth come unto the Gentiles, that the fulness of these things
shall be made known unto them" (see 3 Nephi 16).

The prophet Jeremiah indicates that Israel will be gathered during
the Last Days in a rather unique way. The Lord indicates he will "take
you one of a city, and two of a family, and I will bring you to Zion"
(Jeremiah 3:14).

A great deal of this prophecy has come to pass. The church and
Kingdom of God have been restored to the gentiles. People from all over
the world are finding and becoming members of the restored church of
Jesus Christ. In many cases, those joining the church are individuals.

THE ONLY MEMBER IN MY
FAMILY -NAME WITHHELD

As a convert, I often found myself struggling to remain
connected with my family while living my religion.

One Sunday morning after I finished teaching a Relief
Society lesson, one of the sisters surprised me by saying,
"I sure appreciated hearing about your family." I looked
at her dumbfounded. I had shared a story about how the
family I was raised in had coped with such problems
as divorce and alcoholism. I wondered what she could
possibly have appreciated about the example I shared.

My look of puzzlement prompted her to explain: "Your
family sounds like mine. I was raised by alcoholic

parents, and my home, too, was marked by contention and divorce." (Only Member 2000)

The church understands the blessings and strength that single adult members provide to the church. In 2011, the wards and stakes for single church members ages eighteen to thirty were reorganized. Young single adult wards were realigned and assigned to newly created young single adult stakes.

Church leaders believe this will provide enhanced opportunities for young single adults to serve in leadership positions, to teach, lead, and serve.

After high school, my wife attended college at Ricks College, now BYU-Idaho in Rexburg, Idaho. Her roommate there was a student from Jacksonville, Florida. This young woman learned about Donny Osmond and his religious faith.

She learned about his church, was taught by the missionaries, and joined the Church of Jesus Christ of Latter-Day Saints. She was and still is the only member of her family. She is one of a family who has been gathered.

The single adults who join the church are the one or two of a family that are today being gathered. They are evidence that Jeremiah was a prophet, and his prophecy was true. The final gathering of Israel, and the world, is happening now.

4.7. JESUS CHRIST'S RETURN

The crowning event of the Last Saturday is the return of Jesus Christ to the earth. Disciples of Jesus Christ have been watching for this event since He ascended into heaven after His death and resurrection.

When Jesus comes to earth again, it will be a marvelous, glorious event. Latter-Day scriptures provide some information about what this event will be like, especially for Christians around the world.

> For I will reveal myself from heaven with power and great glory, with all the hosts thereof, and dwell in

righteousness with men on earth a thousand years, and the wicked shall not stand. (Doc. & Cov. 29:11)

For they will hear my voice, and shall see me, and shall not be asleep, and shall abide the day of my coming; for they shall be purified, even as I am pure.(Doc. & Cov. 35:21)

A loud trump will sound when the Lord returns. Will people of the whole earth hear this trump? All the earth shall quake. Will the people of all the earth feel this quake? Will the ground shake? The sun shall be darkened and the moon turned into blood. Have these events happened?

For a trump shall sound both long and loud, even as upon Mount Sinai, and all the earth shall quake, and they shall come forth-yea, even the dead which died in me, to receive a crown of righteousness, and to be clothed upon, even as I am, to be with me, that we may be one.

But, behold, I say unto you that before this great day shall come the sun shall be darkened, and the moon shall be turned into blood, and the stars shall fall from heaven, and there shall be greater signs in heaven above and in the earth beneath;

And there shall be weeping and wailing among the hosts of men;

And there shall be a great hailstorm sent forth to destroy the crops of the earth. (Doc. & Cov. 29:13-16)

Joseph Smith reiterates the Old Testament prophecy about the sun being darkened and the moon turning to blood. The sun and moon, as celestial bodies, have not been destroyed or physically turned into blood. However, we can see people weeping and wailing almost every day.

Boyd Matheson was in Washington DC on the evening after the mass shooting in Las Vegas on October 1, 2017. He says the shooting "demonstrated that evil continues to exist in the world." He also made an interesting comment about the signs of the times:

THE U.S. FLAG REMINDS US THAT
EVIL WILL NOT PREVAIL

> The evening after the Las Vegas shooting, I found myself in our nation's capital …
>
> I began to walk from the Capitol toward the Washington Monument …
>
> The buildings and monuments before me were all in complete darkness, but the sky hung scorched and ominous with clouds red with rage. The visual before me captured the gloom, anger, despair and fear that held the country in what felt like a physical, mental and spiritual war zone. (Matheson 2018)

Matheson doesn't say he saw a red moon. But he did see an angry red sky. Scriptures relating to the Last Days often describe what could be called a "physical, mental, and spiritual war zone."

Scriptures state that a great hailstorm will occur sometime on the Last Saturday. We don't know if this will be a worldwide storm or a major hailstorm in a single location. Intense hailstorms seem to be occurring more frequently throughout the world. Can you remember a major hailstorm that you recently experienced or heard about?

> Wherefore, I the Lord God will send forth flies upon the face of the earth, which shall take hold of the inhabitants thereof, and shall eat their flesh, and shall cause maggots to come in upon them;
>
> And their tongues shall be stayed that they shall not utter against me; and their flesh shall fall from off their bones, and their eyes from their sockets;

> And it shall come to pass that the beasts of the forest
> and the fowls of the air shall devour them up. (Doc. &
> Cov. 29:18-20)

These scriptural verses describe some pretty clear events that will occur before the Last Saturday ends. Most people agree that many (even most) of them have not yet happened. We would prefer to not see some of them first-hand.

Is it possible that some of these events and conditions have been seen in parts of the world where death and violence have occurred? People in countries that have experienced extensive rebellion, war, and famine have seen these horrors to some degree. Perhaps some of these signs have been witnessed and do exist, even if we have not seen them.

In his book Hiroshima, John Hersey describes the horror and suffering he found through his research. He followed six survivors of the atomic bomb dropped on Hiroshima, Japan, on August 6, 1945. We are not concerned with the decision to drop the bomb during World War II. However, here are some of the effects of radiation sickness John found in Hiroshima:

THE EYEBROWS OF SOME WERE BURNED OFF

> The eyebrows of some were burned off and skin hung
> from their faces and hands …

> Mr. Tanimoto found about twenty men and women on
> the sandspit. He drove the boat onto the bank and urged
> them to get aboard. They did not move and he realized
> that they were too weak to lift themselves. He reached
> down and took a woman by the hands, but her skin
> slipped off in huge, glove-like pieces …

> [Father Kleinsorge] got lost on a detour around a fallen
> tree, and as he looked for his way through the woods,
> he heard a voice ask from the underbrush, "Have you
> anything to drink?" He saw a uniform. Thinking there
> was just one soldier, he approached with the water.

> When he had penetrated the bushes, he saw there were
> about twenty men, and they were all in exactly the same
> nightmarish state: their faces were wholly burned, their
> eyesockets were hollow, the fluid from their melted eyes
> had run down their cheeks. (They must have had their
> faces upturned when the bomb went off: perhaps they
> were anti-aircraft personnel.) (Hersey 1946)

Nuclear fallout and radiation sickness can cause flesh to fall off and eyes to fall out of their sockets. The latter-day prophecy of the Lord's vengeance being manifest by flesh falling off of bones and eyes falling out of their sockets, may be fulfilled by nuclear war.

When we see or hear of flesh falling off the bones of men and eyes falling out of their sockets, we can be sure that the Last Saturday is not only here, but it is coming to an end.

WHAT WILL JESUS DO WHEN HE COMES AGAIN?

> He will cleanse the earth. The wicked will be destroyed
> (see Doc. & Cov. 101:24–25).

> He will judge all nations and divide the righteous from
> the wicked (see Matthew 25:31–46).

> He will raise those who have slept in their graves (see
> Doc. & Cov. 88:95–98, Revelation 20:4–5).

> He will usher in the Millennium and reign on the earth
> for a thousand years (see Doc. & Cov. 88:96).

> He will complete the First Resurrection. Those in the
> resurrection of the just will rise from their graves (See
> Doc. & Cov. 88:97–98).

> He will take His place as King of heaven and earth. He
> will rule in peace.

When He comes again, everyone will know who He is.
(Gospel Principles 2011)

As Latter-Day Saints, we should be able to recognize the signs of the times. Those signs are about the Lord's kingdom, the latter-day followers of Christ, and the conditions of the world.

When the Lord comes again, He will reveal many things, not just things related to his church and kingdom.

> Things which have passed, and hidden things which no man knew, things of the earth, by which it was made, and the purpose and the end thereof-
>
> Things most precious, things that are above, and things that are beneath, things that are in the earth, and upon the earth, and in heaven. (Doc. & Cov. 101:33-34)

The Lord has said that he will perform a marvelous work and a wonder (see Isaiah 29:14, Doc. & Cov. 6:1). He has, and He is, and He will.

The restoration and growth of the Lord's Kingdom on the Last Saturday, when the Great Redeemer returns, will be rewarding, as described by prophecy. Brigham Young, second president of the Church of Jesus Christ of Latter-Day Saints, said,

> In the Millennium, when the Kingdom of God is established on the earth in power, glory and perfection, and the reign of wickedness that has so long prevailed is subdued, the Saints of God will have the privilege of building their temples, and of entering into them, becoming, as it were, pillars in the temples of God [see Revelation 3:12], and they will officiate for their dead. Then we will see our friends come up, and perhaps some that we have been acquainted with here ...
>
> And we will have revelations to know our forefathers clear back to Father Adam and Mother Eve, and we will enter into the temples of God and officiate for

them. Then [children] will be sealed to [parents] until
the chain is made perfect back to Adam, so that there
will be a perfect chain of Priesthood from Adam to the
winding-up scene. (Young 1997, 333-334)

In consideration of the number of temples currently around the
world, and the work that is being performed in those temples, we can
easily conclude that Brigham Young's prophecy has come true. His
words are a sign of the times.

The true church of Jesus Christ has been restored to the earth in
these latter days. The church encompasses all the power, authority,
teachings, doctrine, and organization required for the Savior to return.
As Latter-Day Saints, we need to "lengthen our stride" and prepare the
people of the world for his Second Coming.

The Last Saturday will be a day when the Lord gives the wicked
their reward (or perhaps their punishment).

For the hour is nigh and the day soon at hand when the
earth is ripe; and all the proud and they that do wickedly
shall be as stubble; and I will burn them up, saith the
Lord of hosts, that wickedness shall not be upon the
earth. (Doc. & Cov. 29:9)

Have the wicked and proud been burned up? Has wickedness been
removed from the earth? Our current answer would be no, but based
on current events and headlines around the world, it will be happening
soon.

The dispensation of the fullness of times has been ushered in. It is
about to be ushered out. The Last Saturday will soon be over, and the
Millennium and the mortal reign of the Savior will be ushered in.

4.8. FALSE CHRISTS AND PROPHETS

Jesus himself warned us about the Last Days when he walked among
men here on the earth. His words from those days also teach us about
the state of affairs during this last dispensation.

For in those days shall be affliction, such as was not from the beginning of the creation which God created unto this time, neither shall be.

And except that the Lord had shortened those days, no flesh should be saved: but for the elect's sake, whom he hath chosen, he hath shortened the days.

And then if any man shall say to you, Lo, here is Christ; or, lo, he is there; believe him not:

For false Christs and false prophets shall rise, and shall shew signs and wonders, to seduce, if it were possible, even the elect.

But take ye heed: behold, I have foretold you all things.

But in those days, after that tribulation, the sun shall be darkened, and the moon shall not give her light,

And the stars of heaven shall fall, and the powers that are in heaven shall be shaken.

And then shall they see the Son of man coming in the clouds with great power and glory.

And then shall he send his angels, and shall gather together his elect from the four winds, from the uttermost part of the earth to the uttermost part of heaven. (Mark 13:19-27)

These scriptural verses found in Mark chapter 13 describe many events and trials of the Last Saturday. First, these Final Days of wickedness will be shortened, or no flesh would be left upon the earth. Second, false Christs and prophets will teach to seduce and lead the elect away from Jesus Christ. Third, we shall see the Savior coming with great power and glory.

Verse 21 of these scriptures says that if anyone says, "Lo, here is Christ, or lo, he is there," we should not believe them. This sounds a lot like the leaders of the churches as described by Joseph Smith when he was a young boy.

The world today admonishes us to beware of false Christs and prophets. Here are some posted observations by Pastor Tim Challies of the Grace Fellowship Church in Toronto, Ontario.

7 False Teachers in the Church Today

The history of Christ's church is inseparable from the history of Satan's attempts to destroy her. While difficult challenges have arisen from outside the church, the most dangerous have always been from within. For from within arise the false teachers, the peddlers of error who masquerade as teachers of truth. False teachers take on many forms, custom-crafted to times, cultures, and contexts. Here are seven of them you will find carrying out their deceptive, destructive work in the church today. Please note that while I have followed the biblical texts in describing them in masculine terms, each of these false teachers can as easily be female. (Challies 2017)

An article in the *Guardian* about Jonas Bendikson talks about men who claim they are the Messiah and have returned to earth. Bendikson has published a book about his experiences with many self-proclaimed Messiahs around the world.

Jesus Christ Superstars: Meet the Modern-Day Messiahs

David Shayler worked for MI5, Vissarion was a traffic policeman … now both preach as the son of God …

"My mission was to say, 'OK, if one were to accept the prophecy of Jesus's return, why *wouldn't* it be this guy?'" ...

David Shayler, ... the former MI5 whistleblower turned Jesus claimant, is what Bendiksen calls "a digital messiah" ...

The revelation that he was Jesus came to him in 2007 ...

Others, such as Vissarion of Siberia, have thousands of followers ...

The disciples of Vissarion, a 56-year-old former traffic policeman in the Siberian town of Minusinsk, for instance, are photographed side by side at a long, laden table. (Cocozza 2017)

Moses Hlongwane, in South Africa, is known as the King of Kings, the Lord of Lords, and Jesus. His wife is called the Mother of the Whole World. These are but a few of the many self-proclaimed Messiahs in the world.

Scriptures frequently declare that Jesus Christ, the Messiah, will return to the earth. Jesus said that many would come in his name. We may think that false messiahs have not yet come, but they really have. You may learn all about them with an online search. These modern-day messiahs validate prophecies and the Last Saturday.

The title page of the Book of Mormon explains why the gold plates were given to Joseph Smith, why he translated them, why it was published as the Book of Mormon, and why it has been presented to the world.

Which is to show unto the remnant of the house of Israel what great things the Lord hath done for their fathers; and that they may know the covenants of the Lord, that they are not cast off forever—And also to the convincing of the Jew and Gentile that Jesus is the

Christ, the Eternal God, manifesting himself unto all
nations. (Book of Mormon, Title page)

The Book of Mormon has come forth in the Last Days to reveal,
testify, and convince any and all of God's children who Jesus Christ is.

Mormon, the prophet whose name the Book of Mormon bears,
understood the mission and purpose of the Book of Mormon. He knew
and prophesied that the sacred records he had, and his own words, would
come forth in a future day, by the Lord's commandment and wisdom.

> And behold, they shall go unto the unbelieving of the
> Jews; and for this intent shall they go—that they may be
> persuaded that Jesus is the Christ, the Son of the living
> God; that the Father may bring about, through his most
> Beloved, his great and eternal purpose, in restoring
> the Jews, or all the house of Israel, to the land of their
> inheritance, which the Lord their God hath given them,
> unto the fulfilling of his covenant. (Mormon 5:14)

In the Old Testament, Malachi prophesies about two major events of
the Last Days. In the Book of Mormon, Nephi the son of Nephi declares
the same events. Whether he was familiar with the words of Malachi
or not, his declaration becomes a prophetic confirmation of Malachi's
words:

> For, behold, the day cometh, that shall burn as an oven;
> and all the proud, yea, and all that do wickedly, shall
> be stubble: and the day that cometh shall burn them up,
> saith the Lord of hosts, that it shall leave them neither
> root nor branch. (Malachi 4:1--3, Nephi 25:1)

> Behold, I will send you Elijah the prophet before the
> coming of the great and dreadful day of the Lord.
> (Malachi 4:5/3, Nephi 25:5)

Nephi clearly states that specific events will happen during the Last
Days, on the Last Saturday. The Book of Mormon will come forth to the

gentiles, who will then spread the Gospel to the remnant of the house of Israel. The gathering of the Children of Israel to their own lands will take place.

Nephi teaches that the "work of the Father" to gather Israel and fulfill the covenant made with them began with the restoration of the Gospel through the prophet Joseph Smith (see 2 Nephi 21:12). Nephi even reveals that the gentiles who receive the things which he declared would be a free people in the land where Nephi lived: America (see 3 Nephi 21:4).

Ancient biblical scriptures and Last Saturday scriptures support and verify each other. Holy prophets and the fulfillment of their prophecies serve as a banner to the world of the Lord's true prophets today.

John the revelator and Joseph Smith both referred to a latter-day prophecy.

The prophecy states that two prophets will be raised up during the Last Days in Jerusalem. The prophets are to "prophesy to the Jews after they are gathered and have built the city of Jerusalem in the land of their fathers."

These two prophets will also play a major role in the great battle of Armageddon, which will take place just before the Lord's Second Coming. The prophets will eventually be slain. John specifies that the people will not allow their bodies to be "put in graves". The bodies will lie in the streets of Jerusalem for three and a half days (see Revelation 11, Doc. & Cov. 77:15).

Today is the Last Saturday. Prophecies about the Lord's Kingdom have and are becoming reality. When the two prophets lie in the streets of Jerusalem, we may be assured that the "Great and Dreadful Day of the Lord" is not near; it will be here.

Another prophet by the name of Nephi, Lehi's son, also testified that the writings he and others were keeping would come forth to the gentiles. Referring to what would take place in the Last Days, Nephi declares that God would bring forth a book (see 2 Nephi 27).

That book is the Book of Mormon. It was truly brought forth by the power of God.

The Last Saturday will be filled with false Christs, prophets, and other deceivers. Some of them will deceive the world and the church. Some of them even come from within the church.

One of these was Mark Hoffman. He attempted to deceive the church and its members. His actions promoted false teachings and information about the church and its history. Hoffman discovered and promoted many different documents to church members, church leaders, and historical experts.

The First Presidency's Statement

A letter purportedly written by Martin Harris to W. W. Phelps was recently presented to the Church by Steven F. Christensen, its owner. The document is dated Palmyra, Oct. 23, 1830 and has been the subject of much discussion and research.

With the letter was presented a copy of a report which points out factors which indicate that the letter was written about the time of the date it bears and on materials which were likely manufactured about that time. The examiner concludes his statement by saying, "that there is no indication that this letter is a forgery." …

President Gordon B. Hinckley, second counselor in the First Presidency, who accepted the letter, stated: "No one, of course, can be certain that Martin Harris wrote the document. However, at this point we accept the judgment of the examiner that there is no indication that it is a forgery. This does not preclude the possibility that it may have been forged at a time when the Church had many enemies. It is, however, an interesting document of the times."

Actually the letter has nothing to do with the authenticity of the Church. The real test of the faith which both Martin Harris and W.W. Phelps had in Joseph Smith and his work is found in their lives, in the sacrifices they made for their membership in the Church, and in the testimonies they bore to the end of their lives. (Church News 1985, 6)

On June 23, 1985, President Hinckley spoke at a Young Adult fireside from Temple Square. He talked about some of the documents that the church had recently acquired.

CHURCH REACTION TO THE HOFMANN FORGERIES

As most of you know, recently there have been great stirrings over two old letters. One was purportedly written in 1825 by Joseph Smith to Josiah Stowell. If it is genuine, it is the oldest known product of Joseph Smith's handwriting. It concerns the employment of Joseph by Mr. Stowell, who was engaged in a mining operation looking for old coins and precious metals. The other carries the date of October 23, 1830, and was purportedly written by Martin Harris to W. W. Phelps.

I acquired for the Church both of these letters, the first by purchase. The second was given to the Church by its generous owner. I am, of course, familiar with both letters, having held them in my hands and having read them in their original form. It was I, also, who made the decision to make them public. Copies were issued to the media, and both have received wide publicity ...

I am glad we have them. They are interesting documents of whose authenticity we are not certain and may never be. However, assuming that they are authentic, they are valuable writings of the period out of which they have come. But they have no real relevancy to the question of the authenticity of the Church, or of the divine origin of the Book of Mormon. (Hinckley 1985)

Most of the documents and artifacts that were discovered and presented by Mark Hoffman were ultimately determined to be false and clever forgeries. His actions are clear signs and warnings that today is Saturday: the Last one.

Forger Mark Hofmann, Twenty Years Later

> The two murders Mark Hofmann committed that bright October day were cold-blooded, clumsy attempts to divert attention from his life's work—hundreds of forgeries and lies that tampered with LDS and American history. (E-Sylum 2005)

Mark Hofmann created forgeries from Emily Dickinson, Mark Twain, George Washington, and Joseph Smith. His talent and knowledge deceived document experts and others. His success continues to perplex historians and investigators today.

The Lord's Kingdom today is being subjected to deceivers of men and women, acts of violence, and terrorism.

Feminist Raps LDS Sexism

> SPOKANE, Wash. (AP). An excommunicated Mormon author and feminist says a series of personal discoveries made her "realize it is extremely important for women to gain the priesthood" and to "overthrow the patriarchy" of the Mormon church …

> [the woman], born and raised in Utah, said that unlike many women in other male-dominated faiths, women in the Church of Jesus Christ of Latter-Day Saints have not begun to question "the fundamental issue of sexism in the church." (Salt Lake Tribune 1980)

The woman in this story says a series of personal discoveries gave her special insight into some actions that women should work towards. Are personal discoveries the same as personal revelations? Do personal discoveries sustain the claim that the clock will soon sound midnight on the Last Saturday?

In 2018, today's violence not only came to the Church of Jesus Christ of Latter-Day Saints, but it also became deadly right inside the meetinghouse. If today is the Last Saturday, it would be wise to plan and prepare for violent acts like this, in places like this.

LDS SHOOTING WITNESS: "PEOPLE WERE SCREAMING AND HITTING THE GROUND"

SALT LAKE CITY. [A man] sat on a couch in the west foyer just outside the chapel with a few other members of his LDS congregation.

When the sacrament service was complete and as the meeting's first speaker began to talk, [the man], 48, stood up, walked through the chapel's west door, drew a handgun and at point-blank range shot and killed Bert Miller, 61, a man he had known for years, witnesses and police said. (Walch 2018)

The shooting took place inside the church meetinghouse and in the chapel. City officials said the motive for the shooting was unknown. It is also believed the shooter was targeting a single person in the meeting.

In 1979, in Shelton, Washington, two teenagers were charged with the attempted murder of two Relief Society visiting teachers. The shootings took place during a robbery that netted $1 and a brief joyride in the victim's car. Each woman was shot twice in the head and chest. They were then left to die on an isolated logging road.

The assault took place when the women stopped at an intersection. A masked man from a car that was following them jumped into their car and demanded the women's wallets. The youths, including a sixteen-year-old girl, commandeered the Relief Society sister's car, and the vehicles drove to the logging road. A judge set bail at a hundred dollars each for the two suspects, ages eighteen and seventeen (see Deseret News, Salt Lake City, February 23, 1979).

It doesn't matter how many false Christs arise, or how many criticize and express malice towards the latter-day Church of Jesus Christ. Their actions and rhetoric only confirm that it is the end of time, and the Lord's true church is here.

4.9. Church Growth

A true sign that the Church of Jesus Christ of Latter-Day Saints is the Lord Jesus Christ's restored church, and that these are the Last Days, is that the church continues to grow, flourish, and expand throughout the world.

This Week in Church History 25 Years Ago

> The growth of the Church led to a change in administration with six General Authorities called to supervise areas outside the United States. (Church News 2000)

These new General Authorities will live in the new areas and serve indefinitely under the direction of the First Presidency and Quorum of the Twelve Apostles.

Before the church was restored and organized in 1830, and even today, it has experienced many types of ridicule, contempt, and disapproval. In 1839, the growing church paid no heed to such behavior and attacks.

Persecution Has Not Stopped

> Persecution has not stopped the progress of truth, but has only added fuel to the flame, it has spread with increasing rapidity. Proud of the cause which they have espoused, and conscious of our innocence, and of the truth of their system, amidst calumny and reproach, have the Elders of this Church gone forth, and planted the Gospel in almost every state in the Union;

> It has penetrated our cities, it has spread over our villages, and has caused thousands of our intelligent, noble, and patriotic citizens to obey its divine mandates, and be governed by its sacred truths. (Wentworth 540)

Today, as back then, the church moves forward and continues to grow. The church increasingly bears forth good fruit. The good fruit is found in more and more nations of the world. All of this asserts that the church is precisely what it claims to be and is directed by divine power.

CHILE 4TH NATION WITH 100 STAKES

> With the creation of the Puerto Varas stake March 9, Chile joined the elite group of nations with 100 stakes.

> So great was the excitement among the local members that the meetinghouse where the stake was created was filled to capacity. Some 300 additional members stood along the walls or hallways to witness the historic event. Chile's 100th stake was created in south Chile, about 25 years after the first stake in this South American nation …

> Only four nations have 100 or more stakes: the United States, with 1,241, Brazil with 154, Mexico with 152, and now Chile. (Acevedo 1997)

The first stake in the Philippines was created in 1973. Elder Neil L. Andersen created the hundredth Philippine stake in 2017. The Philippines became the fifth nation with a hundred stakes. Church growth continues in old and new areas around the world.

The restored doctrine and teachings of Jesus Christ, the Gospel, have not changed as time passes. The organization, structure, and procedures of the restored church do change. These changes are necessary as the church grows and spreads to additional people and nations. Organizational changes demonstrate that the Lord's return is at the door.

Church growth is happening in historic measures, as members and leaders serve to hasten the work and prepare for the Second Coming of Jesus Christ.

In 1988, Elder M. Russell Ballard, a member of the Quorum of Twelve Apostles, made a historic trip to South America. One stop on his trip was Lima, Peru. While in Lima, the church "multiplied by division."

In one weekend, eleven Lima stakes were divided to create eighteen stakes. Six separate conferences were held over a twenty-eight-hour period. Seven new stakes were created, and fourteen new stake presidents were called.

18 STAKES CREATED FROM 11: 28-HOUR
MARATHON IN LIMA MULTIPLIES BY DIVIDING

[Elder Ballard] spoke at all six conferences. That made for some inventive planning: At some sessions he excused himself halfway through the meeting so he could be driven six to eight miles through congested Lima streets to make the start of the next conference.

He emphasized the historic impact of what was happening during this weekend. "The whole church is watching what is happening in South America," he said. "It's really a miracle what is taking place here. Did you know you are blazing a great trail for the Church?" (Warnick 1988)

The Church of Jesus Christ of Latter-Day Saints has experienced tremendous growth for many years. This growth is not only in church membership, but in all areas of spreading the Gospel around the globe. Since Joseph Smith translated the Book of Mormon from the gold plates, the work of translation has continued.

Translators Help Send LDS Message Worldwide

On the 21st floor of Salt Lake City's tallest office building, linguists, translators, computer technicians and others are busily working to make the LDS scriptures and other writings more understandable to the world.

They're only part of a small army of hundreds of people in many nations who are endeavoring to carry the message of the 9.2-million-member Church of Jesus Christ of Latter-day Saints through scriptures and other translated materials …

The Book of Mormon or selections from the book, which church members believe to be a history of God's dealings with ancient inhabitants of the American continent, have been published in 85 languages. The Doctrine and Covenants and Pearl of Great Price have been translated and published in 29 of the 85 languages, and plans are under way for additional translations. There are more than 6,000 known languages in the world …

The Bible now is printed in more than 300 languages. (Palmer 1995)

The April 2018 General Conference of the Church reveals how the church is growing. Millions of people around the world received all or parts of the conference.

Coverage and News Media Resources from the 188th Annual General Conference

General conferences of The Church of Jesus Christ of Latter-day Saints take place every six months, originating in the 21,000-seat Conference Center in Salt Lake City and reaching a global audience estimated to be in the millions. The spring 2018 proceedings are being interpreted live into more than 80 languages and are available in more than 90 languages via television, radio, satellite and internet.

Five conference sessions are being held March 31 and April 1, 2018. This page is a repository of links to news and announcements from general conference weekend.

News and Announcements

- Latter-day Saints Sustain New First Presidency in Solemn Assembly
- Eight New General Authority Seventies Announced
- New Young Women Presidency Announced
- 2017 Statistical Report
- Changes Announced to Church's Adult Priesthood Quorums
- First Presidency Shares Easter Messages
- "Ministering" to Replace Home and Visiting Teaching
- Seven Temples Announced (https://newsroom.churchofjesus christ.org/article/april-2018-general-conference)

There is abundant evidence of how the church is growing at each General Conference of the Church. The following information is about the many resources available to access the April 2019 General Conference.

HOW TO ATTEND, WATCH OR LISTEN TO THE 189TH
ANNUAL GENERAL CONFERENCE THIS WEEKEND

All sessions of general conference will be streamed live in 31 languages on ChurchofJesusChrist.org. The Saturday and Sunday sessions will also be streamed live on YouTube.

You can also watch general conference through the Deseret News on deseret.com or on the Deseret News app, through KSL on ksl.com or on the KSL app and on BYUtv at byutv.org/watch or on the BYUtv app.

General conference talks will be available in 86 languages on ChurchofJesusChrist.org and the Gospel Library app after the conference. (Lee 2019)

The conference was also available from BYU-TV channels received from cable TV providers. Access to the conference can also be found on KSL and BYU radio stations. The Gospel will go to every nation and people. To a great extent, it already is, at least to those who want to watch or listen.

The Savior will come again soon and reign on the earth for one thousand years. That period is the last Sunday. In the Doctrine and Covenants, the prophet Joseph Smith tells us what happens when Last Sunday ends.

And again, verily, verily, I say unto you that when the thousand years are ended, and men again begin to deny their God, then will I spare the earth but for a little season;

And the end shall come, and the heaven and the earth shall be consumed and pass away, and there shall be a new heaven and a new earth. (Doc. & Cov. 29:22-23)

5

Latter-Day Saints

It's the Last Saturday. What are the Latter-Day Saints doing today? Of all the people in the world, we as members of The Church of Jesus Christ of Latter-Day Saints should be the most prepared for the Last Sunday. Do we even know or realize what day it is?

5.1. SERVICE AND SACRIFICE

A young brother faithfully served as a Temple veil worker for more than fifteen years. He was single during most of this time. I thought giving of his time to work in the Temple would not have been very high on his list of things to do at this time in his life. I expected him to be interested in other activities and pursuits. However, his willingness and faithfulness to this calling was a great example of Last Saturday faith, dedication, and sacrifice.

I discussed it with him once, and he informed me that he knows Latter-Day Saints who have worked in the Temple as veil workers for thirty years. Then when they expressed a desire to be released from the calling, the Temple asked them to work as ordinance workers-and they accepted. How many members, Latter-Day Saints, are willing to sacrifice so much? How many are so dedicated to the Lord and his Kingdom?

A former bishop, stake president, and stake patriarch, many years retired, was called with his wife to serve as Temple workers for two years. They served for over ten years. Today, the Last Saturday calls for such dedication and service on the part of all church members.

Some members of the church outwardly understand what day it is. They have engaged in a unique and reportedly successful missionary program.

Members of the Van Nuys, California, 3rd ward have placed copies of the Book of Mormon in the Best Western Airtel Plaza hotel. Hotel guests are invited to take a book from their room home, as a souvenir. The hotel has two hundred rooms. Books are placed as part of a missionary project. The ward mission leader says that the entire mission is excited about the project and its success (see Church News, March 24, 1985, 4).

Elder Robert D. Hales speaking in the April 2005 General Conference of the Church spoke of the service, sacrifice, and blessings of couples who serve full-time missions for the church.

COUPLE MISSIONARIES: BLESSINGS
FROM SACRIFICE AND SERVICE

Four years ago I spoke in this setting about couples serving full-time missions. My prayer was that "the Holy Ghost [would] touch hearts, and somewhere a spouse … [would] quietly nudge his or her companion, and a moment of truth [—a moment of decision—] would occur." One sister later wrote me about that experience. She said, "We were sitting in the comfort of our family room enjoying conference on television …

As you spoke, my heart was touched so deeply. I looked over at my husband and he looked at me. That moment changed my life forever."

If you are or will soon be the age of a senior missionary, I come to you this afternoon to witness of the blessings that can change your life forever. Your Heavenly Father needs you. His work, under the direction of our Savior Jesus Christ, needs what you are uniquely prepared to give. Every missionary experience requires faith, sacrifice, and service, and these are always followed by an outpouring of blessings. (Hales 2005)

The opportunities to serve and sacrifice for the Lord, and hasten His work, are greater and more diverse than ever before. How and where we serve is not the issue. The issue is that we acknowledge what day it is and the urgency for us to give of our time, talents, and means.

Now is the day we need to friendship, teach, and minister to the children of our heavenly Father. We must do it in every way that our circumstances will allow. It is time for us to help bring to pass "the immortality and eternal life" of men, women, and children. Remember, sacrifice brings forth blessings for those who serve and those who are served.

5.2. Proclaim the Gospel

Today is surely the day and age when the Lord's work must roll, even thunder, forward. As members of the Lord's Kingdom during the Last Days, one of our most important duties must be missionary work. The Second Coming is soon upon us. The time for missionary work by good example only is past. We as members of the church should be actively engaged in sharing the restored Gospel.

We should be teaching and preparing our children to be the Lord's servants. We should all be preparing for His return. We should be preparing ourselves, as married couples, for full-time missionary service, when circumstances allow. Events around the world truly testify that we as a church, collectively and individually, need to step forward to further spread the Gospel. Let the charge to go the second mile in bringing people to Christ be issued and accepted.

Proclaiming the Gospel is not extremely difficult. It generally only requires a single action.

> Open your mouths in proclaiming my gospel. (Doc. & Cov. 71:1)

MERRIE MISS MISSIONARIES

"Now," said Sister Searle, finishing her lesson on missionary work, "close your eyes and think of someone who isn't a member of the Church."

Thea, Annlouise, Michaelene, and Virginia leaned back in their chairs and squinched their eyes shut.

"Imagine yourselves telling this person about the Church."

Thea smiled, Annlouise frowned, Michaelene squirmed, and Virginia sighed.

"Good. Now open your eyes. Your challenge for this week is to do what you just imagined—tell a nonmember about the Church—and report what happened next Sunday."

The next Sunday each of the girls reported on her efforts. (Moore 1992)

The girls had different experiences as they opened their mouths to share the Gospel with friends and neighbors. The friends they invited to learn of Jesus did not all accept the restored Gospel. However, each girl made the effort and had a positive experience. They helped spread the Gospel and further the work of proclaiming the restored teachings of Jesus Christ.

In the New Testament book of Luke, Jesus tells us the parable of the sower. A sower goes out to sow seed. The seed falls in different locations. Some by the wayside, some seeds are trodden down, fowls devour seeds, some fall among thorns, and some seeds fall on good ground and produce good fruit (see Luke 8:5–8).

We should consider the sower as a disciple of Christ, who is proclaiming the teachings of Jesus. Some of those who listen to the sower change their lives and commence to follow the Savior. Many do not. Our command today is to be a disciple and servant of Christ. To proclaim the restoration to others and invite them to come and learn of Jesus Christ. The choice, however, is theirs. If they do not accept the invitation, we should not esteem them as our enemy.

We are not the only Christians in the world who are encouraged to share our faith and knowledge of Jesus Christ.

Sharing Your Faith 101

Maybe you're afraid to share your faith because you don't know what to say. Or maybe you're sharing the Gospel but nothing is happening; people aren't committing their lives to Christ. Are you doing something wrong?

You can't open someone's heart to the truth of the Gospel—but God can, by His Spirit. The Apostle Paul wasn't eloquent, but God used him because he depended on the Holy Spirit to guide him (see 1 Corinthians 2:1-5). God guided many others in the Bible as well …

Remember that God does not call the equipped; He equips the called—and as Christians, we are all called to share what Christ has done. (Graham 2019)

Followers of Jesus Christ throughout the world endeavor to live, follow, and share the teachings of Christ. We, with our knowledge of the restored Gospel and current signs that the Lord's return is near, should feel the urgency and the responsibility to proclaim the Gospel to others.

There are indications and evidence that Latter-Day Saints are striving to live the Gospel and follow the Savior. A study published by Simon and Schuster in 2010 included some positive information and conclusions about members of the Church of Jesus Christ of Latter-Day Saints. The study discloses that many church members are living the way they should on the Last Saturday.

MAJOR NEW STUDY OF RELIGION HAS MUCH
TO SAY ABOUT MORMONS MAY 23, 2014

Recently published under the title *American Grace: How Religion Divides and Unites Us, ...*

Among the study's findings related to Latter-day Saints are the following:

- Mormons are among the most devout religious groups in the country ...
- Mormons are among those most likely to keep their childhood faith as adults ...
- Mormons are unusually giving ...
- Mormons are relatively friendly to other religious groups ...
- Mormons are among the most likely to believe that one true religion exists, *but also* that those outside their faith can attain salvation or reach "heaven." (Putnam and Campbell 2010)

5.3. POWERS OF DARKNESS

As members of the Lord's kingdom on earth, we have some knowledge about the powers of darkness. We are aware of and know about the father of lies, he who continually wages war against God, Jesus Christ, and the plan of salvation. We learn about secret combinations, secret oaths, murderers, and how the influence of evil can blind men and enter into their hearts.

For it came to pass that they did deceive many with their flattering words, who were in the church, and did cause them to commit many sins; therefore it became expedient that those who committed sin, that were in the church, should be admonished by the church. (Mosiah 26:6)

As the church comes out of obscurity, critics, antagonists, and detractors have arisen to rail on and persecute the church and its members. We live in a day when claims and accusations against the church are increasing.

FAKE VERSION OF LDS WEBSITE FOOLS READERS AND MEDIA WITH FAKE APOLOGY FOR RACISM

SALT LAKE CITY (KUTV). A fake version of a LDS Church website with a counterfeit apology about racism caused a ruckus on social media and in Mormon communities Thursday.

The fictitious website closely resembled the authentic MormonNewsroom.org, where The Church of Jesus Christ of Latter-day Saints posts information, press releases, photo and video assets and official statements to the media. The hoax site not only fooled readers but at least one media outlet with its URL that used mormon-newsroom.org, which was differentiated with the hyphen. (Curtis 2018)

The manifestation of the power of darkness against the church is not always criticism and threats. It sometimes becomes violent and physical: the destruction of church property.

UPDATED: MAN BREAKS INTO, VANDALIZES ST. GEORGE LDS TEMPLE

ST. GEORGE. Police were sent to the St. George LDS Temple early Saturday after a man broke in through a window and proceeded to damage furniture and artwork inside …

The man was contained on the fifth floor by temple workers and was ultimately taken into custody …

Preliminary charges... include felony offenses for criminal mischief and burglary,... misdemeanors for assault, interfering with an arrest and disorderly conduct. (Kessler 2018)

Do we understand the extent of the power of evil in our world? The scripture below should alarm us and cause us to seek refuge and peace through Jesus Christ. The scripture could refer to our mortal lives, our spiritual lives, or both. It doesn't really matter. It should, however, motivate us to be true, obedient saints, followers of the only begotten Son of God.

And again, I say unto you that the enemy in the secret chambers seeketh your lives. (Doc. & Cov. 38:28)

The Lord talks to us in the Doctrine and Covenants about the wars we hear of throughout the world. He states that we don't know "the hearts of men in our own land." Then we find these news headlines:

LDS CHURCH RESPONDS TO ALLEGATIONS OF SEXUAL ABUSE BY FORMER PROVO MTC PRESIDENT

Allegations of sexual assault by a former president of the Provo Missionary Training Center against a sister missionary have resurfaced after 34 years ...

"These allegations are very serious and deeply disturbing," the church statement says. "If the allegations of sexual assault are true, it would be a tragic betrayal of our standards and would result in action by the Church to formally discipline any member who was guilty of such behavior, especially someone in a position of trust."

According to the statement, the matter was first brought to the attention of the church in 2010, approximately 26 years after the alleged assault. (Pugmire 2018)

We are looking for evidence of powers of darkness, here in the Last Days. Not whether the accusation(s) against a former MTC president is true or false. This matter was apparently first raised in 2010. How many years after the incident was that?

We don't know how the matter was handled back in 2010, but surely it received some attention, and resolution, in some measure. Now eight years later, in 2018, the accusation has again surfaced. Is this an example of the dark powers that exist today, even against the church?

The Lord has warned us about the darkness that is in people's hearts today. He has also told us how to escape the latter-day power of the enemy.

> I tell you these things because of your prayers; wherefore, treasure up wisdom in your bosoms, lest the wickedness of men reveal these things unto you by their wickedness, in a manner which shall speak in your ears with a voice louder than that which shall shake the earth; but if ye are prepared ye shall not fear.
>
> And that ye might escape the power of the enemy, and be gathered unto me a righteous people, without spot and blameless. (Doc. & Cov. 38:30-31)

Are we as Latter-Day Saints prepared for today? How much fear resides in the hearts of church members? Now, this day, this minute, we should raise our title of liberty and faith. It is indeed time for us to prepare for the Savior's Second Coming and "seek first, the kingdom of God."

Powers of darkness have been found throughout the world in the past, and even today. Germany was in turmoil for many years. This turmoil was the era in which Adolf Hitler became the chancellor. His persecution and execution of the Jewish people fulfilled prophecy and were surely manifestations of powers of darkness.

TREATMENT OF JEWS

Anti-Semitism was an essential element of the Nazi ideology, and Jews were singled out for attack from the first day of Hitler's chancellorship. A law of April 7,

1933, decreed the dismissal of Jews from government service and universities. They were also debarred from entering the professions. Under the Nürnberg Laws of September 15, 1935, marriages between Jews and persons of "German blood" were forbidden, and the Jews were virtually deprived of all rights. Their prewar persecution reached its climax on Kristallnacht (November 9–10, 1938), a pogrom carried out under the direction of the SS. (Britannica n.d.)

Hitler's Nazi regime and crimes against humanity came to a head during World War II. The end of the war did not immediately restore the freedoms and liberties of the German people.

Powers of darkness have been revealed many times in modern history. Take a moment and review countries around the world that have had wicked kings, presidents, or dictators in recent years. Military and other coups have been attempted in many countries of the world.

A coup is defined as "a sudden, violent, and illegal seizure of power from a government." Coups may be attempted by groups and organizations who will liberate the people, or who will enslave and oppress the people. They are sometimes successful, sometimes not.

Some of the countries where unrighteous leaders have been in power: the Soviet Union, East Germany, Hungary, and all of the Eastern bloc countries, the Philippines, Panama, Iran. Remember Tiananmen Square in China, the summer of 1989. After several weeks of demonstrations and protests, Chinese troops entered the square and opened fire on the demonstrators. Death toll estimates were hundreds to thousands killed.

We are not passing judgment on any of these leaders, governments, or nations. We are asking ourselves, do all of these events confirm that it is the Last Saturday?

5.4. The Savior Comes

Prophecies announcing the Lord's glorious return to the earth are being fulfilled almost daily, right in front of our eyes. We as members of the Church of Jesus Christ of Latter-Day Saints should surely lead the forces of Christian righteousness. But are we truly marching forward and onward, as Christian soldiers?

Just how faithfully do church members obey and live the commandments? The last fifty years have seen dramatic changes on Sundays in Salt Lake City. Long gone are the days when Salt Lake City was virtually closed on Sundays. The majority of Utahns, being Latter Day Saints, were in church and kept the Sabbath day holy. Most businesses were closed on Sunday; there were very few things to attract anyone away from accepted Sabbath observances.

Today many (maybe even most) businesses are open. We as members of the church are invited to sporting events, movie theaters, resorts, and recreational sites. It has become increasingly more difficult to keep and revere the Sabbath day. Many members of the church have perhaps found the commandment to keep the Sabbath day holy a little too difficult to obey.

Church leaders recently encouraged church members to improve and strengthen Sabbath day worship and observance.

CHURCH LEADERS CALL FOR BETTER OBSERVANCE OF SABBATH DAY

Leaders of the Church are urging members around the world to improve their observance of the Sabbath day. In local and regional leadership training meetings this year, leaders are receiving instruction on the topic of strengthening faith in God by observing the Sabbath day with greater purpose ...

We're hoping that home activities will be more centered on learning and knowing more about the life and ministry of the Savior and the great plan of happiness that our Heavenly Father has given us to live by." (Sabbath Day 2015)

Church leaders felt a need to enhance and sanctify Sabbath day observance. Church members are encouraged to review and refocus their Sabbath day activities.

Church leaders said Latter-Day Saints need to prepare for the Lord's return. Yes, the church continues to grow rapidly, as predicted on the Last Saturday. But is the righteousness and spirituality of church members also growing? What television programs are we watching and allowing our children to watch? The unrighteousness and darkness of the day have permeated every aspect of our lives.

What movies are we going to see? What videos are we bringing into our own homes and allowing our children to view? What message do we send to our children when we watch questionable movies or videos? The signs of the times witness a need for greater faith and righteousness. We should not be embracing, or even accepting, today's secular standards and values.

Church leaders have counseled us for years to read and study the scriptures. President Russell M. Nelson encouraged us to do more than just read the scriptures. He encouraged us to study them in new and different ways to increase our understanding, faith, and dedication. President Nelson said the following:

DRAWING THE POWER OF JESUS CHRIST INTO OUR LIVES

> Earlier this year, I asked the young adults of the Church to consecrate a portion of their time each week to study everything Jesus said and did as recorded in the standard works. I invited them to let the scriptural citations about Jesus Christ in the Topical Guide become their personal core curriculum.

> I gave that challenge because I had already accepted it myself. I read and underlined every verse cited about Jesus Christ, as listed under the main heading and the 57 subtitles in the Topical Guide. When I finished that exciting exercise, my wife asked me what impact it had on me. I told her, "I am a different man!" (Nelson 2017)

How many church members do this regularly today? How many members in each Gospel Doctrine class have even read the week's assignment for the lesson? How many class members have their scriptures with them in class?

Today's fast-paced society often gets in the way of our sincere desires and intentions. Demands on time, energy, and resources can ambush our desires and efforts of faith and righteousness. Let us remember what day it is and make even small efforts to "bring to pass much righteousness."

Do very many members of the church actively read the holy scriptures? How much less do we actually study them? Elder John A. Widtsoe once stated the following:

EVIDENCES AND RECONCILIATIONS

An effort must be put forth to learn the gospel, to understand it, to comprehend the relationship of its principles. The gospel must be studied, otherwise no test of its truth may sanely be applied to it. That study must be wide, for the gospel is so organized that in it is a place for every truth, of every name and nature. That study must be constantly continued, for the content of the gospel is illimitable.

It is a paradox that men will gladly devote time every day for many years to learn a science or an art; yet will expect to win a knowledge of the gospel, which comprehends all sciences and arts, through perfunctory glances at books or occasional listening to sermons. The gospel should be studied more intensively than any school or college subject. They who pass opinion on the gospel without having given it intimate and careful study are not lovers of truth, and their opinions are worthless.

To secure a testimony, then, study must accompany desire and prayer. (Widtsoe 1943. 16-17)

A quick observation of the world, with our knowledge of the Last Days, should rapidly motivate us to pray and fast with greater faith and diligence. I remember my impressions of the church and its members as a young man. I feel like a gulf is widening in the church. Members are not lukewarm; they are faithful and dedicated, or becoming spiritually lost.

When a spiritual, uplifting, strengthening opportunity arises, many members of the church choose not to participate or attend; for example, Saturday night Stake Conference meetings, General/Stake Priesthood meetings, Special Firesides and programs, and opportunities for service.

It is time to be a real Latter-Day Saint. What or who is a real Latter-Day Saint? Do you decide as you approach each weekend whether you are going to church on Sunday? If you do, you are making a big mistake; you should decide now that you will attend church every week. Decide today, once and for all, to be a real Latter-Day Saint. You will find greater peace and joy on weekends and Sundays.

Believe it. There are real Latter-Day Saints in the church. I see some in my ward every week. Some live in every ward of the church throughout the world. The day, and time, to become one has arrived.

The Latter-Day Saints were asked to build a house to the Lord in Kirtland, Ohio. In March of 1836, that house was dedicated by the prophet Joseph Smith. That dedicatory prayer includes some revelation and counsel to the church and the saints of these Last Days.

> Remember all thy church, O Lord, with all their families, and all their immediate connections, with all their sick and afflicted ones, with all the poor and meek of the earth; that the kingdom, which thou hast set up without hands, may become a great mountain and fill the whole earth;
>
> That thy church may come forth out of the wilderness of darkness, and shine forth fair as the moon, clear as the sun, and terrible as an army with banners;
>
> And be adorned as a bride for that day when thou shalt unveil the heavens, and cause the mountains to flow down at thy presence, and the valleys to be exalted, the rough places made smooth; that thy glory may fill the earth;

That when the trump shall sound for the dead, we shall
be caught up in the cloud to meet thee, that we may ever
be with the Lord. (Doc. & Cov. 109:72-75)

Section 133 of the Doctrine and Covenants also contains exhortation
and admonition to the saints, encouraging the members of the church to
live with faith and prepare for the glory of Jesus Christ.

Hearken, O ye people of my church, saith the Lord your
God, and hear the word of the Lord concerning you—

The Lord who shall suddenly come to his temple; the
Lord who shall come down upon the world with a curse
to judgment; yea, upon all the nations that forget God,
and upon all the ungodly among you.

For he shall make bare his holy arm in the eyes of all
the nations, and all the ends of the earth shall see the
salvation of their God.

Wherefore, prepare ye, prepare ye, O my people;
sanctify yourselves; gather ye together, O ye people of
my church, upon the land of Zion, all you that have not
been commanded to tarry. (Doc. & Cov. 133:1-4)

The Lord instructs the saints to harken to his word. The word of the
Lord who will shortly come to his temple. He will come with a curse
of judgment upon all nations that forget God. He directs the saints to
prepare.

Do we need to prepare ourselves, the Lord's Kingdom, and the world
for the return of the Holy One of Israel?

Nephi, the son of Helaman and son of Nephi, commands us, the
Saints of the Latter-Days, to turn from our wicked ways:

Turn, all ye Gentiles, from your wicked ways; and repent
of your evil doings, of your lyings and deceivings, and
of your whoredoms, and of your secret abominations,

> and your idolatries, and of your murders, and your priestcrafts, and your envyings, and your strifes, and from all your wickedness and abominations, and come unto me, and be baptized in my name, that ye may receive a remission of your sins, and be filled with the Holy Ghost, that ye may be numbered with my people who are of the house of Israel. (3 Nephi 30:2)

It sounds like he is admonishing us to prepare ourselves for the Last Saturday and the Savior's return.

Wilford Woodruff said, "Thrones will be cast down, nations will be overturned, anarchy will reign, all legal barriers will be broken down, and the laws will be trampled in the dust" (Ludlow 1947, 223).

The summer of 2020, in the middle of the Covid-19 worldwide pandemic, we saw a type of things to come. Television video revealed scenes in Milwaukee, Portland, and Salt Lake City that looked like anarchy. It looked like laws were being trampled. Joseph Smith said,

> I saw men hunting the lives of their own sons, and brother murdering brother, women killing their own daughters, and daughters seeking the lives of their mothers. I saw armies arrayed against armies. I saw blood, desolation, fires ...
>
> These things are at our doors. They will follow the Saints of God from city to city. Satan will rage, and the spirit of the devil is now enraged. I know not how soon these things will take place; but with a view of them, shall I cry peace? No! I will lift up my voice and testify of them. (Ludlow 1947, 226)

What did Joseph Smith say in the quote above? "Men hunting the lives of their own sons, and brother murdering brother, women killing their own daughters, and daughters seeking the lives of their mothers." If you don't think this is happening, welcome to the Last Saturday.

Murder Charges: Teen Shooter Waited Hours Between Killing Mother, Siblings

16-Year-Old Told Father He Intended to "Kill Everyone in the House Except Himself," Charges Say

TOOELE, Utah. Over a five hour period, a 16-year-old Grantsville boy waited for each member of his family to come home so he could shoot and kill them, prosecutors say …

He said the killings do not appear to be a case of "I snapped." …

In disturbing charging documents filed late Wednesday afternoon, prosecutors outlined how Haynie stayed home from school on Jan. 17 and waited for each member of his family to come home that day. (Reavy 2020)

The words of Wilford Woodruff and Joseph Smith could easily cause us to shake with fear and trembling. Especially as we see the events they described happening in our world today. Real peace can only be found through Jesus Christ, his restored Gospel, and his Kingdom.

In 1985, the Church News related an amazing experience of a hospital patient. Twelve years earlier, an elderly community leader was laying on his hospital bed at death's door. The leader had undergone major surgery to save him from colon cancer. He communicated to his family that he did not expect to live through the night.

Around midnight, the community leader heard someone quietly and earnestly praying at his bedside. It was his surgeon, kneeling down and pleading with his heavenly Father, asking him to extend the life of the patient, a dear friend. The patient, at that time, was serving in a key church position. His influence for good, through his service, could not be measured (see *Church News*, March 24, 1985, 16).

Oh, that we could all have, and be, friends like this surgeon, this real Latter-Day Saint.

Our current discussion is about Latter-Day Saints in the last dispensation of time. Heber Geurts is an example of a real Latter-Day Saint, even a saint in today's perilous times.

HEBER J. GEURTS, COUNSELOR AT
STATE PRISON, DIES AT 86

> Heber Joseph Geurts, who as an LDS counselor at the Utah State Prison ministered to hundreds of inmates and walked with capital murderers to their executions, died Sunday, July 2, 1995. He was 86. (Deseret News 1995)

In 1957, Heber was serving as a bishop. He started a weekly family home evening program of the Church of Jesus Christ of Latter-Day Saints at the prison. Two members in his ward were sent to the state prison. Bishop Geurts did not forget them.

One of the men was sent to prison for more than twenty-two years. He participated in the family home evening program. His prison "family" helped him become a painter.

A few years later, the former inmate called Bishop Geurts. He and his wife were going to the temple and wanted Bishop Geurts to go with them. A Christmas card said that Heber's prison friend had been called to be the high priests group leader (see *Church News*, Mar. 24, 1985, 16).

It sounds like many years ago, Heber Geurts was a real Christian, a minister for Christ. Here is another example of some Latter-Day Saints today. They have given of their time and energy to serve and minister as Jesus taught. Service and sacrifice should be major efforts by church members to hasten today's work of the Lord.

CALGARY LATTER-DAY SAINTS HELP FIGHT HUNGER

> Volunteers from The Church of Jesus Christ of Latter-day Saints that included missionaries from the Canada Calgary Mission were among 7,000 people who partnered with the Calgary Food Bank to collect hundreds of thousands of pounds of non-perishable food

during the September 15, 2018, city-wide food drive. (Newsroom Canada 2018)

The food drive volunteers always include grandparents, children, and grandchildren. Some say their family member always ask about the event, to make sure they will be able to participate. This Calgary citywide food drive is often the largest in Canada.

Do your beliefs include "selfless service and caring for those in need"?

Many church members know what day it is and know the importance of living and serving as Jesus exemplified. Saints helped save many homes from Hurricane Harvey.

MORMON HELPING HANDS VOLUNTEERS
GO TO HURRICANE-RAVAGED AREAS

The LDS Church is among dozens of groups coordinating help through the Voluntary Organizations Active in Disaster and Crisiscleanup.org, including Texas Baptist Men, the United Methodist Committee on Relief, Catholic Charities and Habitat for Humanity …

More than 10,000 Mormon Helping Hands volunteers worked to save Texas homes damaged by Hurricane Harvey. (Gilmer Mirror n.d.)

The Mormon volunteers spent the weekend removing muck and mold from hurricane-damaged homes. The volunteers were from Texas, Louisiana, and Mississippi.

As we move closer to the midnight hour on the Last Saturday, we see increased righteousness. Church members and Christians everywhere are striving to become more like the Savior. Good honorable people are found everywhere. Here is a story about one of those men:

Halt, Diogenes, Here's Your Man

> Ben P. Price, New Providence garage and filling station
> operator, belongs to that group for whom old Diogenes
> is reputed to have searched. (Leaf-Chronicle 1928, 1)

Many believe that an honest man cannot be found in the world today. But Mr Lewis found one many years ago.

Lewis was driving from Missouri to Florida. He stopped at a New Providence, Tennessee, garage to refuel his car. He continued his trip, unaware that he had dropped his pocketbook. The pocketbook contained a fair amount of money inside.

After Lewis returned home, he received a letter from Mr. Price at the New Providence gas station. Price had found the money and sent the pocketbook back to Lewis. Price declined Lewis's reward offer, saying the Golden Rule is his religion, and that required him to return the item he found.

Lewis wrote the *Leaf Chronicle* newspaper, commending Price and declaring that he is an honest man.

Diogenes was born in Sinope, an Ionian colony on the Black Sea, between 404 and 412 BC. He was known as a cynic and was regularly controversial. He frequently criticized and disputed with the leaders and philosophers of his time. He became known for engaging in unusual stunts, one of which was to carry a lamp during the day and claim he was looking for an honest man (see https://en.wikipedia.org/wiki/Diogenes).

Our world today is filled with violence, deceit, and dishonesty. We should realize that there are still good, decent, righteous people in the world. These honorable and honest people are, in themselves, signs of the Last Days. As evil and wickedness increase, so does the faith and goodness of the Lord's people.

A businessman returned to his hotel after having dinner at a restaurant in Salt Lake City. His room phone was ringing. It was the restaurant manager calling to tell him that his billfold was found in the restaurant. The billfold had a significant amount of money and credit cards.

The man confirmed that his wallet was missing. The restaurant manager told him to wait at the front door of his hotel, and he would return the wallet to him. The restaurant had called all the major hotels in the city until they found him. The man was stunned by the restaurant's actions.

The businessman also found an honest man and says, "Diogenes can put out his light" (see Deseret News, March 29, 1987).

The turbulent wicked times of our day often provide examples of faith and endurance. The eternal truths and principles of the restored gospel of Jesus Christ have the power to inspire, lift, and bless the lives of people everywhere, even in the challenging times of the Last Days.

Helvi Temiseva was born in Finland and contracted polio at the age of eight. When she was eleven, an attack of rheumatoid arthritis crippled her further. Helvi found and joined the Church of Jesus Christ of Latter-Day Saints at the age of twenty-one. She learned that she was a daughter of God and there was no limit to what she could do and achieve.

She became a translator and eventually came to Utah. At Brigham Young University, she studied English, Hebrew, Greek, and religion. She received a master's degree in linguistics. She said,

> Who would expect an almost totally helpless arthritic to graduate from high school without the aid of teachers, to attend college, to speak several languages, to travel across oceans and continents, and to earn a living as a professional translator? (Richards 1973, 27)

Helvi Temiseva passed away in 1985. She is an example of faith, dedication, and sacrifice, personal traits we should all have in our own lives today.

Jane Eyre has moral values in place and is true to those values.

Mr. Rochester, a married man, offers Jane his love, and she responds to him, "Who in the world cares for you? or who will be injured by what you do?"

> "I care for myself …

> "I will keep the law given by God …

> "Laws and principles are not for the times when there is no temptation …
>
> "If at my own individual convenience I break them, what would be their worth?" (Bronte 1961, 356-57)

Jane's words are of infinite worth and wisdom, for us who are living on the Last Saturday. If we break laws, promises, and covenants, their value and benefits are lost. They lose their worth. Jane expresses her moral integrity above her feelings, emotions, and desires.

Once we are convinced that today is the Last Saturday, we understand the importance of developing a faith that will sustain us. We need faith that will withstand times of great adversity and prevalent wickedness.

Is not now, at this last hour, the time to commit ourselves to the laws and principles of the Gospel? To serve with all our faith, energy, and talents? To follow and emulate the Savior of the world?

WWJD? MORMON HELPING HANDS SPREAD OUT THROUGH BIG BEND TO AID HURRICANE MICHAEL RECOVERY

> What would Jesus do? He'd leave his air-conditioned house, drive seven hours to a different city and start with recovery efforts after a disaster, said the volunteers with Mormon Helping Hands. (White 2018)

What would you do? Close to five hundred volunteers wearing yellow "Helping Hands" tee shirts helped with cleanup and recovery from Hurricane Michael. Mormon Helping Hands can be found serving around the world.

Signs that the Savior comes: earthquakes and other natural disasters, followed by righteous, faithful Latter-Day Saints gathering to assist, serve, and help with recovery.

Mongolia is a country that holds an annual marathon and many other celebrations and festivals. It is also the home to many strong, faithful members of the Church of Jesus Christ of Latter-Day Saints. These members serve as shining examples for all church members.

In September 2018, eighty members of the church assisted with the annual marathon in the Mongolian National Garden Park. The event is sponsored by a non-government organization and has more than five thousand participants. Many participants have disabilities (see LDS Church News, January 18, 2018).

These Latter-Day Saints in Mongolia are a shining example for all of us in these Last Days, just before the Lord returns. We should all be more involved with this kind of service and activity.

We never truly know when, or how, we may be able to share the Gospel with others. It is imperative, on the Last Saturday, that we live with faith, listen to the still small voice, follow it, and share the Gospel at every opportunity.

As the Lord's return becomes closer and closer, we will see increased criticism and attacks against the church, its leaders, and members.

CHURCH DEPLORES FORGED LETTERS
ATTEMPTING TO DISCREDIT LEADERS

"We deplore the current distribution of numerous fictitious letters, which are replete with false and insulting information, purportedly from or to highly placed representatives of the Church," a Church spokesman said April 12. (Church News 1989)

The church spokesman said the letters appear to be part of "a months-long campaign of vicious vilifications against the Church General Authorities." The letters were examined and found to be complete forgeries.

Speaking to the Sisters of the Church in October 2015, President Russell M. Nelson confirmed the persecution and disparagement of the church in the Last Days. He also underscored the importance of faithful sisters to the Lord and his Kingdom.

A Plea to My Sisters

> Attacks against the Church, its doctrine, and our way of
> life are going to increase. Because of this, we need women
> who have a bedrock understanding of the doctrine of Christ
> and who will use that understanding to teach and help
> raise a sin-resistant generation. We need women who can
> detect deception in all of its forms. We need women who
> know how to access the power that God makes available
> to covenant keepers and who express their beliefs with
> confidence and charity. We need women who have the
> courage and vision of our Mother Eve. (Nelson 2015)

How emotional and gratifying it is when we have an opportunity
to see and hear the Lord's chosen servants speak. It is time for us to lift
ourselves to greater dedication and commitment to the Lord. Through
faith and constant commitment to the Gospel and the church, we can
feel the joy the Gospel brings.

"Words Can't Describe Feelings" of First-Time Conference Viewers

> As general conference sessions were telecast live for the
> first time to three distant locations–two in Europe and one
> in Central America–emotions of members ran deep ...

> "People had tears in their eyes, saying they now felt so
> much a part of the Church." (Church News 1989)

How important is the opportunity to see and hear the Lord's chosen
servants speak? Does this blessing fill us with such emotion that we
cannot find words to describe the experience? Too many of the Latter-
Day Saints may be feeling complacent about opportunities to see and
hear the living prophets.

The world will soon witness the Savior's millennial descension to
the earth. It is imperative that as Latter-Day Saints, we become true
Christians. We should not become mediocre in faith and worship and

all things that are of eternal worth. We cannot be sitting on the fence. We cannot be lukewarm.

Are there any valid reasons, or excuses, for not participating when church leaders speak? Can we disregard an opportunity to learn about the Gospel or worship the Savior and renew the covenants? Is it enough to only occasionally listen, learn, worship, and renew the covenants?

As a church, and members of the church, we are sharing the Gospel in record numbers and pioneering ways. The Gospel is marching throughout the world even stronger via the events below.

MISSIONARY VIDEOS TO BE TELECAST IN MAJOR U.S. CITIES

"Together Forever," a touching half-hour video that introduces the gospel to non-members, will be televised in eight major cities Jan. 23, and, within the next three months, to every city with a mission headquarters in the United States …

"Together Forever" is a series of vignettes about family relationships produced for the Missionary Department by Bonneville Media Communications. It recently won the Catholic-sponsored Gabriel Award, and received a "very high" 8 (on a scale of 10) on a Nielsen television survey. (Hart 1989)

The world headquarters of the Church of Jesus Christ of Latter-Day Saints is a major destination for the people of the world, especially members of the church. The Gospel needs to be preached to the world. People traveling to the church headquarters is additional proof that we will soon see the Savior.

TEMPLE SQUARE VISITS DOUBLE IN A DECADE

During the past 10 years, visitor attendance at Temple Square has climbed from more than 2 million a year to an estimated 4.8 million at the close of 1990 …

> In addition, the American Bus Association named "Christmas at Temple Square" among its Top 100 Events in North America for 1991. (Dockstader 1990)

People from around the world are coming to Salt Lake City. Church sites and attractions are visited, and the church grows, physically with increasing members, and spiritually with greater faith and knowledge. Many of these visitors are not members of the church. Some are unknowingly led by the spirit, because time is short, and God's Kingdom must quickly roll forth.

TEMPLE SQUARE A POPULAR DESTINATION

> With millions of visitors each year, Temple Square was recognized by *Forbes* magazine in 2009 as the 16th most visited attraction in America.

> The 35-acre area draws visitors from all over the world because of its renowned research libraries, cultural activities and historic buildings—most notably the Salt Lake Temple …

> "Temple Square is a reach-out-and-welcome-the-world experience," said Michael Stewart. (Temple Square 2009)

A sure sign of the Last Saturday would be that the Church of Jesus Christ of Latter-Day Saints is becoming more prominent and recognized around the world. The Lord's restored church would be presented more often and in a more favorable light than ever before. The church is being recognized in an unusual way.

BRAZILIANS RECOGNIZE NAME OF "MORONI"

> Although the name "Moroni" is unusual in Brazil, it is becoming known in the northern Brazilian state of Ceara as it inspires confidence in law enforcement.

The name belongs to Moroni Bing Torgan, president of
the Brazil Fortaleza Stake. In 1987 he was appointed
state Secretary of Public Security. (Moroni 1989)

This faithful member of the church holds the highest office in the
Brazilian government. He was thirty-one years old and the youngest
state-appointed security secretary. As a fourth-generation Latter-Day
Saint, he quickly shares his religion and faith.

The Church of Jesus Christ of Latter-Day Saints is better known
today than ever before. We need not, and should not, be ashamed of the
Gospel of Jesus Christ, or his church.

Most of us do not fully understand how fast and to what extent the
Church of Jesus Christ of Latter-Day Saints is growing. Here are some
statements concerning church growth in 1989, quite a few years ago:

CONVERSIONS INCREASE, REFLECT A WORLDWIDE SURGE IN SHARING TRUTHS

The number of convert baptisms worldwide during 1988
reached an all-time high of 256,515 …

The 1988 total means that 703 people came into the
Church every day of the year, or about the number of
one and a half average-sized wards …

A member of the Missionary Executive Council, said,
"Do you realize that more people are born in a day than
we baptize all year?" (Hart 1989)

News coverage of Utah, Salt Lake City, and the church has increased
significantly in the last twenty years. More of this coverage is positive
than ever before. More people know the word *Mormon* than ever before.
However, time is short; we cannot be complacent or content with half-
hearted personal righteousness.

6

Today

We know the world is filled with evil, wickedness, violence, and chaos. We know the Lord has, and will, increase his knowledge and power in the Last Days. It is quite evident that we need to quickly put our lives in order before he comes. Just what more do we need to consider and know about today?

6.1. THE WORLD

In the Book of Mormon, Alma, the son of Alma, was miraculously converted to the Savior and the Lord's church. An angel appeared to Alma and reprimanded him for seeking to destroy the church and lead people away from Jesus Christ.

Alma then began to preach of Jesus Christ and warn the people of their sins and wicked ways. Surely his words apply to us today:

> And now behold, I say unto you, that the foundation of the destruction of this people is beginning to be laid by the unrighteousness of your lawyers and your judges. (Alma 10:27)

People may feel that many lawyers, judges, and politicians today are engaging in unrighteous judgments and activities. We cannot target legal officials here, however. We can see and should acknowledge the great degree of unrighteousness in the world today. Many of those who lead businesses, organizations, and nations are not on the side of Christians, or religion, or righteousness.

On the other hand, not all lawyers and judges seek to destroy followers of Christ. Alma's words were indeed meant for his day and the people who lived at that time. Nevertheless, can we not see the beginning of the foundation of our destruction today?

The behavior and actions of men, women, and even children confirm that we live in the perilous times described by Paul in his second letter to Timothy. Today, we need to minister to others and help them find the restored Gospel of Jesus Christ.

Today, there are mass shootings and other acts of violence and death, here in the United States and around the world.

In July of 2018, a twenty-one-year-old man was shot and killed when gunshots erupted. The shooting took place in a New York City park that was filled with children. People who live around the park said the park had become a battleground for rival gangs. It is not known if the shooter belonged to one of the gangs (see https://www.nbcnewyork.com/news/local/playground-shooting-brooklyn/523945/).

Isolated neighborhood shootings are just a part of the hatred and inhumanity that can be found today. The world is full of war and conflicts. These conflicts are large and small. They exist between nations and neighbors.

Surprise Isis Attacks Leave More than 200 Dead in South-West Syria

More than 200 people have been killed in a brutal surprise offensive by Islamic State in Syria that involved multiple suicide bombings and simultaneous raids in which militants stormed villages and slaughtered civilians …

The militants are also believed to have kidnapped dozens of people and taken them back to their hideouts. (Shaheen 2018)

Terrorism continues to be found in the world today. It causes fear, dread, and death for innocent people. This is a headline from Reuters in 2018: "Islamic State Claims Responsibility for Attack on Tourists in Tajikistan: AMAQ."

The story reports that some tourists were attacked in Tajikistan. Four Western cyclists were killed, and others were injured. The Islamic State claimed they were responsible for the attack (see https://www.yahoo.com/news/islamic-state-claims-responsibility-attack-tourists-tajikistan-amaq-192049616.html).

The lives of the innocent are frequently and brazenly taken in our world. World headlines and actions should awaken us to this alarming situation. We should be motivated to walk with faith and righteousness in every footstep.

Today, natural disasters occur more frequently and with greater destruction.

HUNDREDS STRANDED ON INDONESIAN MOUNTAIN AFTER EARTHQUAKE

SEMBALUN, Indonesia (AP). Hundreds of tourists stranded on Mount Rinjani on the Indonesian island of Lombok by an earthquake that killed 16 people and triggered landslides are making their way off the mountain, shaken by their experience but mostly unharmed, an official said Monday. (Sembahulun 2018)

6.2. THE LORD'S KINGDOM

The Last Saturday is the day when the Lord's Kingdom will be restored. It will grow and prosper. It will come out of the darkness and become the light of the world. The Gospel will be preached throughout the world. People will even flow unto the Lord's house and his Kingdom. We are witnesses of all this right now.

> The word that Isaiah, the son of Amoz, saw concerning Judah and Jerusalem:
>
> And it shall come to pass in the last days, when the mountain of the Lord's house shall be established in the top of the mountains, and shall be exalted above the hills, and all nations shall flow unto it.
>
> And many people shall go and say, Come ye, and let us go up to the mountain of the Lord, to the house of the God of Jacob; and he will teach us of his ways, and we will walk in his paths; for out of Zion shall go forth the law, and the word of the Lord from Jerusalem. (2 Nephi 12:1-3/Isaiah 2)

In the Doctrine and Covenants, the Lord says that the hour cometh when he will drink of the fruit of the vine on earth.

> Behold, this is wisdom in me; wherefore, marvel not, for the hour cometh that I will drink of the fruit of the vine with you on the earth, and with Moroni, whom I have sent unto you to reveal the Book of Mormon, containing the fulness of my everlasting gospel, to whom I have committed the keys of the record of the stick of Ephraim. (Doc. & Cov. 27:5)

"The hour cometh that I will drink of the fruit of the vine with you on the earth." What is the Lord referring to with these words? Do these words speak of drinking when he walked on the earth in Jerusalem? Or after he comes again? He also says he will drink with Moroni. Has he ever drunk of the "fruit of the vine" with Moroni?

The context of these verses is when he is speaking to Joseph Smith and Oliver Cowdery. Consider the following scriptural verses and the fact that when he does this, there will be many more people and servants present.

Continuing to read in the Doctrine and Covenants section 27, we learn about others who will be present for this meeting:

> Elias who brought to pass the restoration of all things John, the son of Zacharias and Elizabeth, the Baptist Elijah who restored the priesthood sealing power Joseph and Jacob, and Isaac, and Abraham, the fathers Michael, or Adam, the father of all, the prince of all Peter, and James, and John (see Doc. & Cov. 27:6-12)

The Lord indicates that when he returns, many leaders, apostles, and prophets will join him on earth. We know that before Christ returns in glory, there will be a great meeting in Adam-ondi-Ahaman. Many of these prophets and church leaders will be present at the meeting. They will most likely drink of the vine and fulfill this prophecy. We know that the Second Coming of Jesus Christ will occur after this meeting and will be a magnificent event. We also know that it will happen soon.

> Wherefore, lift up your hearts and rejoice, and gird up your loins, and take upon you my whole armor, that ye may be able to withstand the evil day, having done all, that ye may be able to stand. (Doc. & Cov. 27:15)

What is the armor of God?

- loins girt about with truth
- a breastplate of righteousness
- feet shod with the preparation of the Gospel
- a shield of faith
- a helmet of salvation
- the sword of the Lord's spirit

The Lord then says, "be faithful until I come, and ye shall be caught up, that where I am ye shall be also. Amen" (see Doc. & Cov. 27:16-18).

With ever-increasing frequency, the church is being required to voice opinions and warnings about the values, morals, and evils in the world and in our lives today.

The church was honored by the RAAP, a coalition of churches united in battling pornography. The recognition was for church media materials available to all faiths used for fighting pornography.

> CHURCH HONORED FOR ANTI-PORN EFFORTS:
> "INTERFAITH COALITION LAUDS PRODUCTION
> OF VIDEO DOCUMENTARIES AND BROCHURES"

> Underscoring the importance the Church places on the fight against pornography, [one] of the Second Quorum of the Seventy accepted a Media Awareness award in behalf of the Church …

> "When pornography becomes influential culturally," [Dr. Mason] said, "and especially when it begins to shape attitudes and habits, … violence becomes more acceptable, and marital commitments deteriorate. (Campbell 1989)

Today, the restored Church of Jesus Christ of Latter-Day Saints stands as a beacon, light, and fortification of faith, love, service, and Jesus Christ to all the world.

> HEROES EMERGE AMID DEVASTATION
> DISASTER CLAIMS TWO CHURCH MEMBERS,
> SHAKES LIVES OF MANY OTHERS

> While the massive earthquake that rumbled through Northern California Oct. 17 left most area Church members shaken but unscathed, it wreaked extensive damage to many structures, particularly those old and weak …

But the earthquake also shook off estrangement between people and uncovered bonds of humanity where people risked their lives for strangers. This heroic action, coupled with abundant provident circumstances, prevented a much greater loss of life in extremely desperate situations …

"The system works," said San Francisco Stake Pres. "Home teaching and visiting teaching programs just kicked in automatically, and there was a real spirit of community among the ward."

The community spirit also spread beyond, he added. "I received calls from bishops and stake presidents in Texas, Minnesota, Washington D.C., and outlying areas of California offering, 'Anything we can do, we'll do it.'" (Hart 1989)

The Lord's Kingdom continually experiences increased growth, which in and of itself is a witness of the restored Kingdom and the current dispensation. How many countries of the world currently have an official church presence? Enough to provide another witness of the truth and these Last Days.

CHURCH GROWING IN MORE THAN 160 COUNTRIES

In 2004, worldwide Church membership reached 12 million, the Church was ranked among the fastest-growing churches in the United States, and Mexico became the first nation outside of the U.S. to top one million members. Brazil is projected to surpass one million members during 2007.

Growth outside of the United States continues to surpass growth within the U.S. More than half of all Church members live outside the United States. Members of the Church are found in more than 160 countries and territories, speaking more than 178 languages. (Church Growing 2005)

A search of church websites today will provide extensive evidence that the Lord's Kingdom on earth is progressing. The concern is, are we growing, serving, and sufficiently strengthening our faith in time for the Lord's foretold return?

6.3. PERSONAL RIGHTEOUSNESS

The Last Saturday and the return of the Great Redeemer to the earth requires that each of us increase our personal righteousness.

> But behold, I trust that ye are not in a state of so much unbelief as were your brethren; I trust that ye are not lifted up in the pride of your hearts; yea, I trust that ye have not set your hearts upon riches and the vain things of the world; yea, I trust that you do not worship idols, but that ye do worship the true and the living God, and that ye look forward for the remission of your sins, with an everlasting faith, which is to come. (Alma 7:6)

As a youth, I received a card from a Sunday school teacher with a quote on it. The quote is more important today than when I received it many years ago. It is only the size of a business card but has become a guide for my life.

The quote could help you plan, make choices, and live your life on this Last Saturday. Using it, we may plan our daily activities and priorities. We may use it to determine how we can and will give of our time, talents, and resources to do the Lord's work. The quote indicates how we should think, live, and interact with others. We would do well to integrate this thought into our lives every day.

NOTHING
Is as important as my membership in
The Church of Jesus Christ of Latter-Day Saints

Think about and analyze this quote. Ponder the knowledge we have because of the restored Gospel of Jesus Christ. Contemplate with an eternal perspective. Reflect on the purpose of our life on earth and the Lord's plan of exaltation. Is that quote not completely, and absolutely, true?

If there was ever a time for Latter-Day Saints, and people everywhere, to decide which side they are on in the fight for people's souls, that time has come today.

> Who's on the Lord's side?
> Who's on the Lord's side who? Now is the time to show.
> We ask it fearlessly: Who's on the Lord's side? who?
> We wage no common war, Cope with no common foe.
> The enemy's awake; Who's on the Lord's side? who?
>
> We serve the living God, And want his foes to know
> That if but few, we're great; Who's on the Lord's side? Who?
> We're going on to win; No fear must blanch the brow.
> The Lord of Hosts is ours; Who's on the Lord's side? Who?
>
> The stone cut without hands To fill the earth must grow.
> Who'll help to roll it on? Who's on the Lord's side? Who?
> Our ensign to the world Is floating proudly now.
> No coward bears our flag; Who's on the Lord's side? Who?
>
> The pow'rs of earth and hell In rage direct the blow
> That's aimed to crush the work; Who's on the Lord's side? Who?
> Truth, life, and liberty, Freedom from death and woe,
> Are stakes we're fighting for; Who's on the Lord's side?
> Who? (Cornaby and Russell 1998, 260)

Two things seem to be of utmost importance this Saturday. The first is personal righteousness. The Lord, his Kingdom, and his church must be the focal point of our lives. If it is, all other things will be added unto us. Our families, professions, deeds, and hearts will be righteous and in harmony. We will be well at the last day.

This does not, however, mean that our lives will be without trials, temptations, and challenges.

6.4. JESUS CHRIST'S SECOND COMING

Cordell Andersen faithfully followed the spirit and sacrificed to help bring the Lord's truth to part of the world. He indeed may know that it is the Last Saturday.

AWAKENING GUATEMALA

For ten years Cordell Andersen couldn't sleep peacefully. His sleep was haunted by a dream—a dream so big it was overpowering. In this dream he saw two million poverty-stricken Guatemalan Indians pleading for help. He recognized their cry as genuine, for he had personally witnessed their terrible plight in 1957 while serving m[in] their country as a missionary for The Church of Jesus Christ of Latter-Day Saints. Each time the dream came and vanished, Cordell cried out within himself, "Oh God, these thy children have suffered enough! Let the time for their redemption begin!"

But what could he do to give these desperately deserving people a new way of life? He was one lone person, lacking any practical training and having no financial resources. Reluctantly Cordell tucked his dream away and went on working, saving, studying about Guatemala, and waiting.

> Finally he could wait no longer. In August 1967, thirty-one-year-old Cordell sold his belongings, resigned his position, packed his wife, Maria, and their four children into an overloaded camper truck, and headed for Coban, Guatemala, a city of 10,000 people, with another 200,000 in the region round about. (Jacobs 1971)

Cordell developed a plan to bring into being a righteous, self-reliant people. He spent two years becoming a friend to the people.

He was accepted into the Indian homes and taught them how to improve their lives and become successful. Eventually, he introduced them to the Gospel and has brought many into the restored Kingdom of God. He is a prime example of ministering.

When the call goes out to help set up tables and chairs, or clean the temple, we should not start raising trivial, insignificant reasons for not accepting the call and serving. Is the Church of Jesus Christ of Latter-Day Saints true? If it is the Lord's Kingdom on earth, blessings always follow sacrifice.

Many years ago, the play *Saturday's Warrior* premiered in Salt Lake City. Everyone talked about it, and many went to see it. I had two friends born in South America, then living in New York City, come to visit my wife and I that summer. *Saturday's Warrior* was so exciting, we told them they needed to see it, even though their English was limited.

"Who are these children coming down, coming down?"

The message of that play is the message of our day. It is the Last Saturday. Time for all of us, Latter-Day Saints especially, to stand for righteousness. We must rededicate ourselves, our families, and our lives to the Lord, his Kingdom, and his work. We must prepare the world for his coming.

If ever there was a time for the Saints to "gird up their loins" and "put on the whole armor of God," that time is now. We need the faith of Job and the strength of Samson to see the Last Sunday. Can you imagine living today without a knowledge and testimony of God's Eternal Plan?

We read and see prophecies come to pass. We should realize more and more each day that it is time to pray for the Lord to come and reign. We don't know the day when Jesus Christ will return to the earth, but we should live "As if He Comes Tomorrow."

Truly, if we don't find and enter into the Lord's rest today, now, this very moment, the wickedness of the world may well consume us, and it will be too late.

How important is it for us to now step forward and serve the Lord? To not only live the Gospel to its fullest, but truly be engaged in the mission of the church? To minister in some way each day?

We are the watchmen of the Lord's Second Coming.

> Son of man, I have made thee a watchman unto the house of Israel: therefore hear the word at my mouth, and give them warning from me. (Ezekiel 3:17)

We may argue that this scripture is directed to Ezekiel, who at this time the Lord called to be a watchman over Israel. However, in chapter 33 of Ezekiel, the same counsel is given with a noteworthy difference.

The Lord indicates that anyone who is called or given the responsibility of being a watchman, falls under the same judgment. We are the Saints of the Last Days, even the Last Saturday. We are, by virtue of our acceptance of the restored Gospel and our membership in the church, the "Watchmen" of the Last Days.

Let us now apply the scriptures to us. We must succeed in adopting the word of God into our lives. Our time, talents, actions, and words should be fully centered around eternal principles and teachings.

> Seek ye first the kingdom of God, and His righteousness, and all these things shall be added unto you. (Matthew 6:33)

> Choose ye this day whom ye will serve ... but as for me and my house, we will serve the Lord. (Joshua 24:15)

> For behold, this life is the time for men to prepare to meet God; yea, behold the day of this life is the day for men to perform their labors. (Alma 34:32)

> Let your light so shine before men, that they may see your good works, and glorify your Father which is in heaven. (Matthew 5:16)

We may see communities, cities, organizations, businesses, and governments collapse around us today. Let us be unwavering examples of faith and dedication to the Savior of the world and his Kingdom.

LET YOUR LIGHT SO SHINE

Our church does not and will not in any way compromise its position! It never at any time or place falters, hesitates, or shows any reluctance to bear unwavering testimony to the divinity of Jesus Christ. The state of the world being what it is, each priesthood bearer must take advantage of every opportunity to testify of the Savior and teach and exemplify gospel truth, letting his light so shine before friends and strangers alike to perpetuate the truth concerning our Savior, Jesus Christ. (Wirthlin 1978)

Today is the day that we should increase our faith, dedication, and sacrifices to hasten the Lord's work. Now is the time to teach, preach, and serve with all our heart, might, mind, and strength.

The second most important thing is missionary work. The time has passed for good righteous examples alone. We must seek ways to be actively involved in spreading the Gospel to the world, to minister with friendship and love. We have a divine command to warn our neighbors.

They then have the choice of agency to heed or ignore our warning.

6.5. SIGNS OF THE LAST SATURDAY

The current state of the world indicates that the sun has gone down, and it is growing dark as the Last Saturday ends. World events in the last few years should convince us that time is running out. Prophecies of the Last Days are being fulfilled daily.

In 1987, a call was made to a country and government, a call that was highly criticized by many and deemed hopeless by even more. Yet the call was heard, action was taken, and the world witnessed another miracle. The Lord's Kingdom was allowed to spread further around the world.

Ronald Reagan: "Tear Down This Wall"

Behind me stands a wall that encircles the free sectors of this city, part of a vast system of barriers that divides the entire continent of Europe …

Standing before the Brandenburg Gate, every man is a German, separated from his fellow men. Every man is a Berliner, forced to look upon a scar …

As long as the gate is closed, as long as this scar of a wall is permitted to stand, it is not the German question alone that remains open, but the question of freedom for all mankind …

General Secretary Gorbachev, if you seek peace, if you seek prosperity for the Soviet Union and Eastern Europe, if you seek liberalization, come here to this gate.

Mr. Gorbachev, open this gate!

Mr. Gorbachev, tear down this wall! (Reagan 1987)

This was a Last Saturday event that many were sure would never happen during their mortal life.

In 1988, the Church of Jesus Christ of Latter-Day Saints announced that the German Democratic Republic (DDR) had agreed to allow church missionaries into the country. The DDR also allowed church members to serve outside of Germany.

Government leaders in Germany agreed to these policy changes after meetings with Thomas S. Monson, Second Counselor in the First Presidency, Russell M. Nelson of the Quorum of the Twelve Apostles, and Hans B. Ringger, a member of the First Quorum of the Seventy and counselor in the Europe Area presidency.

A German official said that church missionaries serve as goodwill ambassadors for their home countries and the countries in which they serve.

This church announcement advances the church into one more nation, kindred, tongue, and people.

The signs of the times can be readily seen in the USSR and the Eastern Bloc countries of Europe. The dramatic changes in the government of the Soviet Union surprised the world. They are additional indications that it is Saturday, the earth's final one.

We cannot deny that the Lord is extending and spreading forth his hand. The world is awakening to the message of the restored Gospel. Some church leaders have expressed their thoughts on our lives today. Their comments serve as warnings and guidance.

The Destiny of the Church

President Gordon B. Hinckley: "The progress of the Church in our day is truly astounding. The God of heaven has brought to pass this latter-day miracle, and what we have seen is but a foretaste of greater things yet to come."

Elder Neal A. Maxwell: "Special challenges [which] will require of us that we follow the Brethren. All the easy things that the Church has had to do have been done. From now on, it's high adventure, and followership is going to be tested in some interesting ways."

Elder Dean L. Larsen: "I do not believe that you are here upon the earth at this time by accident. I believe you qualified in the premortal life to come into mortality at a time when great things would be required of you." (Destiny 2001)

What is the destiny of the Lord's church in these, the Last Days? Joseph Smith stated it very clearly:

No Unhallowed Hand

No unhallowed hand can stop the work from progressing. Persecutions may rage, mobs may combine, armies may assemble, calumny may defame, but the truth of God will go forth boldly, nobly, and independent, till it has penetrated every continent, visited every clime, swept every country and sounded in every ear, till the purposes of God shall be accomplished and the Great Jehovah shall say the work is done. (Smith 1974, 540)

We are in the earth's period of time when the Lord's promises are being fulfilled. The church is becoming a beacon of faith, a center of righteousness, and a power for good. Through the prophet Joseph Smith, the Lord said,

How long can rolling water remain impure? What power shall stay the heavens? As well might man stretch forth his puny arm to stop the Missouri River in its decreed course, or to turn it up stream, as to hinder the Almighty from pouring down knowledge from heaven upon the heads of the Latter-Day Saints. (Doc. & Cov. 121:33)

The Church of Jesus Christ of Latter-Day Saints will fulfill its destiny. We must each choose eternal truths, righteousness, and obedience to fulfill our individual destiny.

Warnings from the Past

Three great civilizations have occupied the Western Hemisphere. Two have passed into oblivion.

Those that disappeared died by virtual suicide. They brought about their own extinction as they defiled the land and defied their God by extensive crime, sexual deviation, and other loathsome sins of almost every kind.

245

Now our modern nations have succeeded them in the occupancy of this hemisphere. Much of the corruption which is common among us today resembles in striking detail the degradation that afflicted them ...

We do not say that sin in other parts of the world is less reprehensible or to be excused in the least degree, for sin is always sin regardless of the philosophies of men and no matter where it appears.

But in this hemisphere a different situation exists. God has dedicated this land to the work of his Beloved Son, the Lord Jesus Christ, and he will not tolerate continued desecration of it ...

In plain, blunt words, then, we are told that whatever nations occupy this land must serve God or die! (Petersen 1971)

We have been warned in various ways, by many different leaders, and many times, since Lehi and his family left Jerusalem. They arrived in this Promised Land and were taught that all nations, and people, that lived here would be required to serve God.

"In an Hour When Ye Think Not" (D&C 45:2)

President Joseph Fielding Smith noted that "one of the great failings of mankind is to ignore warnings of punishment for sin. In all ages of the world it has been the peculiar belief of men that the sayings of the prophets were to be fulfilled in times still future. That is true of the people today. We have had ample warning of the nearness of the coming of the great and dreadful day of the Lord. The signs are upon us in all their power. ...

In this revelation we are given the warning that the summer is passing and if we are heedless of the warning we will find the summer past, the harvest ended and our souls not saved. While no man knows the day or the hour, yet if we are taken unawares, we will be without excuse, for the signs are ample and we now see them being fulfilled." (Student Manual 2002)

In 1983, the *Church News* expressed the need for Latter-Day Saints to see with our eyes and put our lives in order. The article stated, "Only the blind could fail to recognize that we are living in trouble times; only the careless and indifferent would ignore the warnings that have been given."

Are you blind? Are you careless? Are you indifferent? Are we all? It is late on the Last Saturday. It is time to see, care, and take giant steps with faith and righteousness.

An angel shows Nephi, the Book of Mormon prophet, what will happen to the church when Christ returns. Perhaps we have started to see this prophecy come true. It sounds like some rewarding events for the saints of the Last Days. Have we been armed with righteousness?

> And it came to pass that I, Nephi, beheld the power of the Lamb of God, that it descended upon the saints of the church of the Lamb, and upon the covenant people of the Lord, who were scattered upon all the face of the earth; and they were armed with righteousness and with the power of God in great glory. (1 Nephi 14:14)

In January 2018, the *Washington Post* published an article that indicates the world is also aware that we live in the Last Days. Although the world does not necessarily anticipate or accept the return of Jesus Christ, many people expect that the world will come to an end.

THE DOOMSDAY CLOCK JUST MOVED: IT'S
NOW 2 MINUTES TO "MIDNIGHT," THE
SYMBOLIC HOUR OF THE APOCALYPSE

Alexa, what time is the apocalypse?

Ulp.

247

The Bulletin of the Atomic Scientists advanced the symbolic Doomsday Clock a notch closer to the end of humanity Thursday, moving it ahead by 30 seconds after what the organization called a "grim assessment" of the state of geopolitical affairs.

"As of today," Bulletin president Rachel Bronson told reporters, "it is two minutes to midnight." – as close as the world has ever been to the hour of apocalypse.

In moving the clock 30 seconds closer to the hour of the apocalypse, the group cited "the failure of President Trump and other world leaders to deal with looming threats of nuclear war and climate change." …

The clock, a metaphorical measure of humankind's proximity to global catastrophe, also advanced 30 seconds last year, to 2½ minutes to "midnight." (Bever, Kaplan, and Ohlheiser 2018)

The Doomsday Clock is the brainchild of some atomic scientists; the clock can move forward or backward. It does, however, reflect what these scientists are seeing in the world and what they perceive about it.

On January 23, 2020, the Deseret News reported that the Doomsday Clock "just inched closer to midnight." Atomic scientists moved the clock to a hundred seconds before midnight (see https://www.deseret.com/u-s-world/2020/1/23/21078773/doomsday-clock-midnight-bulletin-atomic-scientists).

The Old Testament book of Joel only has three chapters. But all three chapters describe conditions and events that will precede the Lord's Second Coming. Some of the events are also described by other prophets. Joel describes how nations will be at war, possibly the battle of Armageddon.

Multitudes, multitudes in the valley of decision: for the day of the Lord is near in the valley of decision.

The sun and the moon shall be darkened, and the stars shall withdraw their shining.

The LORD also shall roar out of Zion, and utter his voice from Jerusalem; and the heavens and the earth shall shake: but the LORD will be the hope of his people, and the strength of the children of Israel.

So shall ye know that I am the LORD your God dwelling in Zion, my holy mountain: then shall Jerusalem be holy, and there shall no strangers pass through her any more.

And it shall come to pass in that day, that the mountains shall drop down new wine, and the hills shall flow with milk, and all the rivers of Judah shall flow with waters, and a fountain shall come forth out of the house of the LORD, and shall water the valley of Shittim. (Joel 3:14-18)

Do these scriptures confirm that today is the Last Saturday?

Are multitudes in the valley of decision? The Lord's church has been restored and is spreading around the world. People must decide to embrace or ignore the Gospel message.

Have the sun and the moon been darkened? Violence and evil acts occur both day and night now.

Has the Lord roared out of Zion? His house has been established in the tops of the mountains, and his voice is heard all over the earth. Many more people know the Lord and his restored church.

Have the mountains dropped down new wine, and have the hills flowed with milk? The mountains have dropped down and revealed new Gospel truths. This Gospel milk is flowing to the world by missionaries teaching in many nations of the world. Shittim is located in the land of Moab, where the Israelites were encamped. Is the Gospel being preached there?

In Joel 3:19, the prophet says that "Egypt will be a desolation, and Edom shall be a desolate wilderness." We know where Egypt is, but where is Edom? Edom was an ancient kingdom between the Dead Sea and the Gulf of Aquaba, in southwestern Jordan today.

Is Egypt a desolation and Edom a desolate wilderness? If the restored church has no presence in these places, they could be considered desolate.

T.6.6. REJOICE

The Book of Mormon Nephite prophet Jacob, brother of Nephi, admonished, warned, and pleaded with his people at a time when the Lamanites were more righteous than the Nephites. Although his words were spoken a long time ago, through the grace of God, we have them today. On this day, even the Last Saturday, let us follow his counsel and rejoice:

> But behold, I, Jacob, would speak unto you that are pure in heart. Look unto God with firmness of mind, and pray unto him with exceeding faith, and he will console you in your afflictions, and he will plead your cause, and send down justice upon those who seek your destruction.

> O all ye that are pure in heart, lift up your heads and receive the pleasing word of God, and feast upon his love; for ye may, if your minds are firm, forever. (Jacob 3:1-2)

In verse 11, Jacob further exhorts us to pay attention, remember, and act upon his words. If we do, we will be free from the power and fate of the devil.

> O my brethren, hearken unto my words; arouse the faculties of your souls; shake yourselves that ye may awake from the slumber of death; and loose yourselves from the pains of hell that ye may not become angels to the devil, to be cast into that lake of fire and brimstone which is the second death. (Jacob 3:11)

Section 128 of the Doctrine and Covenants is an epistle from Joseph Smith to the Church of Jesus Christ of Latter-Day Saints. The epistle was given in the final hours of the Last Saturday. Reality may well be that we live in the final minutes, or seconds, of the Last Saturday. There is lots of turmoil, chaos, and wickedness in the world.

The prophet Joseph Smith reminds us of the miraculous restoration of the Gospel, the church, and the Kingdom of God to the earth. The messengers, doctrines, and principles of eternal life testify that the Lord lives and is ready to return.

> Now, what do we hear in the gospel which we have received? A voice of gladness! A voice of mercy from heaven; and a voice of truth out of the earth; glad tidings for the dead; a voice of gladness for the living and the dead; glad tidings of great joy. How beautiful upon the mountains are the feet of those that bring glad tidings of good things, and that say unto Zion: Behold, thy God reigneth! As the dews of Carmel, so shall the knowledge of God descend upon them!

> And again, what do we hear? Glad tidings from Cumorah! Moroni, an angel from heaven, declaring the fulfilment of the prophets—the book to be revealed. A voice of the Lord in the wilderness of Fayette, Seneca county, declaring the three witnesses to bear record of the book! The voice of Michael on the banks of the Susquehanna, detecting the devil when he appeared as an angel of light! The voice of Peter, James, and John in the wilderness between Harmony, Susquehanna county, and Colesville, Broome county, on the Susquehanna river, declaring themselves as possessing the keys of the kingdom, and of the dispensation of the fulness of times! (Doc. & Cov. 128:19-20)

However, with knowledge of the restored Lord's Kingdom, with the realization of the great mercies of God the Father, with an understanding

251

of the signs of the Last Days, with living faith in the Lord Jesus Christ and his love for us, we can find and have peace and joy in our lives. We can rejoice in the great plan of happiness.

> Brethren, shall we not go on in so great a cause? Go forward and not backward. Courage, brethren; and on, on to the victory! Let your hearts rejoice, and be exceedingly glad. Let the earth break forth into singing. Let the dead speak forth anthems of eternal praise to the King Immanuel, who hath ordained, before the world was, that which would enable us to redeem them out of their prison; for the prisoners shall go free.

> Let the mountains shout for joy, and all ye valleys cry aloud; and all ye seas and dry lands tell the wonders of your Eternal King! And ye rivers, and brooks, and rills, flow down with gladness. Let the woods and all the trees of the field praise the Lord; and ye solid rocks weep for joy! And let the sun, moon, and the morning stars sing together, and let all the sons of God shout for joy! And let the eternal creations declare his name forever and ever! And again I say, how glorious is the voice we hear from heaven, proclaiming in our ears, glory, and salvation, and honor, and immortality, and eternal life; kingdoms, principalities, and powers! (Doc. & Cov. 128:22-23)

We know we live in the Last Days. The Lord has restored his church. Prophets and apostles lead and guide us today. We have all the knowledge, authority, and blessings to truly follow the Savior Jesus Christ and bring others to him.

> Therefore, verily, thus saith the Lord, let Zion rejoice, for this is Zion—the pure in heart; therefore, let Zion rejoice, while all the wicked shall mourn. (Doc. & Cov. 97:21)

6.7. THE LAST SATURDAY

The most powerful tool of Satan, on this Last Saturday, is expressed by Paul H. Dunn in his book I Challenge You … I Promise You:

> Satan, troubled by a just man, wanting to throw him off course, asked for proposals.
>
> One imp said, "Let me go up and destroy his testimony of God." No, won't work.
>
> Another said, "Let me go up and destroy his testimony of Joseph Smith." No, won't work.
>
> A third said, "Let me go up and testify to him that all he believes is true, but tell him that there is no hurry to do anything about it."
>
> Yes, you go up. (Dunn 1973, 37)

Last Saturday? Oh, I remember last Saturday well. I got out of bed at 6 a.m. My wife and I went for an early morning walk. We came home, and after taking a shower, we went into each of our children. We gently woke them up and wished them good morning. Everyone went into the kitchen, and we all worked together preparing breakfast. During breakfast, we talked about the plans for the day and reviewed tomorrow's church schedule.

After breakfast, I reviewed my lesson for tomorrow. The family then went to my son's soccer game, where we cheered for him and his team. I spent a few minutes pulling weeds in the garden before lunch. After lunch, we took my daughter and some of her friends to the mall to see a movie. We had to deny permission for the first movie they wanted to see.

When we came home from the mall, my daughter said Brother Brown had called. Some of the members were helping a new family move into the ward. I called my next-door neighbor, and the two of us hurried over to help.

Just before supper, the kids and I played a couple of games of Poison on the basketball court. We had a few neighbors playing with us, as usual. After supper, I helped with the dishes. Then I reviewed my lesson again and read the Church News. We brought the kids in early and played a board game at the kitchen table. After the game, we read a chapter in the Book of Mormon, discussed it, and knelt in family prayer.

I remember last Saturday.

It was an active, rewarding, uplifting day of peace and joy.

> And now, my beloved brethren, I would that ye should come unto Christ, who is the Holy One of Israel, and partake of his salvation, and the power of his redemption. Yea, come unto him, and offer your whole souls as an offering unto him, and continue in fasting and praying, and endure to the end; and as the Lord liveth ye will be saved. (Omni 1:26)

References

Scripture References

<Scripture Text ... > (<Book> <Chapter>:<Verse(s)>)

Scriptures of the Church of Jesus Christ of Latter-Day Saints

Scripture Volumes

Bible (King James Version)

Book of Mormon

Doctrine and Covenants (Doc. & Cov.)

Pearl of Great Price

Each scripture volume contains books, books contain chapters, and chapters contain verses.

Aaron, Charlene. 2016. "'Operation Exodus' Helping Us Jews Return to Israel." CBNNews.com. 08-19-2016. https://www1.cbn.com/cbnnews/insideisrael/2015/December/Operation-Exodus-Prophecy-Fulfilled.

Acevedo, Rodolfo. 1997. "Chile 4th Nation with 100 Stakes." The Church News. Archives. 22 Mar 1997. https://www.thechurchnews. com/archives/1997-03-22/chile-4th-nation-with-100-stakes-131191.

AirSafe. n.d. "Airsafe.Com: Recent US Plane Crashes." Key information for air travelers. Accessed 03/15/2020. http://airsafe.com/events/us_ ten.htm.

Alipala, Julie S. 2011. "Aquino Orders Military: Crush Abu Sayyaf." *Philippine Daily Inquirer.* August 01, 2011. https://newsinfo.inquirer. net/34539/aquino-orders-military-crush-abu-sayyaf.

Anderson, Ryan T. 2017. "The Continuing Threat to Religious Liberty." National Review. August 14, 2017. https://www.nationalreview. com/2017/08/religious-liberty-under-attack/.

AOPA. 2008. "Aircraft Vandalism Highlights Need for Airport Watch." AOPA. July 17, 2008. https://www.aopa.org/news-and-media/all-news/ 2008/july/17/aircraft-vandalism-highlights-need-for-airport-watch.

AP NEWS. 1987. "Eight-Year-Old Charged in Shooting of Playmate." April 11, 1987. https://apnews.com/article/1352d13bc7fe42fbe17dbb5a66ef4a81.

AP News. 1987. "IRA Offshoot Says It Killed Two Former Members in Feud." March 15, 1987. https://apnews.com/article/9c4b7d71ac4492ea50 8f971cce2da96c.

AP News. 1988. "Man Accused of Killing Two Called 'Weird.'" January 16, 1988. https://apnews.com/article/b7b56586b44ebdb5b710c1e02b35195d.

APNEWS. 1987. "Man Faces Drug Charges in Pot-Growing Case." March 14, 1987. https://apnews.com/article/add2f81597230687972fbfe4 46781ae2.

APNews. 1988. "Husband Arrested after Wife's Body Found at Sea during Honeymoon Cruise." February 14, 1988. https://apnews.com/ article/c0b8361d377b0ff8924d201c9b24f5ba.

Articles of Faith. #10. The Pearl of Great Price. The Church of Jesus Christ of Latter-Day Saints.

Augenstein, Neal. 2020. "Doctor Suggests Fairfax Co. Mother Charged with Killing 2 Daughters Could Be Malingering." June 30, 2020. https://wtop.com/fairfax-county/2020/06/doctor-suggests-fairfax-co-mother-charged-with-killing-2-daughters-is-malingering.

Baker, Camille. 2017. "BYU Reflects on Missionary Age Change, Five Years Later." *The Daily Universe*. October 5, 2017. https://universe.byu.edu/2017/10/05/byu-reflects-on-missionary-age-change-five-years-later1/.

Balsamo, Michael, and Kathleen Hennessey. 2020. "Officials Blame Differing Groups Of 'Outsiders' for Violence." May 30, 2020. https://www.boston.com/news/politics/2020/05/30/outside-groups-george-floyd-minneapolis-protests-riots.

Bancroft, Katilyn. 2020. "A Utah Teacher Sexually Abused Children over His 31-Year Career. How Did He Hide So Long?" *St. George Spectrum & Daily News*. Aug. 5, 2020. https://www.thespectrum.com/story/news/story/news/2020/08/05/how-sexual-predator-curtis-payne-utah-teacher-hid-30-years/3227290001/.

Barna Group. 2015. "What Most Influences the Self-Identity of Americans?" Research Releases in Culture & Media. March 19, 2015. https://www.barna.com/research/what-most-influences-the-self-identity-of-americans/.

BBC News. 2015. "Paris Attacks: What Happened on the Night?" 9 December 2015. https://www.bbc.com/news/world-europe-34818994.

BBC News. 2019. "South Africa Funeral Firm to Sue Pastor For 'Resurrection Stunt.'" 26 February 2019. https://www.bbc.com/news/world-africa-47370398.

Beau, Justin K. McFarlane. n.d. "Children Are Being Killed because Some Adults Think Life Is a game." Goodreads. Accessed 02/25/19.

https://www.goodreads.com/quotes/7006927-children-are-being-killed-because-some-adults-think-life-is.

Belgium. 2020. "Ferry Sinks in Belgium. 188 People Drown." A&E Television Networks. Extracted 11/18/2020. https://www.history.com/this-day-in-history/sloppy-safety-procedures-lead-to-ferry-sinking.

Benson, Ezra Taft. 1986. "A Sacred Responsibility." Ensign Magazine. The Church of Jesus Christ of Latter-Day Saints. https://www.churchof jesuschrist.org/study/ensign/1986/05/a-sacred-responsibility?lang=eng.

Bernotas, Adolphe V. "New Hampshire's Adultery Law on Trial." March 12, 1987. https://apnews.com/article/f4d580ec334e6a67b3248932638a309b.

Bever, Lindsey, Sarah Kaplan, and Abby Ohlheiser. 2018. "The Doomsday Clock Just Moved." *The Washington Post*. January 25, 2018. https://gazette.com/news/the-doomsday-clock-just-moved-it-s-now-2-minutes-to-midnight-the-symbolic-hour/article_3db1f3a3-8ad7-5511-bf0c-12b7d5b7d9a9.html.

Bible Universe. n.d. "Stars Fall from Heaven." 7 May-June 1940. 57 https://www.bibleuniverse.com/articles/second-coming-prophecies-fulfilled/id/1934/stars-fall-from-heaven

Biblical Proof. 2014. "Preaching for The Money." Wordpress.com. Mar. 13, 2015. https://biblicalproof.wordpress.com/2015/03/13/preaching-for-the-money-2/.

Bonn, Scott A. 2014. "Serial Killer Myth #1: They're Mentally Ill or Evil Geniuses." *Psychology Today*. Posted June 16, 2014. https://www.psy chologytoday.com/us/blog/wicked-deeds/201406/serial-killer-myth-1-theyre-mentally-ill-or-evil-geniuses.

Bonvillian, Crystal. 2019. "'Mommy. Don't!': Graphic Audio, Video Show Killing of Woman Who Stabbed Son 25 Times." Cox Media Group. https://www.kiro7.com/news/deep-viral/mommy-dont-graphic-audio-video-shows-police-death-of-woman-who-stabbed-son-25-times/1007435230/.

Book of Mormon. Title Page. The Church of Jesus Christ of Latter-Day Saints.

Britannica. n.d. "Treatment of Jews." https://www.britannica.com/place/Third-Reich/The-totalitarian-police-state#ref339231.

Bronte, Charlotte. 1961. "I Care for Myself." *Jane Eyre*. Dell Publishing Co., Chapter 27, 356-57.

Brough, Monte J. 2000. "Living the Law of Sacrifice." Ensign Magazine. April. The Church of Jesus Christ of Latter-Day Saints. https://www.churchofjesuschrist.org/study/ensign/2000/04/living-the-law-of-sacrifice?lang=eng.

Brown, Andrew. 2017. "The War against Pope Francis." The Guardian. Fri., 27 Oct. 2017. https://www.theguardian.com/news/2017/oct/27/the-war-against-pope-francis.

Browne, Malcolm W. 1989. "Growing Hole in Ozone Shield Is Discovered over Antarctica." *The New York Time*s. Sept. 23, 1989. https://www.nytimes.com/1989/09/23/us/growing-hole-in-ozone-shield-is-discovered-over-antarctica.html.

Browning, Paul K. 1998. "Gathering Scattered Israel." Ensign Magazine. July. The Church of Jesus Christ of Latter-Day Saints.

Bruner, Rachel. 2020. "The 3 Guiding Principles of the LDS Church in the Mormon Faith." Learn Religions. Aug. 28, 2020. https://www.learnreligions.com/threefold-mission-of-the-lds-church-2159485.

Bruton, F. Brinley, and Paul Goldman. 2018. "Israel's Government Could Fall over Ultra-Orthodox Enlistment." NBC News. March 6, 2018. https://www.nbcnews.com/news/world/israel-s-government-could-fall-over-ultra-orthodox-enlistment-n853556.

Burney, Melanie. 2016. "NJ Mom Who Set Newborn on Fire Sentenced To 30 Years for Manslaughter." *Philadelphia Inquirer* (TNS). Apr. 23,

2016. https://www.mcall.com/news/breaking/mc-web-nj-mom-who-burned-newborn-sentenced-20160423-story.html.

Campbell, Beverly. 1989. "Church Honored for Anti-Porn Efforts." Deseret News. Nov. 4, 1989. https://www.thechurchnews.com/archives/1989-11-04/church-honored-for-anti-porn-efforts-150272.

Carlin, Paolo Fr. 2018. "The Evil One and Today's Society." Catholic Exchange. September 6, 2018. https://catholicexchange.com/the-evil-one-and-todays-society.

Carlyle, Erin. 2016. "America's Fastest-Growing Cities 2016." Forbes. Mar. 8, 2016. https://www.forbes.com/sites/erincarlyle/2016/03/08/americas-fastest-growing-cities-2016/?sh=45e878421aac.

Cassi, Sarah. 2019. "Ex-Teacher, Coach Accused of Sexually Assaulting Students Faces Trial." Lehighvalleylive.com. Posted Aug 02, 2019. https://www.lehighvalleylive.com/news/2019/08/ex-teacher-coach-accused-of-sexually-assaulting-students-faces-trial.html.

Caulfield, Philip. 2011. "'Amish Madoff' Charged with Fraud Bilking Church Members out of $15 Million." NY Daily News. Feb. 17, 2011. https://www.nydailynews.com/news/national/monroe-beachy-amish-madoff-charged-bilking-church-members-15-million-fraud-article-1.139546.

CBS News. 2008. "Man Decapitated by Seat Mate on Bus." July 31, 2008. https://www.cbsnews.com/news/man-decapitated-by-seat-mate-on-bus/.

CBS News. 2017. "Police: Suspect Kills Elderly Victim on Facebook Live. Manhunt Continues." April 16, 2017. https://www.cbsnews.com/news/cleveland police-hunt-suspect-after-facebook-live-killing/.

CDP Disaster. 2020. "CDP Center for Disaster Philanthropy Disaster 2020 North American Wildfire Season." October 29, 2020. https://disasterphilanthropy.org/disaster/2020-california-wildfires/

Challies, Tim. 2017. "7 False Teachers in the Church Today." January 31, 2017. https://www.challies.com/articles/7-false-teachers-in-the-church-today/.

Christian. 2019. "Christian Eschatological Views." https://en.wikipedia. org/wiki/Second_Coming.

Church Growing. 2005. "Church Growing in More than 160 Countries." *Ensign Magazine.* January. https://www.churchofjesuschrist.org/study/ensign/2005/01/news-of-the-church/church-growing-in-more-than-160-countries?lang=eng.

Church in Need. n.d. "Christian Persecution." Aid to the Church in Need. https://www.churchinneed.org/christian-persecution/. Accessed March 31, 2020.

Church News. 1985. "The First Presidency's Statement." Church News, April 28, 1985.

Church News. 1989. "'Words Can't Describe Feelings' of First-Time Conference Viewers." https://www.thechurchnews.com/archives/1989-04-15/words-cant-describe-feelings-of-first-time-conference-viewers-151569.

Church News. 1989. "Church Deplores Forged Letters Attempting to Discredit Leaders." The Church of Jesus Christ of Latter-Day Saints. https://www.thechurchnews.com/archives/1989-04-15/church-deplores-forged-letters-attempting-to-discredit-leaders-151563.

Church News. 2000. "This Week in Church History 25 Years Ago." *Church News.* https://www.thechurchnews.com/archives/2000-04-22/this-week-in-church_history-br-25-years-ago-119440.

Churchill, Chris. 2012. "Red-Light Anarchy Reigns on Albany Roads." *Times Union.* https://www.timesunion.com/local/article/Red-light-anarchy-reigns-on-Albany-roads-3341829.php.

Coates, James. 1985. "Terrifying Flood Leaves 11 Dead in Cheyenne." *Chicago Tribune*. August 3, 1985. https://www.chicagotribune.com/news/ct-xpm-1985-08-03-8502200639-story.html.

Cocozza, Paula. 2017. "Jesus Christ Superstars: Meet the Modern-Day Messiahs." The Guardian. 1 Sept. 2017. https://www.theguardian.com/world/2017/sep/01/jesus-christ-superstars-men-who-think-theyre-the-messiah.

Collman, Ashley. 2014. "Pastor Jailed for Murdering His Second Wife in Staged Accident Is Now Charged with Killing His First Who 'Fell Down the Stairs.'" Daily Mail.com. https://www.dailymail.co.uk/news/article-2538777/New-details-shed-light-Sinister-Minister-killed-second-wife-waits-stand-trial-wifes-mysterious-death-falling-stairs.html.

Collman, Ashley. 2019. "There Have Been 5 Fraternity Deaths This School Year Alone." INSIDER. Nov. 15, 2019. Https://Www.Insider.Com/Why-Young-Men-Connected-To-Fraternities-Keep-Dying-2019-11.

Condon, Stephanie. 2015. "Supreme Court: Marriage Is a Fundamental Right for Gay Couples." CBS News. June 27, 2015. https://www.cbsnews.com/news/supreme-court-marriage-is-a-fundamental-right-for-gay-couples/.

Cook, Arlene. 1982. "Battling Demons: The Reality of Satan." January 24, 1982. LIVE: Springfield, MO.

Cornaby, Hannah Last, and Henry H. Russell. 1998. "Who's on the Lord's Side?" Hymns of the Church of Jesus Christ of Latter-Day Saints. Second Edition. Intellectual Reserve Inc.

Crane, Emily. 2020. "New Trial Begins for 'Cannibal Who Raped and Butchered His Ex-Girlfriend.'" Daily Mail. 15 September 2020. https://www.dailymail.co.uk/news/article-8735757/New-trial-begins-Indiana-man-accused-killing-eating-ex-girlfriend.html.

Curtis, Larry D. 2018. "Fake Version of LDS Website Fools Readers and Media with Fake Apology for Racism." KUTV.com. May 17, 2018. https://kutv.com/news/local/fake-version-of-lds-website-fools-readers-and-media-with-fake-apology.

Dahlfred, Karl. 2019. "What Is the Difference between the Major Christian Denominations?" Biblword. Mar 31, 2019. https://www.biblword.net/what-is-the-difference-between-the-major-christian-denominations/

Davenport, Justin, Dick Murray, and Daniel O'Mahoney. "Union Boss Calls for Terror Summit after 'Device' Is Blown up on Tube." 21 October 2016. *London Evening Standard.*

Davidson, Lee. 2017. "Utah Ranks No. 2 in Growth of Residents Who Speak a Language besides English at Home." *The Salt Lake Tribune.* October 26, 2017. https://www.sltrib.com/news/politics/2017/10/26/utah-ranks-no-2-in-growth-of-residents-who-speak-a-language-besides-english-at-home/.

Davis, Tom. 2016. "'Miracle' Kids Survive Father's Deadly Leap Off I-287. Holding His 2 Children." Patch. https://patch.com/new-jersey/wayne/father-jumps-n-j-highway-2-children-dies-cops.

Deseret News. 1995. "Heber J. Geurts, Counselor at State Prison, Dies at 86." Deseret News. July 4, 1995. https://www.deseret.com/1995/7/4/19181408/heber-j-geurts-counselor-at-state-prison-dies-at-86.

Desert Sun. 1979. "Stabbing." The Desert Sun. Wednesday, August 15, 1979. https://www.newspapers.com/newspage/244726530/.

Destiny. 2001. "The Destiny of the Church." Church History Teaching Manual. Second Edition. Lesson 49. https://www.churchofjesuschrist.org/study/manual/church-history-teacher-manual/lesson-49?lang=eng.

Detroit. 1979. "Injured Boy To Get $4.9 Million in Suit against Dad, Sister." *Detroit Free Press.* Wednesday, July 18, 1979, 19. https://www.newspapers.com/newspage/98995355/.

Dictionary.com. n.d. "Religion Definition." https://www.dictionary.com/browse/religion?s=t.

Dockstader, Julie A. 1990. "Temple Square Visits Double in a Decade." 22 Dec. 1990. https://www.thechurchnews.com/archives/1990-12-22/temple-square-visits-double-in-a-decade-147706

Dolan, Julia. 1987. "Four Teens Make Suicide Pact, Die of Carbon Monoxide Poisoning." AP News. March 11, 1987. https://apnews.com/article/6e3d4ac9c496ab414af8793e089ca4d.

Domonoske, Camila, and Bill Chappell. 2018. "Hawaii Volcano's Lava Spews 'Laze' of Toxic Gas and Glass into the Air." NPR. May 21, 2018. https://www.npr.org/sections/thetwo-way/2018/05/21/612969472/hawaii-volcanos-lava-spews-laze-of-toxic-gas-and-glass-into-the-air.

Doucette, Chris. 2016. "Video Released of Suspects in Teen's Slaying at Pizza Pizza." *Ottawa Sun*. Oct. 21. https://ottawasun.com/2016/10/21/video-released-of-suspects-in-teens-slaying-at-pizza-pizza/wcm/a8b582b4-f138-4093-a43d-28907793e49b.

Dunn, Allison. 2019. "Ex-Pastor … Gets Life in Prison in Child Sex-Trafficking Case; Victim Speaks." The Blade. May 17, 2019. https://www.toledoblade.com/local/courts/2019/05/17/pastor-kenneth-butler-sentenced-sex-trafficking-case-cordell-jenkins/stories/20190517131.

Dunn, Paul H. 1973. I Challenge You … I Promise You. 5th Printing. Bookcraft, Inc.

Ekurd Daily. 2012. "PKK Claims Responsibility for Turkey Suicide Car Bomb Attack." May 27, 2012. https://ekurd.net/mismas/articles/misc2012/5/turkey3945.htm.

Eric. 2010. "6 Outrageously Wealthy Preachers under Federal Investigation." Avvo Stories. Jun 4, 2010. https://stories.avvo.com/nakedlaw/bizarre/6-outrageously-wealthy-preachers-under-federal-investigation.html.

E-Sylum. 2005. "Forger Mark Hofmann. Twenty Years Later." The E-Sylum, Volume 8, Number 44. October 16, 2005. The Numismatic Bibliomania Society. https://www.coinbooks.org/club_nbs_esylum_v08n44.html.

Evertz, Mary. 2005. "Children Killing Children." *Tampa Bay Times*. Oct. 3, 2005. https://www.tampabay.com/archive/1995/04/09/children-killing-children/.

Fagan, Patrick. 2006. "Why Religion Matters Even More: The Impact of Religious Practice on Social Stability." The Heritage Foundation. December 18, 2006. https://www.heritage.org/civil-society/report/why-religion-matters-even-more-the-impact-religious-practice-social-stability.

Faith. #9. "The Articles of Faith." Number 9. The Pearl of Great Price. Chapter 1. The Church of Jesus Christ of Latter-Day Saints.

Flowers, R. Barri. 2001. "Runaway Kids and Teenage Prostitution America's Lost, Abandoned, and Sexually Exploited Children." Chapter 2, p. 25. Greenwood Press. https://www.amazon.com/Runaway-Kids-Teenage-Prostitution-Abandoned/dp/0275973425#reader_0275973425.

Flynn, Meagan. 2018. "Utah's 'Free-Range Parenting' Law Said To Be First in the Nation." *The Washington Post*. March 28, 2018. https://www.washingtonpost.com/news/.morning-mix/wp/2018/03/28/utahs-free-range-parenting-law-said-to-be-first-in-the-nation/?noredirect=on&utm_term=.c1b913e2dbb3.

Fox News. 2017. "Las Vegas shooting: At Least 49 Dead in Massacre Trump Calls 'Act of Pure Evil." October 2, 2017. https://www.foxnews.com/us/las-vegas-shooting-at-least-59-dead-in-massacre-trump-calls-act-of-pure-evil.

FOX59. 2017. "Court Docs: Mother Charged with Arson, Accused of Getting Daughter to Set Fire to Mobile Home in Lebanon." https://fox59.

com/news/crimetracker/court-docs-mother-charged-with-arson-accused-of-getting-daughter-to-set-fire-to-mobile-home-in-lebanon/.

Friedman, Gillian. 2019. "'I Would Be Afraid of Being Attacked': Why Some Jews Won't Put a Menorah in Their Window This Hanukkah." *Deseret News.* Dec. 21, 2019. https://www.deseret.com/indepth/2019/12/21/21003219/i-would-be-afraid-of-being-attacked-why-some-jews-wont-put-a-menorah-in-their-window-this-hanukkah.

Gathering of Israel. 2019. Wiki. 04/22/2019. https://en.wikipedia.org/wiki/Gathering of Israel.

Gilley, Gary E. 2006. "The Bible Does Not Place a Great Priority." Evangelical Press. June 1, 2006.

Gilmer Mirror. n.d. "Mormon Helping Hands Volunteers Go to Hurricane-Ravaged Areas." The Gilmer Mirror. Accessed 12/19/2019. http://www.gilmermirror.com/view/full_story/27488023/article-Mormon-Helping-Hands-volunteers-go-to-hurricane-ravaged-areas?.

Gitierrez, Felix. 1988. "Parents Beware: Software Is Becoming 'Hardcore.'" *The Daily Herald.* Sunday, January 31, 1988, 5. https://www.newspapers.com/newspage/469493914/.

Gospel Principles. 2011. "What Will Jesus Do When He Comes Again?" Gospel Principles, chapter 44. 2011. The Church of Jesus Christ of Latter-Day Saints. https://www.churchofjesuschrist.org/study/manual/gospel-principles/chapter-44-the-second-coming-of-jesus-christ?lang=eng.

Graham, Billy. 2019. "Sharing Your Faith 101." Billy Graham Evangelistic Association. July 29, 2019. https://billygraham.org/story/sharing-your-faith-101/

Greenville News. 1987. "Saboteurs Derail Train, Hurting 150." The Greenville News. Monday, March 16, 1987. https://www.newspapers.com/newspage/191976712/.

Growth. 1984. "A Decade of Growth." Ensign Magazine. January. The Church of Jesus Christ of Latter-Day Saints. https://www.church ofjesuschrist.org/study/ensign/1984/01/a-decade-of-growth?lang=eng.

Guglielmi, Giorgia. 2020. "Why Beirut's Ammonium Nitrate Blast Was So Devastating." 10 August 2020. https://www.nature.com/articles/ d41586-020-02361-x.

Hales, Robert D. 2005. "Couple Missionaries." *Ensign Magazine.* May. The Church of Jesus Christ of Latter-Day Saints. https://www.church ofjesuschrist.org/study/liahona/2005/05/couple-missionaries-blessings-from-sacrifice-and-service?lang=eng.

Hart, John L. 1989. "A Ripe Harvest: Near Temple Square Converts from Many Lands Join in Record Numbers in Mission Zone Surrounding Salt Lake Temple." Deseret News. https://www.thechurchnews.com/ archives/1989-03-18/a-ripe-harvest-near-temple-square-converts-from-many-lands-join-in-record-numbers-in-mission-zone-surrounding-salt-lake-temple-151783.

Hart, John L. 1989. "Conversions Increase. Reflect a Worldwide Surge in Sharing Truths." Church News. 15 Apr. 1989. https://www.thechurch news.com/archives/1989-04-5/conversions-increase-reflect-a-worldwide-surge-in-sharing-truths-151551.

Hart, John L. 1989. "Heroes Emerge amid Devastation: Disaster Claims Two Church Members, Shakes Lives of Many Others." Church News. 28 Oct. 1989. https://www.thechurchnews.com/archives/1989-10-28/ heroes-emerge-amid-devastation-150313

Hart, John L. 1989. "Missionary Videos to Be Telecast in Major U.S. Cities." Church News. 14 Jan. 1989. https://www.thechurchnews.com/ archives/1989-01-14/missionary-videos-to-be-telecast-in-major-u-s-cities-152114.

Harvard Crimson. 1988. "Televangelist Swaggart Admits Infidelity." *The Harvard Crimson.* February 22, 1988. https://www.thecrimson.com/

article/1988/2/22/televangelist-swaggart-admits-infidelity-pbaton-rouge/.

Hawthorne, Emily. 2019. "These Televangelists Have Some Secrets They Don't Want You to Know." Ninja Journalist. October 12, 2019. https://ninjajournalist.com/entertainment/televangelists-secrets-tb/.

Herald. 1988. "Woman Who Kept Husband's Body at Home Could Be Part of a So-Called Health Cult." *Lethbridge Herald*. February 15, 1988, 4. https://newspaperarchive.com/lethbridge-herald-feb-15-1988-p-4/.

Hershey, John. 1946. "The Eyebrows of Some Were Burned Off." August 23, 1946. *The New Yorker*. August 31, 1946. https://www.newyorker.com/magazine/1946/08/31/Hiroshima.

Hinckley, Gordon B. 1985. "Church Reaction to the Hofmann Forgeries." 23 June 1985. The Foundation for Apologetic Information and Research. https://www.fairmormon.org/answers/Forgeries_related_to_Mormonism/Mark_Hofmann/Church_reaction_to_forgeries.

History Guy. n.d. "Wars, Conflicts, and Coups of the Philippines." Historyguy.com. Accessed 12/18/2020. https://www.historyguy.com/wars_of_the_philippines.htm#.X90c8BZ7ncs.

Holmstrom, David. 1995. "Small Towns Fight Big-City Crime." The Christian Science Monitor. February 9, 1995. https://www.csmonitor.com/1995/0209/09041.html.

Hurricane Harvey. 2017. National Weather Service. Corpus Christi, TX. https://www.weather.gov/crp/hurricane_harvey.

ICE Newsroom. 2017. "3 Arrested in Manila on Charges of Child Exploitation." U.S. Immigration and Customs Enforcement. 03/21/2017. https://www.ice.gov/news/releases/3-arrested-manila-charges-child-exploitation-and-offering-children-sex-undercover-his.

Independent. 2018. "Man Held 10-Year-Old Girl Captive in 'Torture Den' Attic as He Played Out Sadomasochistic Fantasies." Wednesday, 22

August 2018. https://www.independent.co.uk/news/uk/crime/coventry-captive-girl-attic-torture-den-david-challenor-coventry-a8502991.html.

Jacobs, Barbara Tietjen. 1971. "Awakening Guatemala." *Ensign Magazine*. July. The Church of Jesus Christ of Latter-Day Saints.

Jacoby, Jeff. 2019. "'Unplanned' Tells an Essential Truth about Abortion: It IS Violent." *Boston Globe*. May 3, 2019. https://www.bostonglobe.com/opinion/2019/05/03/unplanned-tells-essential-truth-about-abortion-violent/E3mCOyHJqiBQSJ7Nb5WUHO/story.html.

Jameson, Sam. 1985. "517 Believed Dead in Japan Air Crash: Jal 747 Down Near Tokyo; At Least 7 Survive Worst Single-Plane Disaster." *Los Angeles Times*. Aug. 13, 1985. https://www.latimes.com/archives/la-xpm-1985-08-13-mn-1318-story.html

Johnson, Joel H., and Ebenezer Beesley. 1998. "High on the Mountain Top." Hymns of the Church of Jesus Christ of Latter-Day Saints. Second Edition. Intellectual Reserve Inc.

Journal. 1988. "Israeli Troops Wound 15 in Clashes with Palestinians." *The Index-Journal*. Sunday, January 31, 1988. https://www.newspapers.com/newspage/69972138/.

Joy, Bill. n.d. "Why the Future Doesn't Need Us." 04.01.2020. https://www.wired.com/2000/04/joy-2/.

Junker, Kendall. 2018. "Hurricane Elena and Its Impacts on the Gulf Coast (1985)." NickelBlock Forecasting. 7/19/2018. https://nickelblock.com/?p=29293.

Kessler, Mori. 2018. "Updated: Man Breaks into, Vandalizes St. George LDS Temple." *St George News*. May 12, 2018. https://www.stgeorgeutah.com/news/archive/2018/05/12/mgk-man-breaks-into-st-george-lds-temple-vandalizes-inside/#.X4nSqe17ncs.

Kimball, Spencer W. 1965. "Love versus Lust." BYU Speeches of the Year. Jan. 5, 1965.

Kirkland, Justin. 2018. "There Is No God on TV. Only *The Good Place*." *Esquire*. Sept. 26, 2018. https://www.esquire.com/entertainment/tv/a23335805/the-good-place-god-christianity-religion-on-television/.

Koren, Marina. 2016. "The Rising Death Toll in Ecuador's Earthquake." *The Atlantic*. April 17, 2016. https://www.theatlantic.com/international/archive/2016/04/ecuador-earthquake-death-toll/478623/.

Lazarus, David. 1991. "Tokyo Plagued by 25-Year-Old Airport Dispute: Aviation: Narita's Expansion Is Stymied by Farmers and Radicals." *LA Times*. Dec. 29, 1991. https://www.latimes.com/archives/la-xpm-1991-12-29-mn-1911-story.html.

Leaf-Chronicle. 1928. "Halt, Diogenes. Here's Your Man." *The Leaf-Chronicle*. 07 June 1928. https://theleafchronicle.newspapers.com/clip/24175462/ben-p-trice-honest-man/

Lee, Ashley. 2019. "How to Attend, Watch or Listen to the 189th Annual General Conference This Weekend." Deseret News. Oct. 3, 2019. https://www.deseret.com/2019/10/3/20893852/watch-listen-general-conference-schedule-church-jesus-christ-latter-day-saints-mormon.

Lee, Harold B. 1973. "Admonitions for the Priesthood of God." Ensign Magazine. January. The Church of Jesus Christ of Latter-Day Saints.

Lelis, Ludmilla. 2013. "Lake County Mom Who Drowned Her 3 Children." *Orlando Sentinel*. April 17, 2013. https://www.orlandosentinel.com/news/os-xpm-2013-04-17-os-dianne-evers-release-20130417-story.html

Let God Be True. 2000. "Perilous Times." https://letgodbetrue.com/sermons/index/year-2000/perilous-times/.

Lin, Linly, and Lulu Yilun Chen. 2020. "WHO Says Hubei Cases Stablilized; American Dies: Virus Update." Bloomberg. February 8, 2020. https://www.bloomberg.com/news/articles/2020-02-07/coronavirus-death-toll-climbs-near-total-from-sars-virus-update.

Liptak, Kevin. 2017. "Trump Signs Executive Order To 'Vigorously Promote Religious Liberty.'" CNN. May 4, 2017. https://www.cnn.com/2017/05/03/politics/trump-religious-liberty-executive-order/index.html.

Ludlow, Daniel H. 1947. "Thrones Will Be Cast Down." *Latter-Day Prophets Speak*. Deseret Book Company.

Ludlow, Daniel H. 1947. "I Saw Men Hunting the Lives of Their Own Sons." *Latter-Day Prophets Speak*. Deseret Book Company.

Lybdahl, Thomas. 2017. "The Catherine Fuller Case: Eight Young Men and the Murder That Sent Them away for Life." *The Guardian*, US Edition. 23 Mar. 2017. https://www.theguardian.com/us-news/2017/mar/23/catherine-fuller-murder-supreme-court-hidden-evidence.

Maargittay, Richard. 2015. "Carnival Racketeering and Organized Crime." *Crime Magazine*. June 26, 2015. http://www.crimemagazine.com/carnival-racketeering-and-organized-crime.

Malloy, Brian. 1987. "Jury Asks Death for Female Killer of Five." UPI Archives. March 21, 1987. https://www.upi.com/Archives/1987/03/21/Jury-asks-death-for-female-killer-of-five/5872543301200/.

Mashal, Mujib, Fahim Abed, and Jawad Sukhanyar. 2017. "Deadly Bombing in Kabul Is One of the Afghan War's Worst Strikes." *The New York Times*. May 31, 2017. https://www.nytimes.com/2017/05/31/world/asia/kabul-explosion-afghanistan.html.

Matheson, Boyd. 2018. "The U.S. Flag Reminds Us That Evil Will Not Prevail." Deseret News. Aug. 30, 2018. https://amp.dailyworld.com/amp/37657637.

McClure, Tess. 2019. "Dark Crystals: The Brutal Reality behind a Booming Wellness Craze." The Guardian. 17 Sept. 2019. https://www.theguardian.com/lifeandstyle/2019/sep/17/healing-crystals-wellness-mining-madagascar.

McConkie, Bruce R. 1966. "All of the Knowledge." Mormon Doctrine. Bookcraft.

McDonald, Henry. 2014. "Satanic Panic: How British Agents Stoked Supernatural Fears in Troubles." *The Guardian*. 9 Oct. 2014. https://www.theguardian.com/uk-news/2014/oct/09/satanic-panic-british-agents-stoked-fears-troubles.

McGarry, T. W., and Louis Shagun. 1988. "Officials Raid Frozen-Body Lab Again." *Los Angeles Times*. Jan. 13, 1988. https://www.latimes.com/archives/la-xpm-1988-01-13-mn-23823-story.html

Michael, Susan. 2018. "What Does the Bible Have to Say about the Return of the Jews to Their Homeland?" International Christian Embassy Jerusalem. Accessed 06/11/2019. https://int.icej.org/susans-blog/what-does-bible-have-say-about-return-jews-their-homeland.

Miiller, Andrew. 2017. "Why the Trumpet Watches: Moral Decline in Britain and America." *The Trumpet*. September 14, 2017. https://www.thetrumpet.com/15704-moral-decline-in-britain-and-america.

Mitman, Wendy. 1987. "14-Year-Old to Be Charged in Shooting Death of 9-Year-Old." AP News. November 10, 1987. https://apnews.com/article/56ec72668a32a77eaa990b1c93d00b7.

Montgomery. 1987. "Bomb Kills 4, Wounds 39 at Academy." *The Montgomery Advertiser*. March 19, 1987. https://www.newspapers.com/newspage/258091847/.

Moore, Ann Woodbury. 1992. "Merrie Miss Missionaries." The Friend Magazine. May 1992. The Church of Jesus Christ of Latter-Day Saints.

Moroni. 1989. "Brazilians Recognize Name of 'Moroni.'" Church News. Archives. https://www.thechurchnews.com/archives/1989-09-23/brazilians-recognize-name-of-moroni-150564.

Nelson, Russell M. 2006. "The Gathering of Scattered Israel." Ensign Magazine. November. The Church of Jesus Christ of Latter-Day Saints.

Nelson, Russell M. 2015. "A Plea to My Sisters." *Ensign Magazine.* November. The Church of Jesus Christ of Latter-Day Saints.

Nelson, Russell M. 2017. "Drawing the Power of Jesus Christ into Our Lives." *Ensign Magazine.* May. The Church of Jesus Christ of Latter-Day Saints.

Netter, Sarah. 2009. "Dad: Shaniya's Mom Trafficked Her to Settle Drug Debt." ABC NEWS. November 16, 2009. https://abcnews. go.com/WN/accused-shaniya-davis-kidnapper-charged-murder-rape/ story?id=9136407

New York Times. 1987. "2 Buffalo Youths Arrested in Murders of 2 Priests." *The New York Times.* March 10, 1987, 2. https://www.nytimes. com/1987/03/10/nyregion/2-buffalo-youths-arrested-in-murders-of-2-priests.html.

Newsroom Canada. 2018. "Calgary Latter-Day Saints Help Fight Hunger." Newsroom Canada. 27 Sept. 2018. The Church of Jesus Christ of Latter-Day Saints. https://canada.lds.org/calgary-latterday-saints-help-fight-hunger.

News-Sentinel. 1987. "1,000 Held Hostage." Mar. 26, 1987. https://news. google.com/newspapers?nid=2245&dat=19870326&id=3xc0AAAA IBAJ&sjid=qDIHAAAAIBAJ&pg=7223.3090770&hl=en.

Niemietz, Brian. 2020. "SEE IT: Televangelist Claims to Cure Coronavirus through Television Sets." *New York Daily News.* Mar. 13, 2020. https://www.nydailynews.com/news/national/ny-televangelist-cure-coronavirus-television-sets-20200313-wvkb2aqkwzfvzgu3lzw hw6223u-story.html.

Niles, Christine. 2019. "Only a Fraction of Vatican's Charity Fund Goes to the Poor." ChurchMilitant.com. December 11, 2019. https://www. churchmilitant.com/news/article/only-a-fraction-of-peters-pence-funds-go-to-the-poor?gclid=EAIaIQobChMIl-6EpfT47AIVxBx9Ch2ElwsyE AMYASAAEgJYQfD_BwE.

Nozicka, Luke 2019. "Iowa Mother Guilty of Murder in Death of Infant Found in Baby Swing." *The Des Moines Register.* Feb. 6, 2019. https://www.desmoinesregister.com/story/news/crime-and-courts/2019/02/06/cheyanne-harris-iowa-mother-murder-trial-maggot-infested-baby-infant-sterling-koehn-ia-crime-courts/2791443002/.

Ochab, Ewelina U. 2018. "Religious Persecution: The Ever-Growing Threat to Us All." Forbes. Jan. 26, 2018. https://www.forbes.com/sites/ewelinaochab/2018/01/26/religious-persecution-the-ever-growing-threat-to-us-all/?sh=2d76a048e30f.

Official Letter. 2018. "Ministering with Strengthened Melchizedek Priesthood Quorums and Relief Societies." The First Presidency. Official Letter. April 2, 2018. The Church of Jesus Christ of Latter-day Saints. https://www.churchofjesuschrist.org/letters?q= April+2%2C+20 18&lang=eng.

Only Member. 2000. "The Only Member in My Family." Ensign Magazine. July. The Church of Jesus Christ of Latter-Day Saints. https://www.churchofjesuschrist.org/study/ensign/2000/07/the-only-member-in-my-family?lang=eng.

Packer, Rand H. n.d. "Dispensation of the Fulness of Times." Encyclopedia of Mormonism. Brigham Young University. Accessed November 15, 2020. https://eom.byu.edu/index.php/Dispensation_of_the_Fulness_of_Times

Palmer, Douglas D. 1995. "Translators Help Send LDS Message Worldwide." Deseret News. June 29, 1995. https://www.deseret.com/1995/6/29/19179850/translators-help-send-lds-message-worldwide.

Parks, Michael. 1987. "7 S. African Black Youths Slain in Political Feud." *The Los Angeles Times.* March 18, 1987. https://www.latimes.com/archives/la-xpm-1987-03-18-mn-7864-story.html.

Parrish, Alan K. 2007. "Seventy: Overview." Encyclopedia of Mormonism. Brigham Young University. https://eom.byu.edu/index.php/Seventy#Seventy:_Overview.

Parrish, Alan K. n.d. "Keys of the Priesthood." The Encyclopedia of Mormonism. Brigham Young University. https://eom.byu.edu/index.php/Keys_of_the_Priesthood.

Petersen, Mark E. 1971. "Warnings from the Past." Quorum of the Twelve Apostles. General Conference. April 1971. https://www.churchofjesuschrist.org/study/general-conference/1971/04/warnings-from-the-past? lang=eng.

Pew Research. 2012. "Size of Major Religious Groups (Pie Chart)." Pew Research Center. December 18, 2012. https://www.pewforum.org/2012/12/18/global-religious-landscape-exec/.

Pew Research. 2015. "U.S. Public Becoming Less Religious." Pew Research Center. November 3, 2015. https://www.pewforum.org/2015/11/03/u-s-public-becoming-less-religious/.

Pew Research. 2017. "Americans Say Religious Aspects of Christmas Are Declining in Public Life." Pew Research Center. December 12, 2017. https://www.pewforum.org/2017/12/12/americans-say-religious-aspects-of-christmas-are-declining-in-public-life/.

Phillips, Kristine. 2018. "A Father Gets 60 Years in Prison for Trying to Sell His Daughter for Sex. She Was 4." *The Washington Post*. March 24, 2018. https://www.washingtonpost.com/news/true-crime/wp/2018/03/24/a-father-gets-60-years-in-prison-for-trying-to-sell-his-daughter-for-sex-she-was-4/.

Pope, Alexander. 1744. "Vice Is a Monster of So Frightful Mien." Essay on Man, Epistle II. https://poets.org/poem/essay-man-epistle-ii.

Popenoe, David. 1998. "Married and Unmarried Parents: A Research Summary." Parenthood in America. Rutgers University. 1998. https://parenthood.library.wisc.edu/Popenoe/Popenoe-Married.html.

Pugmire, Genelle. 2018. "LDS Church Responds to Allegations of Sexual Abuse by Former Provo MTC President." Daily Herald. Mar. 20, 2018.

https://www.heraldextra.com/news/local/faith/lds-church-responds-to-allegations-of-sexual-abuse-by-former-provo-mtc-president/article_ebd998f1-473e-5a70-841f-7407ca824e34.html.

Putnam, Robert D., and David E. Campbell. 2014. "Major New Study of Religion Has Much to Say about Mormons." May 23, 2014. *American Grace: How Religion Divides and Unites Us.* New York: Simon and Schuster, 2010. https://newsroom.churchofjesuschrist.org/article/major-new-study-of-religion-has-much-to-say-about-mormons.

Rasband, Ronald A. 2020. "Fulfillment of Prophecy." Ensign Magazine. May. The Church of Jesus Christ of Latter-Day Saints. https://www.churchofjesuschrist.org/study/ensign/2020/05/41rasband?lang=eng.

Ratcliffe, Rebecca. 2020. "Philippines War on Drugs May Have Killed Tens of Thousands, Says UN." *The Guardian*, US edition. 4 June 2020. https://www.theguardian.com/world/2020/jun/04/philippines-police-may-have-killed-tens-of-thousands-with-near-impunity-in-drug-war-un.

Reagan, Ronald. 1987. "Ronald Reagan: Tear Down This Wall." Address at the Brandenburg Gate. June 12, 1987. https://www.historyplace.com/speeches/reagan-tear-down.htm.

Reavy, Pat. 2020. "Murder Charges: Teen Shooter Waited Hours between Killing Mother, Siblings." Deseret News. https://www.deseret.com/utah/2020/1/22/ 21077177/grantsville-utah-shooting-haynie-teenager-mother-siblings-murder-charges-adult-juvenile.

Rice, Doyle. 2018. "It's Going to Be Another Busy, Above Average Hurricane Season, Meteorologists Say." *Naples Daily News.* April 5, 2018. https://www.naplesnews.com/story/weather/hurricanes/2018/04/05/another-busy-above-average-2018-hurricane-season/488869002/.

Richards, Paul C. "Helvi Temiseva: Victor in a Wheelchair." *New Era Magazine.* Oct. 1973. The Church of Jesus Christ of Latter-Day Saints.

Sabbath Day. 2015. "Church Leaders Call for Better Observance of Sabbath Day." Newsroom. 30 June 2015. The Church of Jesus Christ of Latter-Day Saints. https://newsroom.churchofjesuschrist.org/article/church-leaders-call-for-better-observance-of-sabbath-day.

Salt Lake Tribune. 1980. "[Director] Doesn't Understand Objections to Screen Sex." *Salt Lake Tribune*. Feb. 19, 1980.

Salt Lake Tribune. 1980. "Feminist Raps LDS Sexism." *Salt Lake Tribune*. Feb. 19, 1980.

Salt Lake Tribune. 1980. "Religious Cults, Sects on the Increase." *Salt Lake Tribune*. Jan. 24, 1980.

Samuelson, Cecil O. 2004. "Perilous Times." Ensign Magazine. November. The Church of Jesus Christ of Latter-Day Saints. https://www.churchof jesuschrist.org/study/liahona/2004/11/perilous-times?lang=eng.

Sanchez, Raf. 2018. "US Will 'Move' Its Embassy to Jerusalem by May." *The Telegraph News*. 02/23/2018. https://www.telegraph.co.uk/news/2018/02/23/ us-will-move-embassy-jerusalem-may/.

Schmid, Randolph E. 1987. "Switzerland Rated Best Place to Live." *The Deseret Sun*. March 16. https://cdnc.ucr.edu/?a=d&d=DS1987031 6.2.64&e=-------en--20--1--txt-txIN--------1.

Second Coming. 2019. https://en.wikipedia.org/wiki/Second_Coming.

Sembahulun, Rosyidin. 2018. "Hundreds Stranded on Indonesian Mountain after Earthquake." *The Seattle Times*. July 30, 2018. https://www.seattletimes.com/nation-world/hundreds-trapped-on-indonesian-mountain-after-earthquake/.

Semerad, Tony. 2015. "Utah Growing Twice as Fast as Nation as Whole." *The Salt Lake Tribune*. May 21, 2015. https://archive.sltrib.com/article. php?id= 2534617&itype=CMSID.

Shaheen, Kareem. 2018. "Surprise Isis Attacks Leave More Than 200 Dead in South-West Syria." *The Guardian*. 25 July 2018. https://www.theguardian.com/world/2018/jul/25/dozens-dead-suicide-attack-syria-sweida-isis.

Siegel, Barry. 1996. "Everyone Knew; No One Talked: Doctor Fondled Patients for 3 Decades." *The Spokesman-Review*. Dec. 1, 1996. https://www.spokesman.com/stories/1996/dec/01/everyone-knew-no-one-talked-doctor-fondled/.

Sill, Sterling W. 1967. "The Earth's Sabbath." *The Improvement Era*. June. The Church of Jesus Christ of Latter-Day Saints.

Sirull, Ellen. 2018. "What Is the Dark Web?" Experian. April 8, 2018. https://www.experian.com/blogs/ask-experian/what-is-the-dark-web/.

Smith, Joseph. 1974. "No Unhallowed Hand." History of the Church, Vol. 4. Second Edition Revised. The Desert Book Company. The Church of Jesus Christ of Latter-Day Saints.

Smith, Lee. 2012. "A 40-Year U.S. Embassy Crisis." Tablet Magazine. Hudson Institute. October 17, 2012. https://www.hudson.org/research/9320-a-40-year-us-embassy-crisis.

Smith, Melinda, and Jeanne Segal. 2019. "Domestic Violence and Abuse." NYS Office for the Prevention of Domestic Violence. https://www.helpguide.org/articles/abuse/domestic-violence-and-abuse.htm.

Smith, Michael L. 1987. "Beset Peru Seeks to Strengthen Courts." *The Washington Post*. March 20, 1987. https://www.washingtonpost.com/archive/politics/1987/03/20/beset-peru-seeks-to-strengthen-courts/3ba0abf0-7cdf-4e8a-8d13-22326afa6ecd/.

Smith, Samuel. 2020. "Televangelist Wonders if Liberal Whitewashing of Sin Is the 'Great Apostasy' before Christ's Return." The Christian Post. Mar. 4, 2020. https://www.christianpost.com/books/

televangelist-wonders-if-liberal-whitewashing-of-sin-is-the-great-apostasy-before-christs-return.html.

Sophocles. n.d. Philoctetes. Accessed 04/27/2019. http://www.notable-quotes.com/s/sophocles_quotes.html.

Soul Intention. 2015. "What's the Difference between a Preacher, Priest, Pastor, Rabbi, Reverend, Deacon, Bishop, Minister, & POPE?" thesoulintention.blog. April 23, 2015. https://thesoulintention.blog/2015/04/23/whats-the-difference-between-a-preacher-priest-pastor-rabbi-reverend-deacon-bishop-minister-pope/.

Spiritual Life. n.d. "The Spiritual Life: Sin." https://slife.org/sin/. Adapted from Wikipedia.

Stewart, Robert W., and David Freed. 1985. "Stalker Suspect Isn't Talking." *Los Angeles Times*. Sept. 2, 1985. https://www.latimes.com/archives/la-xpm- 1985-09-02-mn-22959-story.html.

Student Manual. 2002. "'In an Hour When Ye Think Not' (D&C 45:2)." "Looking Forth for the Great Day of the Lord." *Church History and Modern Revelation.* https://www.churchofjesuschrist.org/manual/doctrine-and-covenants-student-manual/section-45-looking-forth-for-the-great-day-of-the-lord?lang=eng.

Sutton, Candace. 2018. "How Cold War II Could Play Out Now That Russia Has Cryptically Declared It's Ready." news.com.au.world. March 16, 2018. https://www.news.com.au/world/europe/how-cold-war-ii-could-play-out-now-that-russia-has-cryptically-declared-its-ready/news-story/7aff9b739343d2a0f009996ad6678636.

Szczepanski, Kallie. 2019. "The Gwangju Massacre." ThoughtCo. January 23, 2019. https://www.thoughtco.com/the-gwangju-massacre-1980-195726#background-to-the-gwangju-massacre.

Tanner, Lindsey. 1987. "Police Link Two Young Suicides with New Jersey Deaths." AP NEWS. March 13, 1987. https://apnews.com/article/2b336a6089a1a8df0b596f830970cd2f.

Temple Square. 2009. "Temple Square: A Popular Destination." Newsroom. 29 May 2009. https://newsroom.churchofjesuschrist.org/article/temple-square-a-popular-destination.

Thompson, Emily 2017. "Incest & Murder: The Cheryl Pierson Story." Morbidology. 3 December 2017. https://morbidology.com/incest-murder-the-cheryl-pierson-story/.

Times Malta. 2010. "French Mother Relieved after Admitting to Baby Killings." *Times of Malta.* https://timesofmalta.com/articles/view/french-mother-relieved-after-admitting-to-baby-killings.320333.

Uco, Cesar. 2019. "Heavy Rains and Avalanches Kill Dozens in Peru." 28 February 2019. wsws.org. http://209.216.230.86/en/articles/2019/02/28/peru-f28.html.

UPI. 1987. "Battered Wife Gets Six Years for Killing Husband." UPI Archives. March 6, 1987. https://www.upi.com/Archives/1987/03/06/Battered-wife-gets-six-years-for-killing-husband/1230542005200/.

UPI. 1987. "Two More Try in Suicide Garage." UPI Archives. March 17, 1987. https://www.upi.com/Archives/1987/03/17/Two-more-try-in-suicide-garage/9550542955600/.

USA Today. 1987. "Channels the Latest in Psychic Chic." *USA Today.* January 22, 1987, 1D.

Vargas, Ramon Antonio. 2018. "After His Wallet Was Stolen, Man Chased Thief and Beat Him to Death, New Orleans Police Say." nola.com. Aug. 10, 2018. https://www.nola.com/news/crime_police/article_8c1a9883-90bf-5af0-bfff-03ec9a767765.html.

Walch, Tad. 2018. "LDS Shooting Witness: 'People Were Screaming and Hitting the Ground.'" *Deseret News.* July 22, 2018. https://www.deseret.com/2018/7/23/20649571/lds-shooting-witness-people-were-screaming-and-hitting-the-ground.

Warchol, Glen. 1087. "An Air Force KC-135 Jet Tanker Crashed Friday." UPI Archives. March 13, 1987. https://www.upi.com/Archives/1987/03/13/An-Air-Force-KC-135-jet-tanker-crashed-Friday-while/7602542610000/

Warnick, Lee. 1988. "18 Stakes Created from 11." The Church News. 6 Feb. 1988. https://www.thechurchnews.com/archives/1988-02-06/18-stakes-created-from-11-28-hour-marathon-in-lima-multiplies-by-dividing-153896.

Wentworth. n.d. "Persecution Has Not Stopped." The Wentworth Letter, History of the Church of Jesus Christ of Latter-Day Saints. Volume IV, chapter XXXI.

Westside. n.d. "Where Are the Bold, Authoritative Preachers Today?" Westside Christian Fellowship. 15 Jan. https://westsidechristianfellowship.org/articles/where-are-the-bold-authoritative-preachers-today/.

White, Ashley. 2018. "WWJD? Mormon Helping Hands Spread Out through Big Bend to Aid Hurricane Michael Recovery." *Tallahassee Democrat*. Oct. 14, 2018. https://www.tallahassee.com/story/news/2018/10/14/mormon-helping-hands-spread-out-through-panhandle-aid-recovery/1631239002/.

Whitehead, Kate. 2005. "Horror Stories." *South China Morning Post*. 26 Feb. 2004. https://www.scmp.com/article/445882/horror-stories.

Widtsoe, John A. 1943. "Evidences and Reconciliations." Deseret Book Company.

Williams, Weston. 2016. "New Temple Highlights Mormon Church Growth, Bucking National Trend." *The Christian Science Monitor*. September 29, 2016. https://www.csmonitor.com/USA/Society/2016/0929/New-temple-highlights-Mormon-church-growth-bucking-national-trend.

Wirthlin. Joseph B. 1978. "Let Your Light So Shine." *Ensign Magazine*. November. The Church of Jesus Christ of Latter-Day Saints.

World Health Organization. 2020. "Adolescent Pregnancy." 31 January 2020. https://www.who.int/news-room/fact-sheets/detail/adolescent-pregnancy.

Yahoo! News. 2019. "Eight Women Found Dead after 'Police Sex Trafficked Them to Male Inmates.'" Yahoo News Australia. 11 October 2019. https://au.news.yahoo.com/jeff-davis-8-women-raped-trafficked-in-prison-before-being-found-dead-04858232.html.

Young, Brigham. 1997. "In the Millennium: Teachings of the Presidents of the Church." The Church of Jesus Christ of Latter-Day Saints.

Zeveloff, Naomi. 2014. "Britain Puts Mormonism on Trial." Daily Beast. Feb. 08, 2014. https://www.thedailybeast.com/britain-puts-mormonism-on-trial.